For Audrey Meyer

an
account of
our
earliest
pioneers.

Sincerely,

Louis H. Wackerbarth

New Port Richey, Fl

March 29, 1989

THE GUARDIANS

by
Doris H. Wackerbarth

Pioneering in
the CONNECTICUT VALLEY

The
Country
Squire
WINCHESTER CENTER
CONN.   06094

FOREWORD

In 1630, John Winthrop led a Great Migration of over 3,000 souls westward across the Atlantic to establish a new England.

The Massachusetts Bay Company, unlike the lonely band of near-martyrs of the Mayflower Plymouth Company who had come ten years before, was not off-course, nor was it of one mind. Indeed, some members never agreed with anyone.

Winthrop's Puritan company were political refugees. The leaders were men of estate, and the majority were businessmen, tradesmen and freeholders; many had left Old England without permission; the dependent families and single men and women passengers were chosen for the contribution they could make in the new undertaking. From the first, dissenters struck out in every direction seeking like-minds.

In 1675, Hadley, on the Connecticut River, was a pre-planned community, the third fresh start for its chief engagers. When King Philip's War began, they had been secretly and treasonously sheltering in their midst — for eleven years — a pair of old political allies with a price on their heads. They had retreated from not-so-safe-keeping in Milford and New Haven.

The Guardians is the story of the pioneer-settler protectors of two Judges of Charles I, friends who sheltered them at the time New England was coming of age.

ACKNOWLEDGMENTS

In addition to my long-suffering family, thank-yous are due every library person I have called on for assistance, many of whose names I never knew.

Mr. Lawrence Wikander, Chief Librarian at Forbes Library, Northampton, when I began, and his staff, were exceptionally supportive. Springfield, Massachusetts Public Library, my home base, carried on in the same manner. Springfield Library has an outstanding endowed collection on the Period of the English Revolution and Commonwealth government. Miss Dorothy Mozely, the guardian for years of the Genealogical and Historical Reference Room, was unfailingly interested and helpful. Michael Baron, Director of the Western Massachusetts Regional Library System, gave unstinting assistance and encouragement without which many questions would not have been answered.

Mary Frear Keeler of Wellesley and Hood Colleges and J. E. Christopher Hill of Oxford University, showed great kindness to a stranger with their detailed replies that are much appreciated.

I hope they all will find some gratification in *The Guardians*.

TABLE OF CONTENTS

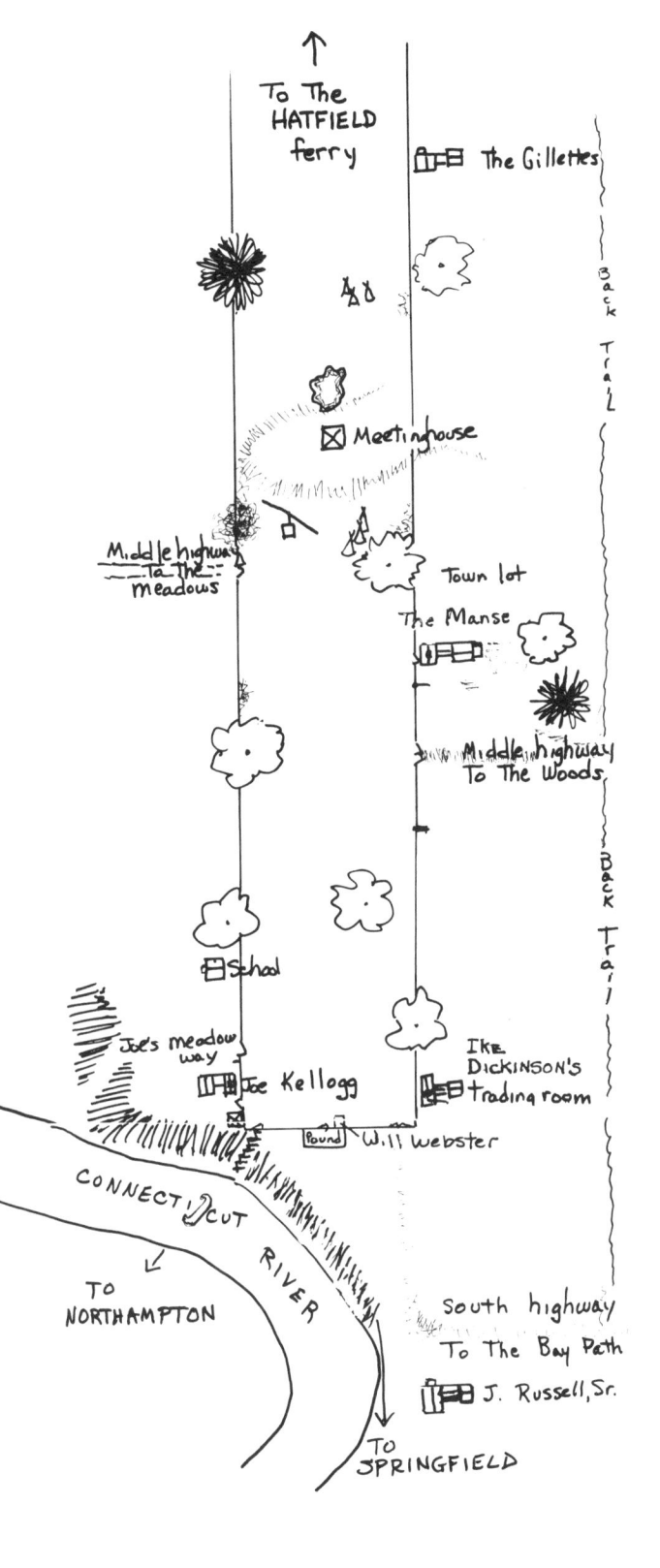

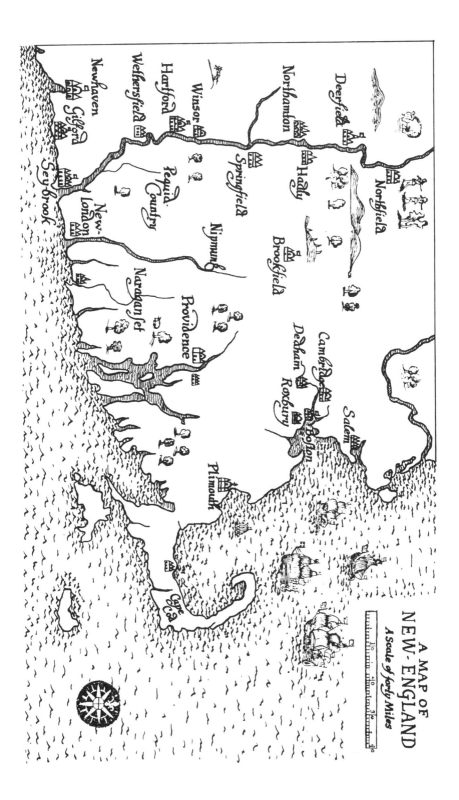

A MAP OF NEW-ENGLAND

A Scale of forty Miles

Newhaven
Gilforad
Wethersfield
Harford
Winsor
Seybrook
Pequia Country
New-London
Springfield
Njmunk
Naraganset
Brookfield
Northampton
Hadly
Deerfield
Northfield
Providence
Cambridge
Dedham
Roxbury
Boston
Salem
Plimouth
Cape Cod

THE GUARDIANS

The GILLETTE FAMILY are composite characters, the only persons among THE GUARDIANS not from the record.

Barnard, Francis	Maltster and head of an independent-minded family
Bodwell, Henry	Militiaman from Medfield
Bull, Thomas	A leading citizen of Hartford
Crawford, Mungo	A Medfield militiaman
Crow, John	Friend of the Judges.
Dickinson, Nathaniel	Father of nine sons, including Hezekiah "Ike" and Az.
Goffe, William	Major general in Parliament's Army and Judge of King Charles I, son-in-law of Edward Whalley.
Goodman, Richard	A would-be dictator
Goodwin, William	Gentleman of large estate, the town's leading citizen
Grannis, Ed	Shoemaker and nonconformist.
Hawley, Joseph	Northampton's schoolmaster
Kellogg, Joseph	Selectman, weaver and ferryman
Mosely, Samuel	Captain of Mosely's Volunteers, riffraff militiamen
Newell, Samuel	Chaplain to Eastern militiamen
Plympton, Jonathan	Militiaman and son of a Deerfield settler
Pynchon, John	Of Springfield, valley's leading colonist
Russell, Philip	Half-brother of Pastor Russell, husband of Mary Terry
Sarah	A Nonotuck squaw in the Tilton household
Savage, Thomas	In charge of Eastern militia
Talcott, John	Connecticut militia officer.
Tilton, Peter, Sr.	Representative to the Massachusetts General Court, father of Mary and "Little Peter"
Treat, Robert	Connecticut militia officer
Wait, Benjamin	Master carpenter and musician
Wappawy	A half-Pocumtuck, half-Nonotuck unfriendly to the settlers
Warrwarrankshan	A Nonotuck sachem friendly to the settlers
Wells, Jonathan	Survivor of the Battle of Turner's Falls
Westcarr, John	Physician, trader and subversive influence
Westcarr, Hannah	His wife, daughter of Francis Barnard
Whalley, Edward	Major general in Parliament's Army, Judge of Charles I and father-in-law of William Goffe
Wilton, David	Northampton's trader and leading citizen

CHAPTER I

"Good - man! Good - man Gillette! Warr - warr — ank - shan at bee tree! Warr at bee tree! Much hon - ey! Much hon - ey!"

Hamblin Gillette turned and stared at Benji, the Nonotuck lad hailing him across his barnyard. He tried not to scowl. "Tomorrow —" he stated flatly and turned back to his half-opened gate.

"Wap - paw - y know bee tree!" Benji warned insistantly.

Ham dropped the heavy chestnut gatelatch back into place and turned again. His glance darted from his new wife, hovering behind her family, waiting to be led from the yard, to his son, Zech, just beyond her. His wife's eyes plainly cried out that they had need of the honey; Zech's pleaded that he not be too hasty. Ham drew in a deep breath. Mid-week lecture was not a gathering to be turned lightly aside — but HONEY! His family had great need of that, and if they did not take it straightway, Wappawy would: no settler would get more than news of the honey, then.

Zech raised his right fist to his chest, silently imploring permission to go with Benji, reminding his father that Warrwarrankshan was waiting — that Warr considered him man-grown, old enough to venture out on his own. Ham considered Zech's message while he drew a deep breath. At last he directed, "Go along," his tone uncertain, his expression grim.

Zech caught back a sigh of relief. He tried to keep his excitement

1

to himself; he kept his expression sober for the benefit of his new stepbrother-cousins crowded by the four-railed fence, studying him. All three lads looked suitably impressed; even ten-year-old Serv, the eldest, never had been beyond a village boundary unattended; Aunt, their mother, looked unhappy, full of doubt. She did not approve of Zech's acting half-Indian. She claimed, only half in jest, that any Gillette could be taken for an Indian. It was their French blood, but of course they kept their hair shorn and were always properly attired so there was no real danger of being mistaken.

Aunt drew a small cheese from her lunchbasket. "You will need something," she told Zech and thrust the cheese at him. Her voice betrayed her relief that the honey would not be lost to them. Only Thankful, her saucy little girl, did not understand the weight of her stepfather's decision. She hopped eagerly in place, her braids bobbing, eager to be off across the Connecticut River to Northampton. Wednesday lecture was a pleasure when you were only six and could play outside while within the mouldering meetinghouse the grown-up villagers discussed the world and all its problems. Lecture was a special adventure when it met out-of-town and meant a ferry ride across the Connecticut in one of Joe Kellogg's long canoes. Until this fall he, too, had looked forward to the weekly gatherings that in good season moved from Springfield to Hadley, to Hatfield, to Northampton; he had especially relished the abundance of tasty fare swapped at the noonings; but now, September 1671, he was fourteen and must attend Wednesday-lecture and try to pay attention to the discussions. In a few years he would be expected to take part. Older folk already were coaching him. Just the thought of speaking-out before everyone tied his stomach in a knot, though. Like his father, he found no fault with others speaking-out for him.

Zech inhaled deeply. His glance darted down the common beyond his father to the scattering of maples, and ash and elm beginning to show scarlet, and crimson and gold. For a moment he forgot the bee tree — his family — lecture — He breathed in the fresh, brisk September air and savored the promising scent of ripening apples; he wanted to shout out the joy that he knew would be his this day: a free day! Just he and Benji! Before he began to exult in the high, high blue sky he caught himself short. This expedition was not to be a mere pleasure jaunt! He turned his gaze back to his father, watching him, his expression shadowed by misgivings. "I will take care —" Zech murmured. His father nodded slowly and turned away, half resigned, half annoyed.

Zech watched his new family fall into step behind Old Thomas Coleman and his wife, shuffling southward toward the ferry. The Colemans began at once to engage their new young neighbors in small talk. They did not see well enough to notice Zech standing at the back of the yard. If they missed him, they would ask where he was and why. Ham Gillette fretted about such matters. Everyone able to be about was expected to attend lecture; he did not like to ask for or allow exceptions.

Zech looked at Benji and grinned. Benji held up three fingers, indicating Warr expected that many bucketsful of honey. Zech's spine tingled when he stepped into the cottage for his father's ax to bring down the honey tree. His father had granted permission for him to go off with his razor-sharp instrument and Benji only because Warr was waiting at the bee tree. He knew of no other village lad who ever had been entrusted with such an assignment. He swelled with pride as he took down the clumsy ax-belt. He glanced at Benji. He did not want Benji to realize his excitement: this was not such a great adventure for *him* —

Benji's black eyes devoured the ax. Zech involuntarily clutched at the axhead . . . Braves could not understand the settlers' unwillingness to share their most choice tools unasked for and at the borrower's convenience . . . Zech almost sighed with relief when Benji did not insist upon taking possession of the ax as some older bucks might have done; though Benji plainly wanted to carry the ax, he turned and led Zech from the cottage at a trot.

Biscuit, Zech's frisky young mongrel, waited in the yard; his cocked head asked what was afoot. Zech motioned toward the wilderness. "Go!" he prompted in high glee. Biscuit yipped and chased himself around in a tight circle three times before he started to scamper ahead along the woods trail. He stopped short after a few flying steps, peered toward the common, then back toward Zech, thoroughly confused. He all but asked in words if they were not crossing the common to the meadows. Were they heading into unexplored territory where he might discover new coveys of quail and heath hens to startle? And groundhogs and rabbits that, unsuspecting, might not escape into their never-ending burrows?

"Go!" Zech ordered again, and Biscuit raced away, eager to find scolding squirrels and chipmunks to whom he could teach a lesson they would not forget.

3

Benji's brindled half-breed, Notchum, large and loosely strung together, disdained such nonsense. He did not race about; he always ranged close to his master and kept his own counsel. Biscuit respected Notchum, who would send him rolling at the least suggestion of play, but Notchum did not frighten him. To be certain that Notchum understood that he was not intimidated, and that his master understood how much he appreciated his being taken afield, Biscuit constantly charged back to give Zech a quick lick by way of a thank-you-my-lad, an attention that pleased Zech, and amused Benji, and Notchum ignored.

Benji headed toward the Highway-to-the-Woods, the trail that led eastward from the common into the wilderness toward The Bay. The bee tree would be beyond the reach of the November fires that the Indians set along their trail each year as soon as the last leaves fell and before snow began in earnest; flames that swept across rolling hills and winding intervals and finally flickered out in the soggy dampness of brookbanks and marshy wastes. The November fires kept pathways free of snaring underbrush and vines, and consumed away old berry brush, making way for more abundant new growth; the burnings kept the woodlands open, provident for deer herds in great numbers. In the night, the flaming countryside brought to mind the Hell-fire that Pastor loved to grimly warn of, the awful scouring that destroyed all that was not strong and worthy. Only stalwart, deep-rooted trees survived each year's scorching, and here and there a sapling saved at the right season by some trick of wind or rain. The bee tree would be in an unburned tangle beyond a brook or swamp; no hollow, dead trees survived in the park-like woods near the villages. Old settlers liked to compare New England's far-reaching, open forests to the walled great parks of the rich and noble that they remembered from their youth. Those preserves they had not dared enter: shadowy pastures for grazing deer and game birds beyond number, a profusion that was the sole property of the lord of the manor, bounty disbursed by his whim and most generally hoarded for his sport. The oldsters liked to remind everyone that here in New England, unlike in Old England, the forests belonged to all.

Benji splashed through a brook that spread wide in the spring, into a young stand of trees beginning to grow up where Hadleymen had cut oak and beech for their cottages and scant furnishings. Zech wondered at Warr's patience and cunning, finding a bee tree. He often had watched Warr start such a search: first watching the

4

bees, following the direction of their departure, intercepting them with a sweet bait of his own concoction, and moving closer and closer to their treasure. He would keep track of the tree, once found; after the queen left, and her bees with her, the honey could be had for the taking.

Benji motioned to the landmarks he had chosen to guide him back to where Warr waited: a towering larch, an oak beginning to change to wine-red, a clump of birch on a protective rise of ledge. Warr had taken Benji to the tree, and then had sent him into town; Benji had used the sun as his bearing, then.

Before Zech entered the tangled wilderness of underbrush and vines, he removed his tow blouse, already limp from sweat, and draped it over a bush in the sun. Sweat would more than just trickle down his back when they got into the close quarters of the woods. He wondered that Aunt had not reminded him not to wear such a good garment; only Phil Smith had owned it before it came to him. It would be dry and warm — comforting — when he returned with the honey. Benji threw off his deerskin trousers. He wore them only because a town ordinance forbade Indian men from appearing about the village unrobed. Benji never wore a shirt or blouse. When the weather got chilly, he would wear a deerskin jacket; but he would disappear for most of winter. In severe weather Indians holed up rather like hibernating bears, gathered around the smoldering end of a vast log, dragged into the wigwam as it was consumed away.

The heavy buckets made passage through the underbrush difficult, especially for Zech, carrying two. Benji, as a brave, would not overburden himself. Zech kept from expressing his relief when Biscuit's bark of greeting indicated he had discovered Warr just ahead. The ancient Nonotuck waited, cross-legged, on a boulder near a tall tree that had been struck by lightning during some past summer's onslaught. He watched his companions flounder toward him, his expression blank. Settlers often wondered aloud what Indians thought about when they sat for long periods of time, as they did, doing nothing.

As a sachem, Warrwarrankshan always seemed to know everything that was going on, but he did not always appear to pay attention. Warr's first trading with settlers had been with Elder Russell, Pastor's father, supplying game, and fish, and brotherly advice. Zech's father had been a youth then, indentured to Elder Russell, clearing land, building fences, and helping to break the rich, alluvial meadow soil for the first time. When Ham became a freeman, and received a grant of his own, and went down to Wethersfield and brought back a bride, Warr had transferred his attention to him. Warr's family had been among those stricken when smallpox wiped out whole Indian villages, in the earliest years of settlement in the lower Connecticut Valley. Warr's fellow-tribesmen were not surprised when, Indian fashion, he adopted Ham Gillette's family to take the place of his own. Warr's hunting and fishing and trapping had supplied his new family with the necessities of life while Ham broke and tilled his first virgin fields; when Zech's mother became ill and could not turn her family's produce to their benefit, Ham would not have been able to continue to farm on his own without Warr's ministrations. Not having learned a necessary trade, Ham would have had to become a laborer, earning wages set at a mean rate by law because in early years laborers, being in short supply, had overreached themselves and demanded exorbitant fees.

Warr had fashioned a long canoe for Ham when Hadley's elders decided that, since his farming could not provide a living for his family, he should take on the task of transporting his neighbors' surplus to market in Hartford. Last year, Warr decided that Zech could take his place in the canoe, and he no longer would go. But he remained indispensible in numberless, silent, immeasurable ways, and continued to live as he chose: stopping in villages of "cousins" along the trails, in Ham's barn, or among his fellow Nonotucks on the common.

"Netop!" Zech murmured the Indian greeting — *Friend* — as soon as he was close enough to greet Warr quietly. Warr did not hold with undue racket, except in council celebrations.

Warr nodded in reply. Zech knew that Warr was as pleased to see him as he was to see Warr. No friend of his was closer to his English grandfather than he was to Warr.

Benji explained to Warr in their tongue why only Zech had come. Warr's curt response when Benji mentioned Wappawy's name warned Zech of Warr's displeasure.

Warr took charge of the ax. After a few solid blows to the base of the long-dead tree it fell where Warr indicated it would. One stroke split it open; never before had Zech seen so much honeycomb at one time: pale gold ribbed with white. Dipping it into the buckets was a messy task. Before they were done, more insects began to beset them than had been attracted by only their sweating bodies.

For the moment, Zech's pleasure in his outing crowded out much thought of Indian ways. He expected that one bucketful of honey would be for Benji's mother who lived on the common; and she would share it with Peter Tilton's family, where her daughter, Sarah, had sojourned since a child. Since Benji was allowed no freedom about the Tiltons' dwelling, whenever the spirit moved him he would feel free to dip into Aunt's supply; an annoyance, to be sure, but a small price to pay for sharing, because the Gillettes would have great plenty: Warr would bestow his bounty upon them. He always did.

Zech and Benji and Warr each carried a bucketful of honey as far as the brook. They plunged triumphantly into a deep pool, and after testing the currents, sat in the sunny shallows and scoured away the stickiness of the honey with fine sand. Stretched out on the grassy brookbank, in the warm, beguiling sun, refreshed, gratified, Zech shared his cheese. They ate in silence, each lost in his own thoughts. Warr caught Zech unaware when he arose and announced: "Me fish," and slipped away downstream, toward some hidden cache of spears.

Zech almost groaned aloud. Two bucketsful of honey to tote all the way home! He should have known! He should have brought his yoke. He turned to Benji, expecting that, Indian fashion, Benji would be leaving his honey for his mother or Sarah to come and fetch . . . What settler would permit such an action? Surely not Hamblin Gillette! . . . Zech watched, amazed, as Benji, his face averted, plucked up his bucket and strode away. Benji's taut carriage as he disappeared signaled his distaste for his task. Suddenly Zech understood Warr's earlier displeasure: Benji had cozened his father. No one but Warr knew of the bee tree. They could have waited another day, or longer, until his father could have come. Warr had ordered Benji to carry his bucketful of honey back to the village as punishment for misleading Goodman Gillette this morning, making him believe that Wappawy would get the honey. Zech did not call out in protest or plead with Benji to wait. Burdened by two weighty buckets, he would not be able to keep up with him and if Benji hurried he would reach the common before the villagers returned. He would not want them to mark him doing squaw's work: if English men and boys took such tasks upon themselves, so be it, that was their way; no Indian would take pride in so demeaning a task.

7

CHAPTER II

As soon as Benji got beyond earshot, Zech groaned aloud. Aside from the interlude in the brook he had not had a single moment's pleasure since his father's unwilling nod. The sun was hot, now. The journey home would be tedious, exhausting, exasperating. The honey could have waited! And Warr's chastisement of Benji was only half as punishing as what he meted out to him! He should have gone to lecture — Grumbling to himself, Zech moved his buckets to a nearby knoll and dropped down on the spongy, musty-smelling earth; he flexed his arms and stretched out his gangly legs. The sun began to feel warm and comforting. He lay back, half-contented; he would return home by degrees, savoring every moment of the time left to him. Biscuit, panting from his explorations, gratefully threw himself down beside him.

Zech tried to put off his resentment at Warr's abandoning him as he had, today. Indians had such strange ways . . . On the whole, Nonotucks were good neighbors. That was one reason Hadley's engagers had dared settle above the falls on the high, mile-wide peninsula formed by the Connecticut's suddenly circling westward, then as abruptly swinging back to its steady, southward flow. Like Northampton, settled five years before, it had not palisadoed as all earlier villages had, because its engagers did not fear their neighbors. Out of habit, though, daunted by the unexplored wilderness that stretched westward beyond the foothills and north beyond knowledge along the majestic Connecticut, Northampton's dwellings clustered close to Lieutenant Wilton's trading post. Like an Old World walled-town, Northamptonfolk lived in each other's pockets, while Hadleyfolk claimed their village to be the most uncrowded in the whole world.

River tribes had watched fascinated as Hadley sprang to life along the Broad Street, a common twenty rods wide across the mile-wide neck of Hadley's rolling plateau. To each of the fifty families that signed their compact agreement, the engagers allotted eight-acre homelots and a share of surrounding meadowland, drawn by lots; they decreed that all dwellings must face onto the street; that no tree could be felled on any ground within ten rods of a highway; that each householder must build and maintain a sufficient fence four-rails high to enclose the common along his boundary; and established a stiff fine for anyone who left a fencegate ajar. In the fifteen years since its founding, the settlement had progressed from a motley collection of rude slab shelters, now used as sheds and barns, to the village as Zech knew it: comfortable cottages and stark mansions, all of weathered clapboard; thick-butted shingles; and glass-paned windows, fired by Pastor Russell's father and purchased by barter. Northampton lay companionably close at hand beyond the south end of the common. To the north, by direction of Captain Pynchon of Springfield, from whom the engagers purchased their land, Hadley's Broad Street continued across the river into uncharted wilderness. There, in a hamlet called Hatfield, dwelled a third of Hadley's engagers. No one envied Hatfieldfolk their often onerous duty crossing the river to attend meeting each Sabbath.

Biscuit began to growl. Zech clutched him around the neck, his fingers gripping handfuls of fur. "Shhhh!!!!" he cautioned. He felt Biscuit respond to his awareness of danger. Hunched motionless, alert, they watched a Pocumtuck brave stride along a trail below them. That brave was a bold one. He would take one of the buckets of honey and deny it — and his father's ax — ! —

The often quarrelsome Pocumtucks lived above the falls up the river; they showed contempt for the Nonotucks' friendliness to the settlers, but they were not hostile in the way of the bloodthirsty tribes that infested the hills to the west. Before the settlers came, murderous Mohawks had swarmed into the valley at will. They had demanded exorbitant tribute of the native tribes and out of pure savagery destroyed crops and left villages in ruins. They carried away captives, too; some they tortured to death, roasted and ate. The Nonotucks had sought the settlers as allies and eagerly learned to use muskets in their own defense. Their new neighbors encouraged them to challenge the overlordship of the western tribes. When the emboldened Connecticut River Indians swarmed across the mountains and attacked the Mohawks in their own territory, though, their war-wise enemies routed them in disorder. The Agawams, the Waranoaks, the Pochassicks, and the Chicopees, with no settlements nearby, repaired to their own campgrounds, but the Nonotucks sought refuge on the commons and in the dooryards of Northampton and Hadley. They set up wigwams, or spread their deerskin or bearskin pallets in barns and sheds, and it did not seem likely that they ever would leave.

Their nonplussed hosts accepted the invasion as a cross that must be borne, but the selectmen decreed that they would force their new neighbors to leave if they persisted in entering village homes without knocking, and taking unto themselves whatever took their fancy; they also forbade noisy games outside the meetinghouse during Sabbath services; directed that about the village braves must wear trousers and the squaws must wear smocks; and also ordered whipping for those who did not cease picking and eating their own lice in public.

Zech's thoughts drifted from the Nonotucks to the busy skies above, to watchful hawks and crows wheeling across each other's paths, and far above them great flocks of ducks and geese winging their way southward. With growing content, he rolled onto his left side and studied the gap the river had worn through craggy ledges to the south. Twice a year he and his father paddled their long canoe through that divide on their way to Hartford, transporting their neighbors' goods to market. Often other ships than those that flew the scarlet ensign of England's Great Union rode at anchor there: carracks and brigs manned by seamen from all the countries that bordered the restless Atlantic and the wind-swept North Sea. Many of the seamen looked fierce, indeed, but he had found that they all meant to be friendly — at least all that he had met up with, anyway. He owned a stout dirk that a seaman had traded to him because he had wanted him to have it. He had traded a moose horn that Warr had given him. Warr had been pleased by the exchange. He claimed that Zech had got the best of the bargain. His father had warned him to be careful of kidnapping, though, so he kept his distance at the wharves.

Tales of such misadventures as kidnapping, such as some old settlers liked to spin, brought to mind the gathering in Northampton's dim, damp, crowded meetinghouse. Zech tried to ignore a twinge of guilt at his pleasure at being so far removed from that scene. He was absent in a good cause, he assured himself, and fastened his attention on an unbelievably long *V* of wild geese beginning to break out of formation and settle toward the Ox Bow. Geese!!! Earth's noisiest creatures! Always quarreling amongst themselves about where they should stop and who should be in charge! Their racket often woke him in the night — great flocks that had started out from feeding places far to the north; sometimes he saw them silhouetted against the moon: hundreds of them. Thousands. During the day, sometimes, he could hear them when they were so high they scarcely could be seen.

Zech sighed. It was getting to *that* time of day. He must be home soon after his family returned or they would begin to worry. Serv, at least, of his new family, would realize what a full day he had put in, with all that honey to tote. He turned his thoughts away from the fact that the effort had been more than he had bargained for. He hoisted himself to his feet and took up his buckets. For diversion he would talk himself home: to that rock, yonder; to that soaring tulip tree beyond; to that patch of huckleberries, unfortunately all gone, now —

Biscuit scampered a furlong ahead of him, sniffing-out prey that had eluded him earlier. At the edge of a hillside meadow, Zech froze in his tracks, his buckets rocking back and forth like weighted pendulums. He braced himself against losing his balance. "Quonounou!" he gasped, and almost yelled out a warning. A full-grown panther was stalking Biscuit, easing himself around an island of scrub-pine and birch, upwind of Biscuit. Quonounou, the Nonotuck word for mountain lion, meant "long one"; that catamount was long, indeed; a tawny male much larger than Biscuit.

The panther loped across the field, watching Biscuit's vain searchings. Beyond the center of the clearing it ran up a slightly-leaning ash tree, its long tail a steady rudder. It would have a fine view — and point of attack — from that perch!

Warr had told him that quonounou do not attack large animals unless provoked. He had said that they do not have lairs, but keep moving, stopping only to rest and sleep in a safe, rocky reach; and they do not travel alone. Not as wolves and bear at this season. Its mate and a half-grown kit or two would be following nearby. They would be on the other side of that island of thicket, or off

11

someplace to the east, probably watching Biscuit, too. If Biscuit came back, he might catch a glimpse of them — he surely would catch their scent. Either way, he would go into action. The panthers would attack to protect their young. They would destroy him —

Warrwarrankshan had warned Zech not to move suddenly if he ever met a quonounou. Move away slowly, he had warned. Slowly. Slowly. Almost too weak to move at all, Zech took one step, then another, in Biscuit's direction. Unaware of his burden, Zech passed the birch thicket where the panther family might be watching him; the male *would* be watching him, now, he knew. As Zech reached the center of the lea, Biscuit stopped ranging bout and turned, planning to race back for a quick greeting. Zech caught his breath. Only dimly aware of the buckets, he broke into a slow, easy gait — He must not stumble and fall! He only knew that he prayed as he trotted toward Biscuit. Biscuit thought Zech was chasing him. He turned and raced away. Zech nearly collapsed with relief. The parent animals — watching — must be relieved, too, he thought. Their enemies, too, had passed them by.

Beyond the next ridge, Zech sagged to the ground, too weak to go on. Biscuit romped back to him, and Zech held him close. Biscuit sensed that something moved Zech deeply. He studied his master anxiously for a moment before he gave his face a quick lick and scampered away, eager to make the most of their outing.

Zech had planned to follow the Middle-Highway-to-the-Woods back to the common, but before he reached sight of the Middle-Highway gate, Biscuit raced away along a path that crossed the trail. At least he was headed homeward . . . The path skirted a finger of swamp behind the manse, Pastor Russell's isolated dwelling. Pastor's African moor had slain a vicious muskrat in that squashy morass last week. With Biscuit in a mood to tackle anything, Zech followed after him. 'Twould be easier to forestall an attack than need to rescue Biscuit, and possibly need to nurse a chewed-up paw and snout in the bargain.

By the time Zech reached the end of the swamp, Biscuit had disappeared completely from sight. Zech felt a surge of relief. 'Twas no matter, as long as Biscuit had reached safety. Perhaps he was at home now, waiting and panting in the dooryard, looking very snug because he had arrived first. Biscuit had no idea what he had missed!

Zech stopped at the edge of the manse garden and set down the buckets. He tried to steady his shaking legs. The small-paned windows of the weathered dwelling seemed to peer at him, questioning his absence from lecture. He was beyond caring. The Russells would be at Northampton, yet; no harm in passing through their yard to civilization.

Zech skirted the cornpiece. An overwhelming scent of tobacco caught his attention. He turned, puzzled, and stopped dead in his tracks, again. Almost within arm's reach an old man — a total stranger — dozed in the sun, his head thrown back against the shed wall. A smoldering pipe dangled from one drooping hand.

Zech stared, dumbfounded.

The old man was no one he knew or ever had seen before, even in Hartford. The shock of surprise held him fast, unable to stir. This could not be! he told himself. There were no strangers in Hadley! No one new had come to town for a long time, not even a French trader passing along the Mohawks Trail to Canada. And this old man was a gentleman. No trader, he!

Zech caught his breath, confused. He could hear his own breathing pounding in his ears. He tried to move along; he began to tremble. At that moment Biscuit sailed past him. He skidded to an abrupt halt at sight of the old stranger, but he did not retreat silently. He began to bark.

Instantly, the old man roused. Irritated, momentarily bewildered, he thrust out his hand to shoo Biscuit from him. In the next instant he swung around, suddenly wide awake, alert, frightened. Wild-eyed, distraught, he stared at Zech, trying desperately to withdraw unnoticed.

Zech never would forget the horror of the old man's trapped expression as their eyes met. He tried to keep backing away, but he could not move. He could only stare slack-mouthed into the wide-opened black eyes that seemed nearly to pop from the parchment-like taut face before him.

The terror in the stranger's bulging eyes changed swiftly to relief. Before Zech could collect his wits, the old man exclaimed: "Ye startled me, Zech!"

ZECH?

Zech felt as if he were whirling about in a vast waste of dark greenness and flashing light. Above the thudding in his head, the stranger's words pounded senselessly through his brain: "Ye startled me, Zech!" *Zech? — ZECH! — ZECH?* The old man had called him by name!

Suddenly the old man wilted. He seemed to crumble where he sat. The hand he had slashed out toward Biscuit dropped limply into his lap. In an instant, Zech became aware of long, tapered fingers, ink-stained but otherwise soft and white, like milkweed silk, fingers that never had engaged in coarsening chores . . . and gentleman's shoes, silver buckled . . . worsted hose . . . broadcloth breeches . . . fine linen . . . His gaze returned, fascinated, to the old man's ashen face, half-hidden by a white, well-trimmed mustache and stately goatee. Weathering had not darkened the fine skin, nor was there any flush of life-like color now that the shock of surprise had passed. Before Zech could catch his breath, the black eyes opened. The Old One drew a deep breath that seemed to come from deep inside him, from the very soles of his well-shod feet. He arose — slowly. He towered above Zech, taller even than Pastor Russell, and just as accustomed to authority. He drew another deep breath, and his gaze looked deep into Zech. Completely composed, now, and severe, he spoke quietly and distinctly. He ordered: "For the good of us all, Zech, never speak of me to anyone — to no one! Ever!" Then he stepped back, his movement one of dismissal.

Zech's knees shook. He felt as if the buckets were frozen into his hands. He caught his breath. Under the old man's watchful eyes, he tried to bow and almost lost his balance.

"Biscuit!" he hissed, with great effort.

Biscuit, silent since the old stranger's first action, but crouched as if holding him at bay, backed up a step or two, yipped twice, then whipped around Zech and frisked away toward the common, homeward bound, concerned now only with Pastor's surly mastiff raising a belated alarm within the manse.

An instant later, not aware how he had stumbled so far, Zech stopped on the far side of the first tree he had come to as he fled up the common. Hardly able to breathe, he put down the buckets and clung to the comforting, sturdy maple tree as if to draw from its strength. When he could breathe more easily, he looked up and down the peaceful common. No life moved along the well-worn paths; even the scattering of Indian wigwams seemed deserted. A few cows resting placidly nearby stared at him, chewing their cuds and looking wise, as if reproaching him for not having gone to lecture. Families should be returning to Hadley, now. No doubt some had, but the only life he saw was a bird, close by, that

14

dropped like a stone from an overhanging tree into a clump of huckleberry bushes.

Zech edged around the tree to where he could view the gaunt, brooding manse. The windows, shrouded against the western sun, stared out at the common, vacant and inscrutable. "Never speak of me to anyone!" pounded through Zech's brain. Over and over again. "That man is a stranger!" he gasped to himself, finally, not quite believing, yet, what had come to pass. What was this all about? No one could harbor a stranger! That was against the law. No one could harbor a stranger! Not even Pastor. Especially not Pastor! And why would anyone — Pastor — want to? What was amiss here that passers-by did not begin to suspect?

Zech glanced about again, suddenly aware how alone the manse stood. All other Hadley dwellings crowded close to a boundary, hard by a neighbor, but the manse stood in the center of its frontage. Beyond the manse boundary, south toward the ferry, lay twenty rods reserved for the seldom-traveled Middle-Highway-to-the-Woods and most of the frontage of the Widow Bedient, the Russells' closest neighbor; her cottage all but shared a relative's barnyard. An eight-acre lot beside the tree he now clung to was pasture. It had been reserved for a school, but a cottage on the opposite side of the common had been willed to the town for school use, so no schoolhouse had been built; Pastor's pair of fine chestnut geldings grazed there now, unmindful of any mysterious stranger, not caring at all about his ordeal. John Hubbard, Pastor's neighbor beyond the pasture, dwelled at least a quarter-mile distance from Goody Bedient, with only the manse between.

Zech tried for a moment to tell himself that the Old Stranger did not exist. He had been under a spell! Fleetingly, full of dread, he wondered if somehow he had conjured up an apparition — a warlock — during his wanderings alone. But he had not entertained any fanciful thoughts today of witches or of magic as he sometimes did. Recollection of the ink stains, and the book, and the silver buckles assured him that the old man was no trick of his imagination. With growing helplessness, he asked himself over and over: "Who is *He*? What does he mean: *for the good of us all*? How does he *know — ME*?"

He closed his eyes and clung to the tree. In desperation, he tried to tell himself that the stranger might have come from Boston to discuss the produce tax that excited the Valleymen so greatly. But, if he had come for that purpose, everyone in town would know.

The old man's warning rang in his ears and with each beat of his pounding heart he heard his name: "Zech! — Zech — Zech —"

Another chill shook him so violently he almost lost his hold on the tree.

He pressed his forehead against the rough bark and wondered what his father would say if he were to ignore the Old Stranger's admonition and tell what had come to pass. What would his father say? First, he would ask how a stranger could call him by name. Then, he would remind him that if Pastor had a guest, he would have taken him to mid-week lecture. Whoever went off and left a guest at home? Certainly not Pastor! Not with lecture across the river in Northampton.

In the next instant, Zech's thoughts turned to the most troubling question of all: Why was the Old Stranger so horrified at being discovered? Was he not under Pastor's protection? Was *that* not enough? Zech shivered . . . The old man's horror went beyond his understanding . . .

Again, he peered around the tree at the closed dwelling. The staring windows seemed to mock him. He rested his head against the tree. Before he could speak to his father of the Old Stranger, he would need answers to at least some of the questions he knew his father would ask. He knew only one person he could approach who would know any answers at all: Sam Russell. Sam was his own age; Sam would know, surely, about the guest at his home. Sam could put his mind to rest.

CHAPTER III

Pastor's family always returned late from lecture in Northampton, and they never sent either Jonathan or Sam on ahead. Zech knew he would not be worth a handful of feathers if he waited until after evening chores, or possibly the morrow, before he sought-out Sam Russell. He decided to go over to Northampton at once and talk with Sam there.

He glanced up the common. Hopeful, his youngest stepbrother, was at home, swinging on the gate. Zech breathed a sigh of relief. He could go over to Northampton without being intercepted by his family. He turned to the buckets of honey that had brought all this confusion to pass. If he took them home, he would not get away again, today. The closure of Annie Husk's nearby wigwam was tied back, welcoming. Annie had been a special friend to his mother. Zech decided that he could leave the honey and his father's ax at Annie's. He hid the ax under a bearskin pallet, and hurried to the west side of the common. The east-side trail would have been quicker to follow, but it passed the manse, and no one could have hired him to pass near the manse right now.

Below the meetinghouse, he met a wave of neighbors returning home; and just above the ferry, Pastor's slave couple, returning from South Meadow, crossed his path. They swung gracefully over the uneven ground, balancing baskets of hops on their heads; they glanced to neither right nor left. They always appeared to be intent on their errands. They spoke a language no one else understood, and though they did not seem to pay attention to anything, Zech had heard many villagers declare that they believed those African moors knew more about what went on about town than anyone else — Peter Tilton, or even Pastor. Sight of them, now, made him uneasy.

17

He reached the river as Joe Kellogg's long canoe slid toward Hadley with another complement of passengers. Joe would know if a stranger had come to town. He often served as selectman and besides hearing a great deal as ferryman, he was the one notified whenever a guest arrived in town. Peter Tilton, Sr., at the front of the approaching canoe, the sun glinting on his silvery head and flashing paddle, would know about Pastor's guest, too, if anyone did. Besides being a deacon and a magistrate of the county court, he served as Hadley's representative to the General Court in Boston. He knew everything that went on about town. But Zech knew he would not approach Peter Tilton.

Behind Peter sat his unfortunate son, called Little Peter, though he had grown taller than his father long before Zech first remembered seeing him. A strong, greying man in the middle years of life, Little Peter could do the work of two men, but he was child-like and could not think for himself. It was because he had Little Peter to depend on that Peter, Sr., could put much time to town affairs. Little Peter usually stayed at home with his invalid mother, in the care of Sarah, Benji's sister, who had grown up from a child in the Tilton household; Sarah was practically a sister to Peter's spinster daughter, Mary. Mary sat next after her benighted brother. A small, solemn woman, she was her father's constant companion about town. She looked like Peter, and directed him in their father's absences, but she suffered none of his infirmities. Joe Kellogg sat behind Mary, and behind Joe sat the handsome Church family: Mary, and her three young ones, like a row of little Indian husk dolls, and behind them three cousins whose parents must have lingered in Northampton. Sam Church paddled expertly at the rear.

As the canoe touched the beach, Peter, Sr., called out to Joe: "Another measure of wheat for you, Joe, on my account!"

Joe cocked his head as if he were puzzled. Pretending to be serious, he asked: "Only one, Sire?"

Peter chuckled. It was a game that he and Joe played constantly. As he assisted Mary to her feet and over the side of the canoe, with all ladies always a time of much pushing and tugging, Peter huffed: "Remember, now, 'tis lecture day and you may charge but one penceworth of wheat to our accounts today, not two."

Joe rubbed his stubbly chin with a long, hard finger and chortled: "A full complement of passengers on lecture day, so I can charge no one full fare? I will make no unlawful profit on you, now will I?''

Mary Tilton and the elder Churches smiled in spirit with the game. Zech helped lift the young ones to the beach; only Mary Tilton and Little Peter paid him any mind; Mary smiled absently, and Little Peter stared unblinkingly. He continued to stare at Zech, turning his head as his father led him away. From the foot of the log stairs up to the common, he called: "Good-bye, Zech!"

Zech waved. Little Peter held his hand close to his face as a very young child does, clutching his fingers open and shut, open and shut. For the first time, Peter, Sr., nodded at Zech. Zech tried to smile. He lifted his hand in greeting. Strange, he thought, that he should get the same chill seeing Little Peter wave like that as he got remembering the Old Stranger.

"Aunt left a package at Wilton's," Zech told Joe, to explain his crossing the river.

"Peter told me he would go back with me, 'til he saw you waiting here. You came in time to save him the trouble," Joe answered. He scowled, angered by the tardiness of his errant son who should be at hand to help man the ferry. Joe did not like to impose on his neighbors. His annoyance tightened his lips, erasing the usually pleasant expression from his weathered face. He extracted a little, worn, leather-covered toll book from his blouse and began to make a charge against the name of each of his passengers.

Zech took a deep breath. Carefully, trying to be offhand, he asked: "Joe, why is it we cannot have strangers about town?"

"Strangers?" Joe repeated, preoccupied, as if he never had heard the word. "Strangers? Strangers?" he repeated, as if he were not thinking. Then he demanded: "Why should there be strangers about town?" He clapped his account book shut. Zech tried to hide his panic. He had not collected his wits about him; he had been caught unprepared. He should have known his curiosity would be challenged!

"Why?" Joe persisted. "What makes you think there's strangers about?"

Zech struggled to appear unconcerned. He had not expected Joe to guess so accurately. But it was plain Joe knew of no one!

Joe tucked his toll book back inside his blouse. "Why do you ask?" he demanded.

19

The Old Stranger's warning chilled Zech again: *"Never speak of me to any —"* Zech stood tongue-tied. He countered lamely: "Well, if there *was* a stranger about —"

Joe's glance darted beyond him; brusquely he ordered: "Git in!"

Zech glanced over his shoulder and gasped. Dr. Westcarr, Hadley's half-Dutch trader, had come upon them too quietly to be heard. He smiled at Zech in a way he thought to be charming, but his eyes were narrowed, watchful, suspicious. Zech tried to smile in return. Fortunately, he could turn his back immediately. He hoped his expression revealed no more than the doctor's.

He wondered how much Dr. Westcarr had heard. " 'Tis too bad he is such a good bonesetter," he thought fretfully. Dr. Westcarr had caused his Dutch mother, now dead, much grief. Since the quarter court meeting had found him guilty of selling kill-devil to the Indians, Old Thomas Coleman, his stepfather, had indignantly disclaimed any relationship with him at all. Dr. Westcarr claimed that the Indians who accused him lied, but Warrwarrankshan said that Dr. Westcarr's accusers spoke the truth. Lately, Zech had heard valleymen claim that they could prove Dr. Westcarr courted favor with the Dutch in Albany; that he was in fact in their hire, making trouble any way he could for English settlers.

Four Hadley men and as many women waited patiently on the west bank of the river. Two of the men puffed absentmindedly on their pipes; the women, more companionably, shared a pipe amongst themselves. On the beach, small children dug holes in the sand with their fingers and watched the water seep into little cups they hollowed out; farther upstream older children played a boisterous game of their own devising, dodging about in the cavernous rooms of swamp willows.

Doctor Westcarr vaulted out of the canoe and slipped past his townsmen with hardly a sign of greeting. Joe saw him on his way, before he turned back to Zech. Zech pretended to be watching the children at play. He gave his paddle to one of the waiting men and did not glance at Joe. He tarried near the beach and waited for Dr. Westcarr to get well ahead of him. By the time he reached the stile into Pudding Lane, Dr. Westcarr had disappeared into the ripening young orchards that spread up the rising Berkshire foothills toward Northampton's clustered gables.

The Russells would be at Lieutenant Wilton's crowded trading room that smelled of tobacco and spice and tanned pelts; they would be sipping tankards of mulled cider and nibbling toasted bread. Pastor would be leading a discussion begun at lecture. Mr. Clark and Mr. Cunliffe, and possibly one-armed Mr. Woodward, would be taking part, and their listening wives often would chime in; throughout it all, Mrs. Russell would be wrapping and rewrapping herself in her voluminous shawl, complaining of the heat or the cold, or of whatever discomfort occupied her thoughts for the moment. Something always did. Somewhere nearby Sam Russell would be reading, or pretending to read, while he waited for his parents. Pastor never allowed his sons to be idle. He preached that the devil never rested from tempting, and with his family's salvation in mind, he insisted that they must keep busy. The Russell boys always appeared to be doing something.

Zech found Sam slumped under an apple tree, half asleep, in his lap a small leather book similar to that the Old Stranger had been reading. Tall and rangy like his father, with a thick shock of kinky brown hair, Sam had grey eyes that seemed to see into things the way his father's did. Zech caught him unaware. Instantly, Sam pretended to be reading. When he realized that Zech was not going to pass by, he hitched himself into a sitting position against the tree. He wrapped his long arms around his drawn-up legs and reminded Zech: "You were not at lecture, today!"

"No," Zech admitted. He doubted that Sam would have any interest at all in why he was absent. He hesitated, wondering how to get on with what he had in mind. He looked about, bothered, bewildered. Sam watched him, puzzled. Zech had planned to work around to the subject of the Old Stranger. He drew a deep breath. He decided suddenly, his palms wet and his throat dry, that he would need to approach Sam directly. There was no other way. To stop his knees from trembling, he dropped into the well-trampled grass beside Sam. A wary expression suddenly shadowed Sam's face.

"Sam —" Zech hesitated, baffled, unable to put his thoughts into words. Words just would not come. He had no idea how to begin. "Have you ever thought — does it not seem strange to you —" he floundered, "that we never have strangers about town?"

"Oh —" Sam gasped, and Zech knew he had touched a tender spot. He stared at Sam, fascinated by his sudden paleness. The trapped expression that sprang into Sam's eyes changed their cool grey to a dark wildness. Suddenly, Zech discovered that he had learned more than he was prepared to know.

He groped helplessly for words. "Ahhh — Sam — the *stranger* —" he blurted out, half choked.

"Stranger?" Sam repeated blankly, his tone unbelieving. The word was only a strained whisper. His face suddenly flushed wine red, as if he were strangling. His eyes darkened with horror.

"Aye, Sam —" Zech insisted, hardly able to whisper. "Ahhh — *the* — stranger — I —" His words stuck in his throat.

"Stranger? STRANGER? —" Sam gasped, stalling; he pulled his head back; his expression began to take on a maddening air of amusement. He was going to laugh and deny the Old Stranger existed!

"Aye, Sam! The stranger — the old one —" Zech protested.

Sam lunged at Zech. He snatched at Zech's blouse, hanging onto him as a hawk clutches its prey. He wrenched Zech close to his distorted face and whispered hoarsely: "There are no strangers in town, Zech! None at all! None! Never! Never! There are no strangers in town, and don't you darst to tell anyone there is! Not ever! Ever! EVER!" With each word Sam's tone became more violent and shrill.

For a moment, Sam held Zech close to him with the surprising strength of panic; then he hurled him backward as if he were unspeakable and must not be touched. Zech sprawled flat on his back and stared up at Sam, on his knees, hanging over him. Shocked beyond speech or the will to protect himself, Zech expected Sam to assault him further, but he could not move to defend himself.

Sam continued to hang over Zech, staring down at him, speechless, his eyes fierce with hate and terror; finally, certain that he must do something, he spit on Zech. Then he scrambled to his feet and spun about. He stumbled headlong through the snarled grass for a few yards, half sobbing, before he caught his balance and began to gallop toward the post. As if he were hastening to spread an alarm.

Zech lay stunned, unmoving, and stared after Sam. His heart pounded and his head throbbed as wildly as it had in the barnyard at the manse, but he had not been as utterly confused then.

Finally, Zech struggled to his knees. Sam had dropped his book. Zech picked it up, wondering what to do with it. He could not take it up to the post to Sam. Not now. Carefully, he laid it back in the grass exactly as he found it. Sam would remember where he had left it. No doubt of that.

Zech glanced up at the post. His heart rose in his throat. Dr. Westcarr was watching him. Boldly he stepped out of the shadows east of the stable and stared down at Zech, stretching his neck as if to take in every detail below, his insolence in every way a threat.

CHAPTER IV

Later, Zech recalled only his relief that Joe Kellogg was gone and Young Joe ferrying a small canoe when he returned to the river. Otherwise, he had no recollection of returning to Hadley until he saw Warr sitting by Annie Husk's fire, watching for him and pretending not to be. Annie had brought his buckets to Warr's attention, and Warr, concerned by such an unusual action on Zech's part, had waited anxiously for his return.

The ancient Nonotuck sat cross-legged, sharpening willow withes for arrow shafts while he kept an eye on everything and waited; nearby, Annie cleaned a string of magnificent trout, Warr's afternoon sport. Zech guessed, from the way Warr's glance swept over him, that Warr thought he had gotten into a brawl with an older boy. He no doubt looked that spent. He wished with all his heart that he could talk to Warr about what had happened. He could trust Warr with every detail, but Indians just did not comprehend many English ways. For one thing, there were no strangers among them in the way the old man he had seen was a stranger to him. Just the way a brave plaited his hair or shaved his head revealed his tribe and his station. Indians considered all other tribesmen to be their cousins, too. Thought of trying to make Warr understand the significance of his discovery overwhelmed him. Chagrined, without making any small talk or explanation, he took up his buckets and started homeward.

Warr touched his arm, signaling for him to wait. He picked up a half-dozen of the fish that Annie had gutted, and laid them carefully in a shallow basket; then he fell into step beside Zech. Zech's heart swelled with thanksgiving. With Warr along, he would not have to make an excuse for not getting home earlier. His father and Aunt would think that he had been with Warr when he did not return with Biscuit. He knew that was what Warr had in mind. He hung his head, and took several deep breaths and blinked hard. He told himself that there were so many things about folks that went beyond his understanding —

His father and Aunt were resting on the doorstep following supper, watching for him. They both saw him and Warr at the same time. Their concerned expressions changed to instant relief and pleasure. Everything was all right with Warr along!

"See!" Warr directed Zech's family, as soon as he and Zech entered the yard. He stuck his finger into one of the buckets of honey and licked it with great ceremony. "Much good! Much good!" he crowed, and beamed his approval, as if Zech had been the one to discover the bee tree.

Zech watched his father and Aunt smile and nod at Warr's bidding. They were pleased that Warr doted on him. Aunt accepted Warr's basket of fish, thanking him properly as she did so. Zech saw a look pass between her and his father. They *thought* they understood: they thought Warr was demonstrating to them that no one else would take Zech's place in his affection. Zech ducked his head to hide a grin of pleasure.

"I saved you some supper," Aunt told Zech as if she spoke for Warr's benefit, too. "There's fire yet to fry the fish, too —"

Warr nodded that he, too, would appreciate that. He and Zech took his father's and Aunt's places on the doorstep and ate the tasty trout and the vegetables Aunt had saved. Zech had to make himself eat. He hoped that Warr would not notice his lack of appetite. The others had gone about their chores and would not have noticed if he slipped his portion to Biscuit, as he would have if Warr had not been present. As soon as Warr left, Zech crawled up into the shed loft. His father and Aunt thought his day's foraging had exhausted him, but he knew he would not sleep. He just wanted to be alone.

He pretended to be asleep when the boys finally crept in next to him; he knew that he would hardly sleep at all, this night.

* * * * *

25

"We'll be husking maize this afternoon, Zech."

Zech spooned up samp from the fireplace kettle and nodded that he understood Aunt's message. If they were going to husk maize, he had to make but one trip to the well, three homelots away.

"Are you feeling all right, Zech?" Aunt asked anxiously.

Zech glanced at her, alarmed; his father, eating at the end of the table, looked up quickly, at first worried about Zech's health. He looked pleased, too, by Aunt's concern.

"I'm all right," Zech protested.

"You look peaked," Aunt went on, and glanced at his father, prompting him to agree with her.

"Perhaps you stayed too long in the sun yesterday, or drank too much water," his father suggested, worried by Aunt's concern.

"You looked dragged out when you got home, yesterday," Aunt persisted, " — and worse this morning."

" 'Twas that screech owl last night," Zech cried out. "And a wild cat was screaming most of the night, too. Did you not hear?"

He hoped to change the subject.

"Well, if you don't perk up through the day, I'll fix you something," Aunt promised.

Her two oldest lads, Serv and Gracie, exchanged knowing looks. They made weird faces and gagged fiendishly. Aunt gave them a hard look, and turned her head quickly, trying to keep them from seeing her grin. Zech's father chuckled. "Better not let her make an invalid of you, now, Zech," he cajoled. His voice lightened by relief, he went on: "I am going down to borrow Tim's ox, now. I'll be down in the meadow."

Zech nodded.

As soon as he finished eating, he plucked up the smooth oaken buckets resting upside down on the bench outside the door. He hung their sturdy leather straps from the hooks on the end of his shoulder yoke; swinging the yoke around onto his shoulder, he started out on his first chore of the day.

For a moment, appreciation of his new family made him forget yesterday's plight. His mother had begun to grow weak when he had been very young, and Granny Felton, the village nurse, had come to live with them. Granny was kind enough, but she grumbled and complained constantly the way some contented folks sing to themselves; she never was cheerful or encouraging. On the Sabbath and when lecture met in Hadley, when his mother could not leave her bed, Granny tended to him, seeing that his hair was combed proper, and that he was brushed off before going back into the meetinghouse for the afternoon. He had not moaned and groaned about such ministrations as his friends did with their relations; Granny might not understand that he really did not mind the attention. Sometimes someone who KNEW, who once had experienced the same emptiness when young, patted his shoulder, or teased him a bit to cheer him up for his mother's absence. More than once he heard someone whisper, " — it makes a difference; 'tis not the same." They were right. By the time his mother was laid to rest, he was old enough to care for himself, but her going had pained him as if he were still a child. His father had told him how it would be. That loneliness. They wept together, just that once, trying to give to each other the strength needed to watch the one they loved depart this world for the next. Zech groaned, remembering. A long-drawn-out recollection.

Everyone had expected his father to marry the Widow Gorse, since gone from the village. She had a boy his own age, a wily one that he did not cotton to, and three girls. Martha, the eldest, a bossy scold, began to tease him right away, threatening that soon they would be kissing relations. Every time they met someplace where no adult was about to admonish her, and she felt moved to amuse her friends, she pinched a piece of his blouse between her fingers and made a face, indicating his linsey-woolsey was a sleazy piece of goods not fit for wearing; one Sabbath noon when he and Dan Crow were off by themselves eating their lunch she poked through his sack and smirked and raised her brows at Hannah Marsh, as if to say he depended on slim pickings. When Hannah told her to mind her own business she simpered and threw her shoulders about as if to say that she was. He bore her disdain with as good grace as he could manage until she began to pick on Biscuit. Once at the well she turned a bucket of water over on him, but he did not complain to his father until she began to 'accidentally' step on Biscuit's paws no matter how close he got to Zech for protection; especially when she made it a point to stumble over him when he was lying quietly watching the militia drill.

At first he had worried that his complaint might only serve to annoy his father, but he soon realized that his protest had had its effect. At catechism soon afterward Martha banged him on the head with her psalter and he realized for the first time that his father was not continuing his hesitant courting of Martha's mother and her *family*. His father seemed to understand everything.

On their next trip to Hartford, his father had hired a horse and they had ridden down to Wethersfield. By law no one could maintain a dwelling alone and Granny wanted to move on. Zech's grandparents had been brought to the colonies as indentured single folk by Wethersfield's first engagers. Zech had visited his grandparents' farms there as a small boy, but after one and the other of them had died, and his mother was taken sick, his father could not take time to make the journey. This spring, he had taken Zech directly to the farmhouse in which his mother had grown up, and had courted his widowed sister-in-law.

A month later, he and Zech returned to Wethersfield, but that trip they did not go southward by canoe: they drove Ensign Wilton's ox team to Hartford. Southward, they carried barrels of hides and furs and wheat and cider for Ensign Wilton. On their return, in addition to supplies for Northampton's trading post, they brought back their new family: Aunt and her four children, and a collection of kettles, featherbeds, sheets of tow and linen, and woolen blankets, and, in a crude chest Aunt's father had fashioned a generation earlier, their Sabbathday garments.

Granny left then to live with a family in Hatfield.

From the first, he had been flattered by the awe of his four young cousins who never had been far from home. The older boys never had paddled a cargo canoe, or even rowed a scow. Preserved, the eldest, nine, and Hopeful, four, had taken after their father. They were red-headed, freckled, and as a rule friendly, though often impatient. Hope was in part short-tempered, too, because he was so tongue-tied no one understood him when he tried to talk. Freegrace, called Gracie, boney, blond and deliberate, resembled his mother. It had been a relief to Zech to have the boys take some of the load of chores off his shoulders. Secretly, he liked Thankful, his stepsister, best of his new family. A blue-eyed, pigtailed six-year-old, she was a busy, merry chatterbox not at all interested in being a kissing relation.

Zech stopped to adjust the yoke across his shoulders, and Thanky skipped from the kitchen doorway to the gate; she grinned impishly at him as she swung the gate open for him to pass through. Zech pulled one pigtail as he swept by, as he knew she wanted him to do. She squealed in protest, as he expected she would. He chuckled to himself, but sobered a moment later. The familiar scenery of the common brought to mind the Old Stranger, and made him miserable, again.

28

CHAPTER V

Before Zech reached the well, within easy sight of the manse, his heart began to pound and leave him short of breath. The Old Stranger might be watching! That could be how he knew who he was. If the Old Stranger watched the common from the manse he would know all the townfolk.

Zech put his buckets down and, while he awaited his turn, moved to a clump of elderberry. He pretended to be looking for a bird's nest until he maneuvered to where he could peer through lacy protection and study the manse. He watched, puzzled, as Peter Tilton and Small Pockets Lewis rode from their yards and Old John Crow cantered across the common to join them. Peter rode one of his chestnut geldings that were the envy of everyone who knew horse-flesh. He and Pastor each had a pair of matched chestnuts that never were turned loose for the sake of economy and rounded up only as needed, nor had they ever been branded on their left shoulder with Hadley's *H,* as an ordinance required.

Pastor appeared around the corner of the manse and stood at his gate, watching his friends ride up the common toward him. The other men glanced about, marking whether anyone other than the few children in sight paid them any mind. They looked grim. Wizen Will Lewis, secretly called Small Pockets because he was so stingy, never looked pleased, but Zech never had seen him look so solemn. The horsemen reined up before Pastor; Old John swung down from his frisky roan. No one spoke. Not a word passed from one to another until Jonathan Russell strode out to them carrying a blanket bundle across his shoulders. Old John extended his hand to Jonathan and spoke then. They shook hands gravely and Jonathan tossed his blanket roll across Old John's horse. Peter Tilton leaned down and shook Jonathan's hand, too. Jonathan was going away! But a trip such as this was talked of for days! What of all the messages and errands neighbors entrusted to travelers?

Zech gasped. Whatever was going on must concern the Old Stranger, yet Sam Russell denied that he existed! He could hardly breathe by the time Jonathan turned his mount southward. With Small Pockets at his heels, he cantered down the common at such a clip Zech decided they must be headed for the Bay Path and going clear to Boston.

Baffled, beginning to feel frightened, Zech returned to the well. Younger children, their buckets lined up behind his, were waiting for him to be gone.

As he loped toward the meadow after leaving the water for Aunt, he broke off a birch switch and lashed furiously at swaying grass and flowers and innocent, passing butterflies. He could make no sense of what was going on. In the meadow, he found Hope riding astride the broad back of the ox, and his father and Serv and Gracie tossing corn into the cart, the bottom already covered.

"Could you not find your way to the well?" Serv asked too sweetly when Zech halted to catch his breath before taking up his pruning knife.

"You were not there when we went to Nash's," Gracie volunteered.

Zech glanced quickly toward his father, afraid perhaps he should have thought up some excuse for his delay, though it was but slight. His father looked annoyed by Serv's harping; he was pretending not to be paying any mind, so Zech said nothing.

"Did you see Peter yet, Ham?" Aunt asked anxiously when Zech and his father maneuvered the cartful of corn into the yard just before noon.

Zech's father came to attention.

Aunt told him: "He was here looking for you, just after you left this morning. He seemed so upset, I thought he might have gone down to the cornpiece to see you."

Zech's heart stopped an instant. Of course Sam Russell had reported him! A coldness began to spread out from his spine. He watched his father try to decide why Mr. Tilton wanted to see him. "Did he say what he had on his mind?" Ham asked slowly, thoughtfully.

"No —" Aunt answered as if she were saying more than a single word of denial; it seemed to Zech that she and his father exchanged a strange look. "He seemed so resolved —" Aunt went on. She sounded troubled. "I told him where you were working, and he started off as if he was going to ride down to see you."

"Well," Ham decided, though his tone sounded uncertain, "Perhaps something about 'porting down to Hartford. I'll see him later." As an afterthought, he asked, with sudden urgency: "He did not say I should look him up?"

"No — but — I did expect that he was going after you," Aunt repeated. Her uneasy, insistent tone indicated that she was more than just passing curious about Mr. Tilton's call.

Ham twisted his mouth in a way that Zech recognized as his father's deciding that he did not know what was going on but would find out. He announced: "I'll stop over to Peter's after I take the rig back to Tim's."

Zech's stomach slowly tied itself into a little hard knot; a chill shook him once and was gone; for a moment he thought he might vomit.

Ham tipped the load of corn out of the cart. "You and the boys start husking as soon as you eat," he directed Zech. He downed a dipper of water from one of the buckets Zech had filled earlier and swung Hope astride the ox, again. Absently, he nodded permission for three of the Welles young ones who had come wandering by to climb into the ox cart. Munching a huge chunk of bread, he started out for Tim's. From there he would go directly to Peter Tilton's.

Zech nibbled on an ear of boiled corn, but could not bring himself to eat enough to provide the strength he needed to face the remainder of the day. Feeling almost numb, he dropped down by the piled-up corn.

"Did you see Wappawy this morning?" Serv asked him.

Zech, distracted, did not realize Serv addressed him.

"I said: Did you see Wappawy this morning?" Serv shouted at him, exasperated. "And don't tell me you did, 'cause we know you did not! — He wa'n't anywhere near the well!"

Taken aback, Zech stared from Serv to Gracie. He raised his brows, admitting he had not heard, but he was listening, now.

"Well! You never saw such a mess of eels as Wappawy had — at this season!" Serv announced, pleased, in a loud voice.

"Yeah?" Zech answered, trying to show interest. Dismayed, he realized his distracted reply sounded like a jeer. He looked from one lad to the other. They were exchanging sour glances.

Serv made a face at him. "You'd think that you was the Valley's greatest eeler, yourself!" he scoffed angrily.

Zech bit back the retort that sprang to his lips. No point in asking for more trouble right now. He wished he could pretend interest in anything, but he could not . . . His father would be arriving at Peter Tilton's about now; soon he would be berating him for his inquiries about the Old Stranger . . . Could he then ask about whatever was going on that they should not be mixed up in, in the first place? His spirit rose and fell instantly. He rubbed his stomach. The pain almost made him groan aloud. He tried to work. He felt as if he did not move at all. He glanced up, once, watching furtively for his father's return. He caught a glimpse of Dr. Westcarr beyond a turn in the trail across the common. He was peering toward him, studying him — watching him —

Zech cringed and looked quickly away; an instant later, when he screwed up courage enough to look back again, Dr. Westcarr was gone.

Dr. Westcarr *had* heard him ask Joe about strangers in town!

Zech's stomach tied into another knot as he tried to put the doctor's peering figure out of his mind. He glanced at Aunt. She was peering down the common, watching anxiously for his father. Zech dreaded his father's return. He would take him to task for not following the Old Stranger's admonition to speak to no one — He and his father almost never had wordy flare-ups such as he had witnessed, appalled, in other families. He prayed that Joe Kellogg had not given further thought to his questioning. Joe might mention his interest to the wrong persons — whoever they were —

Finally, Zech caught sight of his father. In ordinary times he would have rushed out to inquire about his unwonted haste and anxiety; now he pretended to be busy and unaware. When his father burst into the yard, he sat where he was and felt hopelessly sick at heart.

Ham did not look right or left. He hurried across the yard, his face a careworn mask, and herded Aunt into the house ahead of him.

Serv and Gracie, suddenly aware of something amiss, stared after them. "What's the matter, Pa?" Serv cried out, and started to scramble to his feet.

"Sit down! Sit down and mind your business!" Zech ordered.

Serv stopped halfway to his feet. He stared at Zech, his mouth opened wide with disbelief.

"Sit down!" Zech repeated.

Resentfully, reluctantly, Serv dropped back to the ground. Pouting, he stared toward the cottage, suspecting that a fascinating account was taking place inside and he was missing it all. He did not start to husk again.

Suddenly Zech began to comprehend a half-forgotten incident that had mystified and haunted him. Just after his father and Aunt were married he had wandered into the yard, barefoot as usual. His father, crouched on the broad stone doorstep, whetting a kitchen knife, did not hear him. He continued rubbing the blade against the pudding stone, his grey-peppered, kinky head drawn close to his thick-set, coarsely-clad shoulders; just inside the door, Aunt was discoursing on Pastor's refusal to serve as a trustee for Governor Bellingham's estate. The honor included a stipend and two expense-free trips to Boston each year. Townfolk could not understand why Pastor refused such an opportunity. From in the kitchen, Aunt pressed: "Now, Ham, why should Pastor feel he cannot accept? He should welcome getting to The Bay and having a chance to visit with his friends there."

His father did not answer; the rasp of the steel blade went on and on. "Now, why, Ham?" Aunt persisted. "Ham!" she warned, impatiently. His father stopped whetting the blade. He ran the side of his thumb experimentally along the razor-sharp edge before he said: "Well —" dropping his voice to a confidential tone, "I s'pose 'tis as good a time as any —" He glanced quickly about the yard as if he were about to divulge some sort of secret, and caught sight of his hovering son; he stared, speechless.

He had expected his father to be surprised; he had expected him to laugh in spirit with the game, too, once he got his bearing, but a distressed expression flickered across his face, and for an instant his grey eyes darkened — with fear? and he flared with anger, before he caught himself. Then he tried to smile. His tone was a rebuke, though. In a choked voice, he blurted, "I did not know that you were about, Zech!" As if he had no right to be there at all!

Then, Aunt poked her head through the opened doorway; something about his father's expression as he faced her caused her lips to form a small *o*. She withdrew into the kitchen and said no more. While he watched, baffled, his father dragged himself to his feet and went into the house as if he were weighted down by an almost unbearable burden.

Zech tried to put the recollection from his thoughts; he turned when he heard his father shuffling toward the door. His father's daunted expression stopped the questions that had sprung to his lips. Finally, he found his tongue and prompted: "Well?" and got to his feet. He tried not to tremble as he waited to be invited to a secluded corner and told the facts of the matter: if Sam and Jonathan knew about the Old Stranger because their father knew, then he should, too; especially since he had discovered as much — or as little — as he had. But his father's eyes were full of regret — and fear, and disappointment, too. That showed. His father's expression rebuked him because he had not heeded the Old Stranger's warning and had not kept his discovery to himself.

"What did Zech do, Mum?" Serv wheedled, and eased himself toward his mother.

Unnerved, Aunt lashed out at him: "Nothing! Nothing! Nothing *wrong!*"

Serv stared at his mother, speechless. He turned slowly toward Zech. His shocked expression sharpened from blankness to a wrathful, narrow-eyed glare. "What did ye do?" he taunted. He put his hands on his hips and cocked his head, and in a syrupy tone mocked: "What can *you* do that's wrong, but not wrong, heh?"

"What will *I* do — to *you* —" Zech snarled, and thrust himself toward Serv. His hands worked convulsively. He wanted to make Serv pay for all his own confusion; he wanted to thrash the little troublemaker to within an inch of his life. Never had he felt so distracted, so mortified, so angry, so ready to go to battle. Gracie scrambled to his feet and moved up close to Serv. Serv drew a deep breath, heartened by his brother's support. In that instant, Zech felt lost. He tossed his head and turned away, almost overcome by a wrench of regret . . . They were brothers, the brothers he never had, and now he was not one of them; they were brothers and he was shut out . . . all because of a stranger he was supposed to believe did not exist!

His father looked defeated, too. They had been closer than most fathers and sons — Had a stranger dispelled that closeness by accident in a moment's time? Silently, Zech implored his father to give him an explanation — *now*. His father looked at Aunt, and after a gesture of helplessness, moved slowly to the pile of corn. He dropped to the ground and started to husk as if he could do nothing else. Zech choked. He was going to be told *nothing*? As if he were as unaware as Serv and Gracie? This was *today*! Today he had a right to know more than he had before Wednesday.

"Shall I tell everything I know?" he suddenly yelled out to his family in the barnyard, to the common, to the world. The boys stared at him, shocked. After their first startled "Hush!" his father and Aunt said no more. Throughout the afternoon, the younger boys worked in flint-hearted silence, rejecting Ham's awkward attempts to lighten the mood. Zech hardly worked at all, finding himself time after time staring off into space with a half-husked ear of corn in his hand.

When they finished husking, the boys left to go for the cow. Zech no longer could control himself. "Pa!" he warned, much as Aunt had that afternoon when his father had decided to tell her something. He could not keep his voice from trembling, even on that one word.

Aunt and his father exchanged a hopeless look: after a moment's consideration, his father nodded for Zech to follow him.

Ham went into the house and walked slowly into the bedroom beyond the fireplace. When Zech entered the little room, hardly larger than the low, broad bed with its puffed-up feather mattress and neatly-quilted coverlet, his father unfastened the drapery at the door though there was little likelihood they would be heard. Aunt would take care of that.

"Zech," his father said, his voice weary and full of sadness: "I cannot tell you what would be too much for you to know." He sighed. "Sometimes we only know in part — and 'tis better that way. I — we —" The way he said *we* meant more than just he and Aunt — that *we* included the Russells, and Peter Tilton, and Old John Crow, and Small Pockets Lewis, and whoever else knew; even the Old Stranger, himself. "We wish you could have been spared the burden you now have." Zech waited. He stared at his father, waiting for him to go on. He gasped in disbelief when he realized his father did not intend to say more. He had been led in here for that? *He* was going to be told *nothing*?

His father squared his shoulders. "For your own sake, Zech, do not try to find out more than you should know. Someday — *someday* — I will tell you all. That I promise. That will have to be enough — for now."

Desperately, Zech protested: "But Sam knows, and Jonathan!"

"Aye, 'tis sad that they do," his father mumbled unhappily. "I would not want to have to guard you as they must be, and believe me, if you knew all there was to know, as they do, I would need to."

Zech steadied himself against the rough board wall. Sam's constant pretending to be studying — his never being alone — that was all part of hiding the Old Stranger? Was Sam really quite different from his father — from what the other boys thought him to be?

Ham reached out almost timidly, and laid his hand on Zech's shoulder. Zech could feel the weight of his father's burden. It shocked him. "I want to tell you just one thing, Zech," his father said softly, carefully, firmly: "We oft owe debts we know naught of. Sometimes men are entrusted with serving those who dared much . . ." Zech could not believe the pain in his father's eyes, the desperate grip pleading for understanding. Ham inhaled deeply and stared up at the smoke-darkened ceiling as if he hoped for divine guidance. At last he shrugged, as if admitting that he knew that his words were not enough, but he had no others to help him. "I never wanted to know all that I do," he said simply. "But I can not reveal what has been entrusted to me." Quietly, he concluded: "Ask me no more, Son. Forget yesterday afternoon —"

"Pa!" Zech protested, anguished.

They stared at each other a long moment; the sorrow in his father's eyes was as deep as when they'd lost his mother. Zech blinked back tears. His father turned and tied the drapery back from the doorway. Zech watched him scuff away.

Zech realized, watching him, that if, as a lad, his father had stumbled onto the Old Stranger, he would have been relieved to be told to forget the whole affair; beyond moments of recollection, he would not have troubled himself further. But he was not his father. He wanted to know all about the Old Stranger. Who he was — where he came from — why he was in Hadley. Regardless of any admonitions, he knew he could not put the Old Stranger out of his mind.

CHAPTER VI

That night, after the watch had strolled down the common calling his midnight round, when Serv's and Gracie's easy breathing assured Zech that they were safely asleep, he eased himself out of the loft. Biscuit jumped about excitedly in the barnyard. Zech knew that if he tied-up Biscuit and left him, he would bark in protest and rouse everyone. He knew, too, that if he tied him and talked him into being quiet and staying behind, that in record time Biscuit would chew himself free and catch up with him. With misgivings aplenty, he let Biscuit trot along ahead of him. They moved silently down the common in the unfamiliar moonlight. From across the way, a dog barked, announcing their passage, as if duty-bound; knowing Zech and Biscuit, he did not protest so much as inquire. Other dogs relayed their special intelligence along the common with less and less interest; Biscuit made no response. On such an unusual occasion, he did not range far ahead, either.

Zech crossed through Pastor's school-lot pasture toward the woods; no doubt the most interesting activity at the manse took place at the back.

At the corner of the manse barnyard, Nero, Pastor's devilish mastiff, silently hurled himself upon Biscuit. Biscuit screeched the banshee scream that always startled an attacker and gave him a flicker of time in which to gain distance and make good his escape.

Zech, frightened nearly out of his wits, took instant refuge in the nearest tree. He had believed that Nero always was kept chained to the doorpost, or in the house. He hardly had his legs drawn up safely out of reach before the mastiff abandoned his pursuit of Biscuit and charged his haven. Snarling fiercely, Nero leaped so high Zech could have touched him had he wanted to. Zech groaned when Nero settled down at the foot of the tree to prevent his escape. The mastiff made himself comfortable, growling every now and then, grumbling to himself because he had not caught either intruder. He warned Zech that he would not get away as Biscuit had.

Zech waited breathless, expecting at any moment that Pastor, or Sam, or even the Old Stranger, might come out of the darkened house to investigate the dog's warnings. He stared unhappily into the silvery night, and studied the sombre manse, stark even in the soft, still moonlight. He tried to scheme how he could get away ahead of the mastiff, and clung to his perch not sure he could muster the courage and the strength he needed. It would not do for him to be discovered; somehow, he must risk the cur's displeasure and make up a good excuse to explain whatever would happen to him while he tried to get away. He worried, too, that he might be missed at home. Would Biscuit go back and whimper 'til he roused someone?

The hackles on his neck rose when he thought he heard horses. There should be no one abroad in the dead of night! But horses *were* cantering along the Middle Highway! Zech thought first of marauding Mohawks, but no one would hear *them* approaching! And no Englishman would be about at such an hour. Where would riders be coming from along a trail with no civilized settlement beyond?

Nero tore off silently in the direction of the horses. Zech knew that he should make good his escape immediately, but he could not move. His own breathing deafened him. He prayed for strength as dark shapes, distinct in the gleaming moonlight, turned into the manse cartway from the highway trail. The mastiff trotted dutifully beside the men. One was Pastor, but the other was no one Zech ever had seen before, and he was not the Old Stranger, either. He was an old man, though, and very like him, but without the mustache and goatee. Zech assured himself that it was not the same gentleman, newly shaven. He watched, on the point of expiring, as the men dismounted in the dooryard. Pastor took both horses into the barn; his companion, tall and rangy, stalked directly to the house. He talked softly to Nero, who kept tearing away from him to leap up at the tree where Zech roosted. Quietly, the second stranger assured Nero that what disturbed him was a raccoon or possum. Zech breathed a sigh of relief when the stranger took Nero into the house with him.

As soon as the door closed, Zech dropped to the ground and fled.

The next morning, Zech managed to meet with Tom Bedient at the well. Tom's mother had inherited the cottage south of the manse from her brother. She and her two sons had come from Old England only last year. They had a lively interest in all that went on at the manse though, like most Hadleyfolk, they did not visit the Russells as freely as they did other neighbors.

"What errand of mercy takes Pastor from town?" Zech asked Tom as soon as he became engaged at the well.

"Pastor — gone?" Tom asked, amazed.

"You should know better than I, should you not?" Zech challenged carefully.

After a moment's thought, Tom corrected: " 'Tis but — Jonathan — who is gone," he got a good grip on his bucket handle, ready to leave, not being one to idle about and gossip.

"Oh?" Zech prompted, hoping he conveyed a proper degree of doubt.

"Aye. Jon's to enroll at the college, Mum says," Tom defended.

"But he was not going so soon —" Zech protested.

"Aye," Tom agreed. "Something must have come up."

Zech stood silent a moment; then, his heart hardly beating, he said carefully: "The tall one is still at the manse, then, or did he go, too?"

Tom scowled, perplexed. He eyed Zech skeptically. "Tall one?" he repeated, before he reprimanded coldly: "You cannot mean Pastor!"

Hastily, Zech explained: "Oh — oh — no — I meant the one riding with Jonathan yesterday morning. I did not know they were going to the East. Nor did I see who 'twas."

Tom snorted, as if to say Zech had no need to be so curious. "Well, 'twas Mr. Lewis went with Jon," he announced smugly.

"Small Pockets?" Zech echoed, pretending disbelief.

"Aye!"

39

"Is he planning to enroll at Harvard, too?" Zech teased.

Tom looked annoyed. "Of course not!" he snorted, and added unexpectedly: "Perhaps he went along to get Old John another wig!"

Zech cackled appreciatively and let his bucket down into the well. He felt a bit of satisfaction knowing that at least Pastor's nearest neighbors did not know everything that went on at the manse.

Friday, the day Dick Montague fired up his outdoor ovens and baked his neighbors' bread for them, Zech watched for Sam Russell to arrive and claim his family's supply. He expected Sam would be disturbed for a moment when he confronted him; perhaps even resentful. But once that hurdle was past, Zech expected he could approach Sam again. This time, he would not be taking Sam by surprise. Before yesterday, Zech had wondered how anyone could abide being as restricted as Jonathan and Sam were — they were not close to any other boys of their own age. He had thought that they wanted to be scholarly, and acted as they did, not only because their father required them to set an example for the rough and tumble boys about town, but because they were indeed bookish. Since talking with his father, though, he had come to realize how much Sam was hovered over: like Little Peter, never permitted away from home alone except in sight along the common. Zech believed that if he approached Sam, now, and let him know he understood how much the Old Stranger had limited his life, that Sam would be happy to unburden himself and enlighten him a bit, in the bargain. Zech reached Dick Montague's gate just as Sam did. He hurried to open the gate for Sam, loaded down with basketsful of fragrant loaves.

Sam's wintery stare checked his expectations. "Stay away from me!" Sam ordered evenly under his breath, his tone a dire threat. A look of dread in Sam's troubled eyes, a fear that seemed to cause him real pain, disturbed Zech.

Zech hesitated. "I have talked with my father — Sam —" he stammered.

"He told you nothing that wasn't any affair of yours, I'll grant!" Sam retorted coldly.

Zech's gore began to rise. He felt his face flame. He had not expected to be insulted.

"I — I —" he stammered.

"Only attend to your own affairs, lad!" Sam ordered hatefully. "What you know, you learned by accident, not because you could be trusted! As — as you have proved — you can not be!"

Zech's knees began to tremble and sag.

" 'Twill be in your favor if you do as you have been instructed," Sam advised, his lips drawn into a maddening sneer. "Be sure in future that you do not speak of what you have seen to any of your — ignorant — wrestling companions."

Zech clenched the gatepost. His head reeled. He told himself, amazed, that Sam really did not mind being restricted. And Sam was jealous! For the first time, Zech realized that those who knew about the Old Stranger had set great store in Sam and Jonathan; now they had to include him, too. That galled Sam! Now he and Jonathan would not have all *that* honor just to themselves!

Zech stared at Sam. Sam's gaze wavered, and Zech guessed that Sam was aware how much he understood. That pleased him. He stepped back suddenly, and bowed low, mocking Sam, motioning for him to step through the gate. He was astounded by his own behaviour. So was Sam. Sam caught his breath, as if he were about to sob. He tossed his head, and swung a basket of still-warm loaves so abruptly that one loaf flew from under the linen cover and skidded along the grass on the common. Zech grinned with fiendish delight. Sam awkwardly retrieved the errant loaf; hugging it too close, he stamped homeward.

"I hate him! I hate him!" Zech told himself fiercely, gleeful that, though Sam had rejected him, he had not humiliated him as he had intended to do. "I hate him!" Zech repeated bitterly, and turned homeward, too. But even as much as he savored knowing that his discovery exasperated Sam almost beyond endurance, he could not escape admitting to himself that the horrid dread in Sam's eyes came from his knowing that, somehow, everyone who knew about the Old Stranger was in danger; and Sam really cared about the secret guests, too, whoever they were.

CHAPTER VII

Sunday morning at the closely crowded Sabbath service, Pastor's tone of voice wrenched Zech to attention. It was as if Pastor had called him by name. Slowly, emphatically, Pastor recited: *"Thereby some have entertained angels unaware —"* Zech realized Pastor was repeating himself. He stared up at Pastor, unbelieving. Pastor went on, as if issuing a warning: *"Let brotherly love continue. Be not forgetful to entertain strangers: for thereby some have entertained angels unaware. Hebrews thirteen, verses two and three —"*

Zech's glance fell from Pastor to Mr. Tilton, and Old John, and Mr. Goodwin, sitting as stiff as lot markers in their honored, front pews. He realized that his father, beside him, had become as rigid as a post, too. He stole a glance at his father. He was not staring up at Pastor, but straight ahead, his jaw set, his hands gripped so tightly together in his lap that his knuckles shown white. Every muscle in his own body ached, too, now. He glanced at the other men and boys about him; their expressions betrayed their dreaming, or boredom, or distraction; just the way many slumped in the shallow pews showed that they had stopped listening. Here and there a head nodded abruptly and came back to life; some older men looked to be asleep; at the back of the meetinghouse, some oaf shuffled his feet and creaked his bench. Zech leaned slightly forward and stole a glance across the meetinghouse to the women's side where Aunt sat; her head was bent, her face flooded with scarlet, her shoulders drooped. Knowing was a burden!

Well, Zech told himself fiercely, only half-knowing was worse! Why would Pastor want him to believe that he had seen an angel? Sam Russell had not acted as if angels were in any way concerned, nor had Peter Tilton, or his father. Would Jonathan and Small Pockets have ridden off to Boston because of an angel? Would angels need the ministrations of mortals? No one was going to mislead him! He had not promised anyone that he would not find out all that he could. For his father's sake, for everyone's, he would tell no one anything he learned, but for his own information he intended to find out everything he could discover no matter what Pastor preached about angels being about as strangers.

Pastor droned on and Zech began to wonder if some of the other boys about town knew of the Old Strangers and were keeping the secret from their friends as he was doing. He decided to test Dan Crow. If anyone his age besides Sam Russell knew, it would be Dan. Surely his father, Old John, and his grandfather, Squire Goodwin, knew all about the Old Stranger. They spent a great deal of time at the manse and Old John had seen Jonathan off on his mission last week. Dan did not go to the manse at all that he *knew* of, but he might know a deal of what went on there.

"What do you suppose an angel looks like?" Zech asked Dan at the nooning, and managed to walk him out of earshot of their neighbors scattered about the common, eating their lunches in the sun, enjoying the crisp, sunny air that soon would not be so comfortable; clouds were beginning to scud in from the west.

Dan recalled Pastor's mentioning angels. He liked Zech's addressing him as a font of knowledge. With an important air, he informed Zech: "My father has told us that back in Old England many parish churches had windows of colored glass that showed scripture in the likeness of people. 'Twas for the benefit of those who could not read, you know. If you can read, you do not need such —"

Joe Field recorded remarkable likenesses of animals and birds on his slate sometimes, but the master always advised him curtly that he would be better off to spend his time on his conjugations. Other than Joe's interesting likenesses, and sketches made by absent-minded adults while listening to a speaker drone along, neither lad ever had seen a picture.

"Did the windows show angels?" Zech asked, truly impressed.

"Oh, aye, I suppose," Dan tried not to sound doubtful. "Papa said that in one, 'Peter by the Sea of Galilee,' the fishing boats were like those on the Thames, and Peter looked like an uncle of his."

"Then the people, then, looked like us, too?" Zech asked, awed. "Would angels look like us, too?"

Dan frowned. "They would have to look like us, would they not, if we could not tell who is an angel and who is not?"

"Well —" Zech conceded lamely, "I would think an angel would be something more — I would think an angel who might appear amongst us would be taller than Pastor —" and he found himself describing the Old Stranger. He wondered that Dan did not hear his heart pounding as he talked. Nothing he said roused any response, though, or even much interest. Dan could not claim to be knowledgeable about angels, so he wanted to change the subject. Plainly he knew nothing of the Old Stranger. To be sure, Zech explored one more point: "Pastor would entertain such a one at the manse, Dan. Do you suppose he ever has entertained strangers? Should he? You know that none of the others of us ever has strangers in our midst."

"Anyone who comes to town comes because he knows someone here," Dan advised wearily. "All visitors go to the manse to call, you know. All except hired help, I mean. There might be angels about, Zech, but there are no strangers."

"Aye," Zech murmured, feeling weak from his effort. "Strangers are in rather short supply." He was not certain whether he was relieved or disappointed that Dan did not know anything about the strangers at the manse, either.

Rain began to fall as the afternoon session began. It increased steadily to a punishing downpour. At the close of meeting, Hatfield's families stopped off with friends and relatives to wait for the showers to let up, but rain that begins after noon seldom abates for long; before dusk shrouded the countryside, the last Hatfield family plodded homeward, sodden and complaining, protesting their ill fortune in not having a meetinghouse of their own. Each stormy Sabbath more and more folks agreed that Hatfield should have that comfort. Crossing the river in foul weather tested anyone's faith to the utmost; only the hand of Providence had stayed disaster; besides, Hatfieldfolk pointed out, no one should travel on the Sabbath. For them 'twas surely no day of rest.

Ham had planned to leave on his fall trading expedition to Hartford early Monday morning, but when Zech woke in the night and heard the rain's drumming on the roof, he knew they would not be leaving for at least another day. The rain let up after noon, but clouds hung low, hiding the mountaintops, a sign the rain would continue. Tuesday afternoon, little wispy clouds that hung alongside the hills began to lift and blow away. This rainy spell was past: on the morrow they could go to Hartford.

As dawn lightened the sky, Ham and Zech made their way down the common to Ike Dickinson's trading room, a lean-to on the back of his brother Tom's dwelling. The ground squnched moistly beneath their moccasins. The dampness was chilling, but the sun would warm everything up shortly; the world soon would be dried out. It would be a beautiful day.

Ham had to plan his trips according to the crops and the weather, and nature's ways, too. In the spring, he had to start out as soon as the swollen river subsided within its banks, when danger from cruising ice floes had passed, and before the fish runs began. In the first few weeks of the fish runs, transporting was out of the question. In early May, salmon and shad and eel began to all but clog New England's rivers. In dark and silvery waves of teeming life they crowded upstream to spawn. Above them crane, geese, heron, and teal hung in great drifts, seeking prized specimens, honking and screaming warnings and triumphs at each other, and indignantly protesting the settlers' sharing in their bounty.

Within a day or two of the beginning of the overwhelming fish migrations, Valley men and boys set out with ox carts and basketed horses to harvest fish. Barelegged, they flung themselves at the surging tide; soon soaked to the skin, they worked furiously, attacking their wriggling, gasping prey with pitchforks and hoes and shortened pikes. They intended to cast ashore only those females that ran to six pounds or more. At home, they culled accidentally gathered light-weights and humped-back, pithy-skinned males, good only for fertilizer, and cast them aside. The tasty females and their roe they salted, and smoked, and pickled for winter use; the entrails they threw to the pigs. Depending on the weather and the demand of their home chores, every householder soon acquired all the fish wanted or needed to be preserved until the runs began again.

So many silvery scales shimmered along the cart tracks in the spring that householders referred to The Broad Street below the meetinghouse as Silver Street South, and above the meetinghouse as Silver Street North. Valley families would take the name Silver Street with them when they moved out into the hills. In future generations, the name Silver Street would fall to the rutted cartways that wound among hardscrabble farms in the new villages. There the glittery fish scales betrayed the luckless landowners whose rocky acres could not provide for their families between the season of hay and grass. Hard-luck farmers had to take time from important spring chores to repair to the rivers for their food supply or their families would go hungry. The better-situated neighbors liked to claim piously that farmers who left home to go fishing in the spring would rather fish than farm, anyway.

In the fall, trading trips had to be scheduled between harvest time and sudden cold that could glaze the river shut.

Ike was in the barnyard fastening a blanket about Rosie, his brother's mare. "There's not so much but she can handle things this time," Ike explained. He stroked Rosie's thick-set neck. In the fall, when the carting was considerable, Ike engaged Will Markham's enormous shire, Naseby, to transport Hadley's goods to the beaching place below the thunderous falls, five miles down the Valley. With the falls so high, and the current above and below them treacherous, journeys down-river began a safe distance below the falls to save portaging.

Ham and Zech followed Ike the few steps to his trading room, pained as always by the sight of Ike's effort to get about. His left leg had been withered by a fever that had struck him as a lad of ten. It had stopped growing then. Most of those stricken that summer had not survived. It was because he could get around less than others that Ike had been granted the opportunity to do Hadley's trading, just as Ham had been sent on the transporting expeditions because he did not have much land to tend to, or a necessary trade to take his time. Until Hadley began to prosper, Ensign Wilton had taken care of Hadley's trading needs, but times had changed. Now trading made both Ike and Ham good livings.

Ike leaned his crutch beside the doorway; with his right hand he motioned toward the inside darkness. He breathed deeply a few times, to catch his breath following his latest exertion. "There's six sacks of peas and beans there, going for Ben Wait," he explained.

Ham nodded: a surplus of the wages paid to Ben by neighbors for his being the best carpenter in the Valley.

"He wants the usual," Ike explained, still short of breath. "I've got it all down on my list. Nails — and flints — and a lute string, again."

Ham nodded, again. He pointed toward a leather bucket in the doorway, full of round, hard cheeses. "Mary Goodman's?" he asked.

"Aye — they're marked," Ike answered. "The list is in there on the table, Zech. Fetch it for your father."

Zech studied the list inscribed on a piece of white-birch under-bark. In addition to the wares Ike had mentioned, he had listed in his careful hand: molasses, calico, duffel cloth, papers, pins, and rum. The rum would be paid for, in part, by Mary Goodman's cheeses, but none of the other goods would be for her. Her husband, Deacon Dick, was niggardly. One reason he had been licensed as keeper of the ordinary was because he doled out rum as sparingly as he shared anything at all; the too-thrifty way in which he provided for his family caused much grumbling among the womenfolk. Beyond Mary's buckets of cheese lay a pile of flax skeins. With this year's yield coming in heavy, several women must have decided to market what they had left of last year's crop, skeins not yet bleached and prepared for weaving. They would be the ones ordering the cloth, and pins, and needles for what they had ready to work-up. Ham studied the list a minute before he tucked it into the top of one of Ben's sacks of dried beans, then he and Zech tied the bags of goods in pairs and hung them across Rosie's back, one bag dangling down each side. "Got any letters?" he asked, ready to go.

"Oh — aye. Zech — they are on the table, too. That packet. Two for Windsor, the others for Hartford."

Ham examined the names on the folded and sealed pieces of paper before he put them in a deerskin pouch hanging at his side. He already had four, given to him at meeting.

"Hope you'll find new stock in," Ike commented.

"Well, like I told you, they were expecting a deal of pewter and some hourglasses, last time," Ham reminded.

"There'd be takers for those," Ike allowed, and asked, "Do you think I should send Naseby down to meet you?"

"With the rum, I'd say you should," Ham answered. "Someone coming down for Rosie, or do you want me to stake her out 'til Will brings Naseby down?"

"I 'spect Az will be down for her shortly, this morning," Ike sighed, resigned. "All he needs is an excuse, you know —"

Ham nodded, again, and decided: "Well, then, guess we are ready to be off." He shook Rosie's loosely tied reins free of the hitching post ring, raised his left hand in farewell to Ike, and led the mare out of the yard.

Ham halted while Zech closed the gate. He grinned at Zech as he turned to join him — a ritual look, a quick glance of kinship, father-to-son and son-to-father, a gesture never acknowledged but never omitted; a pact renewed at the beginning of each trip, avowing their special relationship and their pleasure in each other's company and their undertaking. Obsessed by the Old Stranger, Zech could not keep his reproach from his gaze. His father's brows rose slightly, as if asking Zech why he must continue resentful. Anxiety darkened the first light of pleasure. Ham sighed as he turned away.

Zech closed the gate and ran to catch up with his father and Rosie. The thrill of excitement he felt starting out on the expedition was just as keen for a moment as when he had started out for the first time. He breathed deeply, savoring his pleasure and satisfaction. They had not needed to have a horse meet them upon their return when he first went with his father. Now, with debts paid off, and more fields cleared and ploughed, and orchards bearing well, their neighbors produced a surplus beyond what they needed for payments among themselves and for taxes; they wanted all sorts of truck they had not been able to afford before; more than could be lugged in back packs from the beaching place. Poking about Hartford's trading post and wharves for new goods was a fascinating bit of business, and today he had another reason for being anxious to get to Hartford.

CHAPTER VIII

Zech caught his father's groan before he saw Will Webster waiting by his slab hut. Ike probably had refused to accept whatever Will had in the bulging sack leaning against his gate.

"Hamblin!" Will called quite grandly. "I thought you would be happy to trade these off for me down the river."

Ham strained to be polite. "What you got?"

"Chestnuts — Ahhh! De - li - ci - ous chest - nuts!"

Ham sighed. Chestnuts were in great supply throughout New England's forests and Will's would be last year's. In the spring when chestnut trees blossomed out, some mountainsides looked as if piled-up with snow. It was a breathtaking sight. In good seasons — and this year the whole Valley would be well-supplied — every family would gather all that could be used with little effort. Chestnuts were a pleasure in so many ways; few aromas matched that of roasting chestnuts, but there was no reason to transport such an ungainly load to Hartford, except that Will had nothing else to offer. There would be takers only if a foreign ship was in port and a supply not laid in. "What you expecting in return?" Ham asked, his tone full of doubt.

Will blinked the sleep from his eyes and tried to look alert, as if he had not made a special effort to intercept Ham at such an un-earthly hour.

"Perhaps some new books have arrived," he replied a bit loftily. "Mr Stone could advise you."

"Books!" Ham reproved. He glared at the bulky sack. "You know they don't bring much —" he reminded tartly.

Ben Wait, who played the minstrel, in one of the ditties he tossed off, had dubbed Will "Unwillin'," and the name had stuck. Will, huddled in an impressive coat he had donned for Ham's sake, blinked in the early morning light and looked more unable than unwilling, not at all like an heir of Squire Webster who had been Governor of Connecticut Colony and a Commissioner of the United Colonies. Governor Webster had left his two youngest sons a thriving farm blessed with thrifty gardens, orchards and cattle, and a well of its own. But Will and Tom, not as inclined to work as to read, were not able to farm, dependent upon rude, indentured youths — troublesome street waifs sent over from Old England. Tom sold his inheritance to John Taylor who had come to town indentured, and married the daughter of a prospering Northampton Welshman who put him to what use he could. For a time, Will tried to contend with Hadley's disinterested schoolboys, until dismayed by the pranks of some, he too sold his patrimony to John Taylor and moved in with his sister, Ann Markham. Quite unexpectedly, he married her snappish hired girl, a Springfield spinster who shared his love of reading. When her elevated station made Will's wife too disruptive a burden for the Markhams to bear, the selectmen, unable to devise an occupation given mainly to reading and discourse, put Will and his wife in charge of the pound, tending stray cattle for their keep. They had little to do except when Az Dickinson or Jonathan Marsh let out neighborhood beasts just to make mischief.

Ham swung Will's sackful of chestnuts up onto Rosie's load. "We will take them this time," he grumbled. "If you could salt-down a barrel of shad, or pickle some eels — there's plenty of market for them, you know," he counseled.

Will looked offended. He never could understand how a simple yeoman like Ham Gillette could feel free to make suggestions to one of his station: after all, Ham's parents had been indentured servants; it was *his* father who had been Governor of Connecticut and Commissioner of the United Colonies! *He* was the one who had been the schoolmaster.

Before Ham and Zech reached the edge of the bluff above the beaching place, they could feel the steady beat of galloping behind them. For a moment, recalling the horses a few nights before, Zech felt a cold chill slide down his spine. But this time he knew who was coming: Az Dickinson. No one rode the way Az did. His recklessness irritated all the older men. Old Nathaniel, his father, a horse fancier of considerable reputation in the Midlands back in Old England, had had the first blooded stallion brought to Hadley. Zech had been young then, but he could recall plainly the wild way Az rode that powerful creature. Az's older brothers and the neighbors all protested, but to no avail. In Old Nathaniel's eyes his youngest son could do no wrong; and they both loved horses with the same pleasure in their speed and power. Now Az had a black Barb that his father had had sent over from Bristol. The indulgence alone exasperated Nathaniel's eight other sons, and vexed others, too. Old Nathaniel claimed that he had nothing but improvement of the Valley's stock in mind, but many questioned the qualities for which Az seemed to be breeding. Valley men did not require speed from their mounts so much as endurance. For the most part, an ox served their purpose better than colts and fillies such as Az doted over. But he was earning a reputation for breeding fine riding horses. He had bred Peter Tilton's, and Pastor's, and Captain Pynchon had bought one of his high-stepping bays; and leading men in Hartford and New Haven had put in requests for future deliveries.

Zech stopped to watch Az sweep toward them. His lank hair streaming back from his lean, taut face, Az seemed one with the horse as they bore down on him.

"Judged it just right!" Az bragged, yelling above the roar of the falls: "I bet myself that if I let you have an hour's start, I would catch you before you reached the river!" He pulled Midnight up onto his hind legs and turned him aside. He rode off slowly, cooling him down while Ham and Zech carried their lading down the steep riverbank to the beach, well below the swirling eddies churned up by the plunging water. Any other able-bodied man or boy would have pitched in to help, and would have lent a hand uncovering the long cargo canoe, too. Another pair of hands would have made turning over the ungainly canoe a deal easier; and Zech and Ham could have used another strong back shoving it across the sand to the water's edge, but Az disdained such assistance. He did not care at all what anyone else thought. He seemed to like to fret folks. While Ham tucked the tarpaulin about the goods stowed in the middle of the canoe, Zech scrambled back up the bank to look for Az. He tied an extra knot in Rosie's reins. He had tied them loosely to a young sapling when they arrived. He had expected, then, that Az would start back immediately, but Az had disappeared from sight and sound. He might have gone on down to Springfield. No telling what Az might do. Rosie would be safe

51

enough if they just left her where she was until they got back Wednesday afternoon. That was the way his father used to do when he and Warr had first made trading trips.

Wild geese hovered noisily above favored feeding spots near the river, preparing for the day's long flight southward; they continued their strident discussion as they found their places in long, graceful formation and disappeared over the horizon. Glancing up at the geese, Ham remarked that he was grateful the good Lord had spared the Valley an invasion of passenger pigeons of late. Great hordes of those senseless creatures sounded like the roar of the November fires when the wind came up unexpectedly; sometimes they cut off the sunlight for hours, darkening the earth as they streaked along. They left the countryside as desolate as fire wherever they stopped to feed.

Beyond the divide, after they passed a just-rousing Chicopee campsite, they met a Nipmuck brave paddling a Springfield canoe. Ham muttered his dissatisfaction regarding Indians from afar who had begun to gather a campsite together on the high bluff across from Great Meadow. Their presence made Warr uneasy, too. Ham fell silent, and Zech watched the sun steal away the mist, the only sound, the lapping of water at their bow and their dipping paddles; here and there a fish leaped through the air, and unexpectedly, off in the distance, a bull moose trumpeted.

Captain Pynchon had visited Hadley last week and had carried messages back to Springfield for those who had any to send, so they had no need to stop there. Within hailing distance of Windsor's wharf, a family turning their retting hemp saved Zech's needing to run up to the palisadoed village on top of the hill with messages from Peter Tilton. To get the family's attention, Zech let out a piercing Indian war whoop. He chuckled at the startled response. They must have thought he was a rum-soaked Mohawk on the warpath!

The relieved gardeners waved in greeting and one of the larger lads loped toward the wharf when Ham motioned for him. It was Gregory Gibbs. He waded into the water, saving them the trouble of beaching.

"You be sure you do not lay that message down and forget it!" Ham admonished. Panting and grinning, Gregory promised. "Pa is with us —" he explained. Zech recognized the glint of awe, tinged with envy, in Gregory's glance as he grinned in his direction.

Every lad along the river would like to be in his place. Every trip made him more appreciative of his special privileges.

Zech caught his breath as they swept around the last riverbend above Hartford. Sight of the stockaded village on Assylum Hill and the weathered buildings spilling down to the wharves always excited him. Two foreign ships rode at anchor near the middle of the river. "Guess we'll be able to get shut of Will's chestnuts, Pa," Zech reminded.

Two coastwise sloops tied up at the wharf flew the Massachusetts Bay Colony's pennant. Zech always experienced awe and fear as the long canoe, so insignificant compared to the larger vessels, ground up onto the beach. Local men hailed Ham, and strangers from far countries leaned on the rails of their ships and talked to each other about the arrivals from up-river. One yelled at them, but neither Ham nor Zech paid him any mind, and the sailor's friends laughed. More than likely the comment was about their checked shirts. Nobody anywhere but in the Upper Valley ever had checked cloth like Joe Kellogg turned out. Joe said weaving checks made his work more interesting. Checks certainly created plenty of talk. Their shirts were years old, and had been washed often, and the dyes had run quite a lot, but the checks still were well-defined. Zech did not like to wear Joe's cloth to Hartford, but until Aunt loomed yardage enough, and had time to make him a new shirt, he had no choice.

When Zech finished helping his father tote their lading to the river-front trading post, he hurried up the hill to the village tavern on the far side of the rutted common. On his last trip, he had become acquainted with Jack, the stable boy, an orphan sent to the colonies at the expense of a London congregation. Jack would know everyone who came through Hartford publicly.

Zech helped Jack rub down a traveler's horse. As he worked, he prompted: "You are in a right spot to see all the important people who come to town, are you not?" He spoke as if full of awe, as if envious of Jack's advantage, being from so large a village.

Jack had grown up in London's tangled streets. To him Hartford was so small and isolated he could not believe it was real. At first, New England's wilderness — wildcats screaming in the night; in the day, bear and wolves crossing distant meadows — had frightened him nearly out of his skin. He still would not dare venture out of the village alone. But Zech spoke as if this little port, so far up the quiet, forest-enclosed river, compared to Southampton, the busy city from which he had been shipped. "Governor Winthrop comes in often with his visitors," Jack told Zech with a glow of pride. "They are all important men — come here — of course."

"Of course," Zech agreed wistfully. He added: "Men like your guests send messages up the river to us. They do not come in person. Passage would be too difficult — not that they could not manage — but — well —"

Jack looked at Zech, his expression one of compassion that Zech should be deprived of such pleasure as watching the important men of the colonies coming and going, or taking care of their horses.

"Who comes through — *actually* —" Zech asked, pretending awe, and Jack, his spirits beginning to soar, went into detail about everyone he had seen, many of whom he had not properly appreciated before.

"I have heard that an important visitor from London arrived — this summer —" Zech tried to be offhand. He must not make the Londoner so memorable Jack would inquire of others about him.

"To stay?" Jack inquired doubtfully, but eager to be of help.

"I do not know — really —" Zech could be honest about that. "A relative of some, I think. I just heard the elders talking — that's all —"

"Well — " Jack thought a moment. "New families have come. But not many, any more, now, you know. But I know no one — important — from London — or of any of England — of late."

"I think you would remember him if he came, from all I have heard," Zech explained. He was quite composed, at ease with his ruse, now. "I believe he is one you would recall. Men in Hadley speak of him —" and he described the Old Stranger in detail.

Jack shook his head. "No one like that has been in Hartford, I am sure." He added, proudly: "Like you say, I see 'em all, here." Suddenly he did not mind the quiet to which he had thought he never would become accustomed. He had thought of going aboard ship when his indenture was over, but now he realized he had not been hungry or ill-clothed since he landed, though in winter he did mind the cold. Given the choice between the uncertainties of the hurly-burly life he had known beyond the valley, and staying on, he thought now he probably would cast in his lot with New England.

Certain that the Old Stranger had not come through Hartford, Zech took his leave of the stuffy, dusty stable. Jack, well-primed now, would remember the Old Stranger and tell him if he ever saw him. Keen to get back to the excitement along the river, Zech jumped in one triumphant leap from the stable's threshold ramp almost to the end of the barn. A figure slumped there moved suddenly and collided with him as he landed. Zech lost his balance, and pitched headlong down the hill.

He grabbed as he fell, and tried to protect himself, to throw himself sideways and break his fall. But the man he had fallen against carried him to the ground: they rolled over and over, and Zech, suddenly panic-stricken, tried to shake himself free. At the same time they stopped rolling, strong hands grasped his shoulders from behind, and held him securely as they yanked him to his feet. A woman and small boy passing by with a tethered calf stopped; she stared concerned. She looked ready to call for help for Zech, as if she believed he needed assistance from an attacking bully.

"He's all right! He is not hurt. He's my boy! I have him." The man's voice dismissed her brusquely.

The strength in Zech's knees melted like butter on a warm griddle: Dr. Westcarr!

For an instant Zech sagged, completely helpless. The woman and child tugged the calf along and Dr. Westcarr's huge left hand slid quickly, roughly, expertly over Zech's mouth. The elbow of the doctor's sinewy right arm tightened against Zech's throat. He dragged Zech downward to the back of the barn. Zech, half strangled, felt as if he were going to lose consciousness altogether. In the solitude far below where he had been talking with Jack but an instant before, Dr. Westcarr jerked his head back. "Where did you see that stranger in Hadley?" he growled. He slipped his hand from Zech's mouth to his left ear. He gave it a sharp tug at the same time he wrenched Zech's right arm behind him, until Zech felt it would be pulled from his shoulder.

"Where did you see that stranger?" Dr. Westcarr repeated.

"Stranger?" Zech repeated in a whisper, hardly able to breathe. The doctor's piercing torture sapped all his strength. He tried to ease himself into a position that would save his shoulders or elbow from cracking, his ear from bursting asunder. He knew there was little chance anyone in the barn would hear them, or if they did, would investigate. No one bothered with every tussle in a seafaring town.

Zech's strength began to ebb. The doctor jerked his head further backward and bent close above him. His unblinking eyes narrowed. "That stranger you talked of to Joe Kellog — at the ferry —" he reminded with an excruciating tug at Zech's ear.

"O — *then* —" Zech gasped. "— Leave off — " he begged, panting. The Doctor eased his grip just enough to allow Zech to speak. He warned: "Don't yell or I'll stick your head so far into that manure pile you never will see Hadley, again!"

"— 'Twas only — Old John — Old John Crow," Zech panted, "— in his — new broadcloth — and — new — wig —" He prayed that the Doctor had not lurked so close to him at the stable that he had overheard his conversation with Jack.

Dr. Westcarr hesitated.

" 'Twas only — Old — John —" Zech repeated weakly.

"Come clean, or I will break every bone in your body before burying you —"

Words of a strange language — angry words — a command — interrupted Dr. Westcarr. Zech found himself sprawled on the manure pile. An enraged, burly seaman from one of the vessels riding at anchor in the river had shaken him free of Dr. Westcarr's grip. The sailor was shaking Dr. Westcarr as if he were a bundle of old rags.

Dr. Westcarr wrenched himself free of his attacker. The two men snarled at each other — guttural sounds like mad dogs — before the brawny foreigner lunged for Dr. Westcarr's collar, again. Dr. Westcarr tried to dodge. He slipped; he fell trying to bargain. The seaman pulled Dr. Westcarr to his feet, and at the same time deftly yanked a moneybag from his waistcoat. He threw Dr. Westcarr away, then; a mighty heave that landed the outraged doctor on his hands and knees, one arm up to his elbow in manure. He tried to scramble away; he looked like a giant spider, slipping and sliding, all arms and legs. The seaman aimed a swift kick that shoved his victim to his feet and sent him tottering toward the end of the barn. Dr. Westcarr stopped there, and turned back, poised for further flight if pursued; he shook his fist at Zech: "I shall get you, yet!" he snarled before he disappeared.

Zech's rescuer watched the corner of the barn expectantly a moment before he turned to Zech. He reached down a calloused, burl-like hand; the middle finger was missing above the first joint. He pulled Zech to his feet, then shook his fist after the departed doctor, muttering an explanation that he knew Zech could not understand. He grinned and shrugged, and looked at his hands; he made a face, pretending to be exasperated by the manure Zech's hands had smeared on him. He wiped his hands thoroughly on his neatly patched pantaloons before he opened the bag of coins he had taken from Dr. Westcarr. He spilled a collection of gold and silver pieces into his leathery palm. Zech gasped at the sight of so much money. The seaman winked at him. Zech feared for a trice that he might start to cry or burst into wild laughter. He looked helplessly at his stalwart deliverer, his lips clenched between his teeth, and drew a deep, unsteady breath.

The man's grin broadened. He studied Zech's besmeared appearance and shook his head, teasing him, pretending that all was lost with Zech in such wretched condition. Zech tried to stammer his thanks. The sailor waved his hand, dismissing any debt. He motioned toward the brook, suggesting Zech go down and clean himself off. With a companionable clap that rocked Zech, he started him on his way.

Zech limped to the brook and tried to make himself presentable. He did not want his father to suspect the danger he had been in. He kept telling himself that Dr. Westcarr might have believed what he had called-out about Old John. He thought that surely Providence had provided a deliverer as well as the inspired vision of Old John in his wig at the moment of attack.

Zech found his father talking with friends he could hardly discern in the dingy and pungent warehouse. He stood in the cooling draft of the open door and blinked toward the men lounging about on bales, and barrels and hogsheads of goods recently arrived from The Bay, and Virginia, and Barbados and farther overseas. His father's mouth dropped and he stared at Zech, unbelieving, when he realized who Zech was.

Zech thought that he had made his appearance quite presentable. "I was rasslin'!" he protested, when he realized he had failed. In his anger and bewilderment, he almost burst into tears. His father's friends took their pipes from their mouths. A few exchanged covert glances amongst themselves, but no one said a word. Most of the astonished men looked, though, as if they did not believe what he said. They knew him well; they knew that he could take care of himself, that he very plainly had suffered indignities that went beyond having his shoulders pinned to the ground.

Ham's expression sharpened from disbelief to alarm as he stared. He struggled to show no emotion at all. He peered closely at Zech, but Zech pretended not to be aware of what he knew frightened his father. He hung his head as if completely abashed by his defeat; he scuffed his toe in the dust and said no more.

His father did not press for an explanation, though Zech knew from his thoughtful expression the rest of their trip that his father did not believe his excuse and would not put the incident out of his mind, either.

CHAPTER IX

Hadley youngsters always watched eagerly for Ham's return. About mid-afternoon of the second day after his departure they began to walk out of town along the trail to the beaching place to meet him. As soon as Ham's expected parade hove into sight, a few self-appointed town criers raced back to the common and ran about announcing his approach. Those for whom Ham had done some particular errand arrived at Ike's about the same time Ham did; others joined them out of curiosity: to see what Ham brought back, and to learn the latest news of the world. More than a dozen townsmen waited at Ike's by the time Ham and Zech reached the common.

"We have news for *you,* this time!" Ed Grannis, the town's busy newsmonger, announced grandly before Ham reached the gate. He winked at John Markham, resting on the chopping block just inside the fence.

Ham looked from one teasing face to the other. Sometimes the men waited, sobered by some tragic Act of God, but the children already had regaled him with word of the arrival of *important* visitors from the East. He pretended ignorance. "Deacon Dick's cider blow up, did it?" he countered, his expression purposefully blank.

The men laughed, delighted, and Sam Church volunteered: "Small Pockets is back already, and brought Governor Leverett with 'im!"

"And Dan Fisher! Don't forget Dan!"

"And a lady —"

59

That last, of course, was cause for excitement; even more so than the unexpected visit by the governor. Ham only answered "Oh?" His flat tone surprised Zech. He snatched a quick, guarded look at his father. Why was he not much interested? Did he know more than the other men about this sudden arrival?

"Is Dan married, now?" Ham asked suddenly, as if he realized he should make some response.

"If there'd been bans published of Dan's bein' married, we would have heard," John Markham muttered. He always chewed a willow twig to keep his head from aching, so his words often ran together and his meaning had to be guessed at; no one could miss the worried sound of his voice, though. He would like to spare Mary Tilton the pain and embarrassment she would suffer if her long-time suitor appeared suddenly at her door, wed to someone else.

"We do not know who *she* is," Ed complained. "They got to Peter's 'fore most of us knew they was about."

Ham looked at Ike and shook his head, pretending he felt sorry indeed for the way their neighbors had been outsmarted. But he was not in the same mood as the other men.

Zech guessed that his father knew more than they about what was afoot. He scanned the concerned expressions about him. Not one of these innocent stay-at-homes knew about the Old Strangers! Little did any of them suspect how Dr. Westcarr had attacked him yesterday because of what *he* knew —

Ham passed out the goods he had brought on request, before he reached inside his blouse and withdrew a small white kidskin sack. He passed the package to Ike. For a moment Ike looked puzzled, then his lean face broke into a wide grin. "Finally come, did they?" he asked. A smile began to play around his lips.

Instantly, Zech forgot the burden of the Old Stranger.

Fascinated, the men all moved close to Ike. He fumbled with the bag, his big, clumsy fingers not accustomed to delicate, silken drawstrings. Carefully, he extracted a small, highly polished box; he weighed it thoughtfully in his hand, teasing those around him before he cautiously lifted the top of the box.

"Gold buttons!" Ed Grannis gasped.

"Eight of them!" Nehemiah Dickinson breathed, shocked.

Eight round, gold buttons, each the size of a large kernel of corn, and just as bright, lay jumbled together on a tiny silken pillow inside the box. Grandpa Phillips reached a twig-like finger forward and moved the buttons about. Finally, Ike looked at Frank Barnard and asked: "You want to deliver these, Frank?"

Frank gasped, surprised. His tongue clicking, he reached out a huge whitened hand. At this time of year, with barley ripe and brewing recommencing, lack of grime on his hands was the badge of his profession as village maltster: he and his family exuded the pungent aromas of brewing beer and ale all year round. "Hannah's?" Frank finally asked, pleased, already knowing the answer.

"Who else?" Ike replied with an amused snort.

Frank's daughter, Hannah, wife of Dr. Westcarr, could afford luxuries as well as any lady in Boston or New Haven. Frank moved the box about, catching the light. "We're a way, yet, from bein' a city — but there's no sayin' we're not civilized —" he began. A cloud of smoke rose from the pipes of the men hanging transfixed above his treasure. Everyone had known the turn Frank's comments would take. He talked about civilization the way other men talk of the weather, or their crops, or ill-luck, or of God in their lives. He did not just encourage Hannah Westcarr to teach the dame school at his house so that Hadley's girls and small boys could learn to read and write and cypher: he kept slates and slate pencils on hand so that none need feel discouraged from want of supplies; he had been known to persuade some parents to spare their young ones from chores by giving them such advantage in trade that he put them in his favor. He had even argued, when a schoolmaster had not been available, that Hannah should be allowed to do the honors for the older boys until a master could come. The elders thought Hannah's classes good for the village — and for Hannah, too, burdened as she was with such an unfortunate marriage, and with no young ones of her own — but Frank had no one so much in his favor that anyone agreed with him regarding a female schoolmaster.

John Markham backed away from the circle of button admirers. He stared icily at Ike, the willow twig standing straight out from between his clenched teeth. "I can see where you are going to have requests for more such choice merchandise —" he admonished, speaking quite distinctly.

Ike shrugged. "We will get what we can, of what folks require."

"They are going to be a cause of much covetousness —" John warned.

"What worldly goods have you great travelers brought, now, the crown jewels?" Ben Wait asked as he burst into the yard, his approach unnoticed.

"Not quite," Barnabas Hinsdale answered, impressed by Ben's guess. Frank held out the buttons for Ben to admire.

Ben whistled. "I was only partly right, this time!" he chuckled. "And I don't have to ask whose they are!" He swung his ever-present lute around in front of him, and began to sing:

"You promised me gold, and you promised me fee,
    In the Neather-lands —
Your eldest daughter my wife she must be,
    In the Neather-lands —
And your eldest daughter, my wife she shall be —"

He broke off, humming to himself. Everyone expected Ben to go beyond a familiar ballad with jingles appropriate to the occasion. He could not get away from the minstrel in him that in generations past had earned his family the name Wait. Waits, professional musicians and rhymesters in Old England, led processions and at smaller entertainments versified rhymes of their own making, sometimes for a half-hour without pause.

Ben looked from the buttons to Ike. "Beautiful! Beautiful!" he exclaimed, truly impressed. He looked up at Ike, and ordered: "Git me a set, for Martha — next trip!"

The men all stared at him, taken aback, before the younger men burst into laughter and shook their heads. Will Markham stumped out of the yard. He had not stayed within speaking distance of Ben in the five years since Ben had composed verses making light of Liza Hawkes, Will's heedless young sister. Liza, a young widow with crow's-wing black hair, and mulberry eyes and a complexion all women envied, lacked judgment of any kind. When her frivolous ways escaped chastisement that had been dealt a bound girl, Ben took matters into his own hands. He had been keeping bad company at the time, but no one doubted the idea was his own. He not only put a telling rhyme about Liza on paper, he sailed the offending missive into her dooryard. Will Markham took Ben and his rhymes to law. The court ordered five stripes well-laid upon his naked body and £4 cost of court. Only Ben's much-needed skill as a carpenter had saved him from being drummed out of town along with riffraff involved in the matter, rowdy moss troopers taken prisoner during England's Civil War: homeless, able-bodied derelicts sent to the colonies because England's jails had room for no more. But Ben had settled down, now.

"So long, Willy-boy! See you a-round!" Ben called impudently after his offended neighbor. His companions sighed and looked pained. They wished that Ben would behave.

Ben turned back to the buttons. "I'm not funning," he promised, looking about, challenging the others. "I will get Martha gold buttons if she wants 'em, and there's not a Man Jack in the colony is going to tell me nay!"

The other men's silence admitted that they knew he could afford gold buttons; he did not realize, though, that his intention caused little anxiety; Ben was going to incite no one's jealousy: Martha was not one to fancy gold buttons.

Frank closed the box carefully, returned it to the kidskin bag, and dropped the bag inside his worn blouse. He gathered up the sundries Ham had brought for his family. "Hannah'll be pleased you got these for her," he assured Ham, and hurried out of the yard.

Tom Welles could hardly wait until Frank stepped out of earshot before he remarked: "Hannah'd have to get them for herself. John may pay for 'em, but he wouldn't give 'em to her —"

"You get my lute string, Ham?" Ben interrupted. He always turned aside the futile litany men recited regarding Dr. Westcarr. Dr. Westcarr had misled Ben at the troubled time that had shadowed his life, and Ben had his own way of dealing with such evildoers: not idle talk that lost interest with repetition, but rhymes that ridiculed, lines that men remembered and repeated with relish.

Ham nodded that he had gotten the lute string. While he rummaged through a bundle of goods in search of it, Ben strummed on his lute, his chords lighthearted and melodious; a missing string never totally disadvantaged him. After a moment's thought he had a verse ready for his waiting audience:

"What gold is that on your bodice, lass?
What gold is that, pray tell?
Now, do you buy but for notice, Ma'am,
Be - cause life goes not so well?
Your husband is rich — and a blackguard, Ma'am,
And we *all* know what you won't tell!
But buttons o' gold won't change any o' that
Though 'twill drive other maids' lovers to — debt."

Again, his companions shook their heads and grinned, admiring his skillful teasing.

"You getting Mary buttons like Hannah's?" Ben suddenly asked Ike's brother, Nehemiah. He added, bitterly, unexpectedly: "They won't be so fine as what her sister's got already, you may be sure. No matter what you get her! Esther will always beat everyone out — you can be sure of that!"

For a moment Ben's companions stared in disbelief, caught unprepared. Never before had Ben spoken to anyone of Esther Cowles, Mary Dickinson's sister to whom he had once been betrothed.

Esther was a saucy minx and everyone had agreed, a likely match for Ben's jocular, vexing ways. Ben, a carpenter trained by a master in Dedham, had come to town recommended by Squire Leverett. Built like a young bull, with all the strength and agility needed to handle the demands of his trade, his craftsmanship had won the admiration of the valley men and his gifts for song and mirth had turned every girl's head. In record time, he won the consent of John Cowles, one of Hatfield's chief engagers, to wed his youngest daughter.

While Ben fulfilled his contracts and started to build a cottage for Esther, her father sent her to Hartford to help her eldest sister, Sarah Goodwin, with a new baby. In only a matter of weeks, word reached Hadley that Esther's bans were being read in Hartford for her marriage to Thomas Bull, Junior, one of Connecticut Colony's best-provided-for young men.

Ben and John Cowles swept down the river to protest. John stated that, though no bans had been published in Hadley, he had given his promise that Esther would wed Ben; he would not dishonor his word; Ben protested that Tom's wealth and the excitement of living in a large town had helped turn Esther's head; he was sure he could change her mind. But Esther would not be moved. Ben took his case to court. The Hartford magistrates, sympathetic to his cause, suspended Esther's bans for a month. They directed Ben to win back her favor. His efforts came to naught. John Cowles forbade Esther ever to return to his hearth again for any reason.

Ben took his jilting hard. For a time, when he played his cornet in the quiet of evening, so much torment poured out in his music that he brought tears even to the eyes of flinty old Magistrate Clarke. For a season, nothing seemed to go well with Ben. When his music began to enthrall Hannah Lewis, Small Pockets' visiting granddaughter, her grandfather unceremoniously gave Ben short shrift. Small Pockets claimed that Hannah was too young to be courted, but Ben said the the old miser had his mind set on a suitor as rich as Tom Bull. At that time, pews were assigned in the meetinghouse that Ben had supervised in the building; he had been unstinting with his time and skill. To his consternation, since he was not a family man, he received no pew assignment, but found himself shunted to the back of the hall with indentured men and servants. In his outrage, he quoted loudly without regard to respect due some present: "Remember: 'tis better to be a doorkeeper in the house of the Lord, than to sit in the seats of the scornful!"

Too buffeted about, he had fallen under Dr. Westcarr's evil influence and into bad company and trouble. But last year he had married Martha Leonard of Springfield, a sister to one of his and Az Dickinson's more rambunctious companions. Everyone agreed that Martha, independent though she was, was not a turbulent spirit like her brother. She was helping Ben to settle down. He was building her a finer house than Small Pockets', where Hannah now lived, married to Samuel Crow.

Nehemiah, startled by Ben's outburst regarding his wife's sister, stared at him speechless, before he protested, confused: "I always wanted fancy buttons, Ben. For myself. Silver ones. I always wanted some like Pa's. His will go to Az — sure as the sun comes up in the morning — but I am going to have my own." He turned abruptly to Ham and directed: "Find out about some silver buttons and buckles for me — and for Mary, too, next time, Ham, and —"

"Guess you don't know about the new lass that's come to town, Ben," Tom Welles interrupted, wanting to divert the conversation.

"New lass?" Ben echoed, only half-interested, still smarting from the hurt fresh in his mind.

"Aye — with Gov'nor Leverett and Dan Fisher."

"Dan in town, is he?" Ben asked, his interest aroused. He and Dan had grown up together in Dedham.

"Aye. And brought a maiden with 'em, too."

"Suppose he's married, Ben?" Ed Grannis prompted uncertainly.

Ben shook his head. "No. No. Not so sudden. Dan ain't giving no mind to nobody but Mary — he's told me so, himself. And besides, there ain't that many ladies to wed now, is there?"

"Well, who is she, then?" Ike challenged. "Why's she here?"

"Is she red-faced like Dan?" Ben asked, ignoring the question.

"None of us knows. We did not see her."

"Well, 'tis more than likely one of Dan's sisters," Ben guessed. "He's got two not yet wed that I know of."

Everyone looked disappointed.

"Can you imagine any of the Leverett ladies coming out here for any reason?" Ben demanded, heartened because his friends were heeding his counsel. "If Dan ain't married, and I'll wager he is not, that's who she would have to be. What other lass could travel so far with strangers, staying overnight along the way?"

The men all nodded solemnly. Zech noticed that as his father listened to Ben's reasoning, he unconsciously nodded that each statement Ben made was correct. He had known this lass was coming! Governor Leverett and the Fishers had something to do with the Old Stranger, somehow, too!

CHAPTER X

When Ben Wait's familiar drum roll signalled the approaching hour of meeting on the Sabbath, most villagers turned out eager to see the lass who had come to town with the Governor and Dan Fisher. It was presumed by then that she was Dan's eighteen-year-old sister, Lydia. Those who called at Tilton's reported they had seen no sign of her there, though, and mention of her got put off. Only a few folk did not linger outside the meetinghouse watching for Peter Tilton's entourage to arrive: Dan Fisher beside Mary Tilton, followed by next-door neighbors Hannah and Samuel Crow, behind them Peter, Senior, and Small Pockets and, at the rear, Squire Goodwin and the Governor. The lass was nowhere to be seen.

While the expectant congregation murmured amongst themselves, perplexed by the unsettling circumstances of Lydia's strange non-appearance, Frank Barnard's family emerged from their nearby dooryard. Hannah Westcarr stepped along sedately, her face a carefully-composed, expressionless mask. She wore a new dress of a soft shade of blue; narrow braid trimmed the neck and wrists. The material was of much finer stuff than Hartford provided, and down the front of her bodice her new gold buttons glistened like small flames. Across her shoulders she wore an India shawl that had been Dr. Westcarr's mother's. It was a thing of beauty, heavily fringed, of an intricate pattern faded to a pastel loveliness. It had been folded away years ago, unsuited for wear in

67

the wilderness. Dr. Westcarr, in town for the nonce, strolled coolly at his wife's side; Goody Barnard marched behind them and tried to appear unaware of her gaping neighbors' shocked interest in her daughter's gala display. When, before, had anyone ever blossomed forth in a new frock at this nearly-frantic time of year? Sally Barnard, fourteen years old, betrayed her family's pretense of being unaware of the effect of her sister's appearance. She wore a new frock, too, of the same piece as Hannah's, but untrimmed. Though she must have been warned beforehand against showing such pride, Sally looked as if she would burst from trying to contain her excitement. Frank Barnard, puffing matter-of-factly on his pipe, herded his womenfolk along. He made no attempt to hide his pride in his family. Ever. He felt that he owed no one any excuses for what he provided. His four sons, aware of the consternation their family was creating, suddenly found something wrong with their gate and hung back, examining it with great care.

Dr. Westcarr swept the disconcerted crowd with a vaunted look. His smug expression roused as much emotion as his wife's galling finery. Zech wanted to pull back behind Dan Crow, next to him, to avoid Dr. Westcarr's darting glance, but Dr. Westcarr found him in the crowd. Their eyes met for but a trice, yet he signalled: "Wait! Just you wait!"

Zech heard Aunt gasp, alarmed. Since his skirmish with Dr. Westcarr, he had come to respect what his father had said about the fear and dread that guided Sam Russell's every move. He no longer dared go dashing around the corner of a building; now he moved cautiously, staying clear of any obstacles that might shelter a threat. On any chore away from home, he calculated his time and the presence of others so that he never would be alone. He gave up all thought of devising ways to spend Wednesdays more profitably for the family than at lecture. He had decided, too, that Serv and Gracie were a worthy form of protection; he let them tag along wherever he went. They enjoyed that, though it was a cross to bear. At least it made his father and Aunt happy.

A surprised murmur attracted attention to Pastor Russell's approach. In Pastor's wake followed Madame Russell, leaning on a lass who must be Lydia Fisher. She was slight, and almost fair, like Dan; her naturally high color was heightened because she was blushing, knowing that she was the center of attention. She kept her head bent low; her hood almost hid her face. She did not glance to right or left. Sam Russell stalked behind her, somehow able to appear removed from the scene.

"That *her*?" Dan Crow demanded of Zech in a loud whisper, the only sound in the staring silence. When Zech half-nodded his head that he thought so, Dan muttered, louder than he intended: "She ain't much to look at —" Lydia must have heard him.

Zech glanced about, mortified. Ike, leaning on his crutch by the meetinghouse steps, gave him and Dan a baleful look.

No one had suspected that Lydia had been escorted to the manse. Last Sunday, Madame had not appeared at meeting, and Pastor had explained that she had had a fainting spell, but such announcements were nothing new; Madame had appeared in robust health at lecture, and had said not a word about household assistance being in the offing: with their slave couple, few in Hadley were as well attended to as the Russells. Many resented Becky Russell's standoffishness. Since Mistress Lewis had died, she welcomed to the manse only Susannah Goodwin and her daughter, Old John's young wife. She spent an entire afternoon each week at the Tiltons', too, sewing and reading, a social time to which no one else was bid come, then at noonings and lectures she expected all other women to relish her company.

Encouraged by their mothers, at the nooning the more forward girls Lydia's age — Rebecca Graves, the Montague sisters, Sarah Welles — tried to make overtures of friendship. Mrs. Russell turned aside their invitations to share their lunch or to walk about and view the village. Lydia, flustered and discomfitted, huddled at Mrs. Russell's side. No one doubted that she yearned to join the girls. Ordinarily, even as plain as Lydia was — and she was not *that* plain — the competition for her attention among the young blades would have been fierce. But Mrs. Russell's coolness put them off. It was a new experience for village swains accustomed to rushing each new arrival brought from Connecticut or The Bay. Az Dickinson, Joe Barnard, Sam Gardner, Eph Hinsdale — all viewed the prospects and made not a move to make Lydia's acquaintance. No one except Ike.

While Lydia ate her lunch as if it were sticking in her throat, her unhappy glance met Ike's. Her downcast spirit responded to his affliction. She smiled at him, quickly, kindly, a smile that, like the sun bursting through a cloudy day, seemed all the more radiant. Ike, overwhelmed, without second thoughts such as stayed the others, lurched forward and introduced himself. Lydia glowed.

Ike, thoroughly smitten, did not acknowledge Madame Russell's authority. He tried to join the Russells following afternoon meeting, but to no avail. Lydia's hosts warned him off.

That evening, Zech braved his father's displeasure; he asked him directly if Lydia's being at the manse had anything at all to do with the Old Stranger. His father stiffened instantly, as if he would take him to task for disregarding his bidding. For a moment Zech thought that his father intended to ignore him; then, unexpectedly, his expression unfathomable, he murmured, "Aye —" and turned away.

Hadley folk urged Ike to press his suit and court Lydia. It had been obvious to everyone that she had been especially interested in him. Tom Dickinson's wife decided that she would prepare Ike's way. She was a Crow, one of Old John's first family. Her father went to the manse often; the friendship between the Crows and Russells went back to the Good Old Cause that for generations had bound families together in Old England, and had brought them together to the New World. But Becky Russell did not receive Anna cordially. Nevertheless, Anna told Ike that Lydia knew well who he was, and that, in spite of Becky's coolness, he should take heart and take matters into his own hands.

At the next Sabbath nooning, Lydia kept her eyes downcast and spoke to no one. The next evening, clean-shaven and dressed in his Sunday blouse, Ike sallied forth to the manse. Pastor Russell received him more graciously than his wife had received Anna; but neither Lydia nor Madame Russell appeared. Pastor was direct. He explained that with Jonathan away his wife needed someone like Lydia for companionship; loneliness surely had been a reason for her recent sinking spells. Also, Mr. Leverett, who had managed to persuade Lydia's parents to permit her to come to Hadley, had promised that the Russells would see to it that she made no permanent ties in Hadley. They expected to lean on her in their old age; under no circumstance would they consent to her settling far from the home in which they were content to end their years. Pastor advised Ike that if he wished to try to persuade Lydia's parents to change their minds he should ride out to Dedham and do so; no doubt he would need to remove to Dedham in the bargain, if they agreed. Since Lydia was young and at an impressionable age, he and Mrs. Russell believed that the best way to insure keeping Mr. Leverett's promise on their behalf would be to ask their neighbors to leave Lydia alone. He prayed Ike would not think him and his wife heartless. He asked Ike if others had not mentioned the marked improvement in his wife's health since Lydia had come. She seemed much less melancholy, and Lydia had been with them but a few days.

The townswomen agreed that Lydia's company appeared to improve Mistress Russell's state of mind, though they all grumbled that she enjoyed poor health. The villagers, in general, chafed at Lydia's "entombment," and many chided the Russells on their own young people's behalf, but henceforth Lydia confined her public appearances to Sabbath meetings and to lecture when it met in Hadley. She saw no one in private.

Zech went back to the manse again the next clear, moonlight night. Biscuit made no effort to go along. Zech took with him a ripe venison leg he had hidden away for the occasion. He dragged it along the ground for a rod before he got to the sheltering tree, then he hurled it with all his might toward the pasture. He had himself comfortably in place by the time Nero charged into the yard and toward his refuge. The scent of the venison bone distracted him, and he bounded in eager pursuit of it. Zech watched him, pleased with himself. He had no idea how long he waited; it seemed an eternity before Nero left the bone and wandered back toward the manse. Zech had seen or heard no one emerge from the house or sheds, but Nero's wagging tail, when he stopped in the half-light of the shed door, indicated someone there was petting him. Zech waited, certain no one suspected his presence. Presently, the barn door swung open and Pastor led his two chestnut geldings into the yard. He and the same tall rider that Zech had seen before started toward the Middle-Highway-Trail. They walked slowly so the horses would make no more sound than they would walking in the pasture where they often spent the night. From somewhere up the common came the sound of a cantering horse. The men halted and listened intently. Not *a* horse — *horses!* Instantly, the stranger retreated to the house and Pastor hurried to Nero to quiet his protests. As soon as he pushed Nero into the house, Pastor mounted his horse; he rode down the common, away from the sound of horses dying away to the west. Zech guessed that he was hurrying to rouse Peter Tilton, at least.

Zech dropped from the tree and started along the common, moving from shadow to shadow in the direction taken by the night riders. They must have turned down the Middle-Highway-to-the-Meadows. He paused at the edge of the ridge to catch his breath and get his thoughts in order; with all the excitement and exertion, he hardly could breathe. He peered out over the unnatural night landscape and tried to discern where the riders had gone. He had been so taken up with the Old Strangers that he had not been aware of much else, of late . . . Had the men at Ike's been discussing these night riders when he and Az arrived about the same time, yesterday? When Az complained that he would like to get his hands on the brave who was riding his horses at night, he had expected that everyone would be as attentive to what Az said as he had been. But Ike had turned instantly to Ed Grannis and asked him of some matter between them, his jaws working in a way they did when he was angry; while Ed spouted his response to Ike, Az sauntered away and his intriguing subject seemed to have been passed-over. As soon as Az was through the door, though, Ed stopped in mid-sentence and exclaimed: "Say, Ike, Az don't look like he's gittin' much sleep these moonlight nights —" Ike, in a rage, had knocked over a stool with his crutch and stumped away from Ed. He had not understood Ike's anger. If Ed thought that Az was out-about trying to catch the culprits he complained of, why should Ike — "Oh-hhh —" Zech moaned aloud to himself, suddenly aware of all he had not understood . . . Az was night-riding, and Ed was letting Ike know that he knew, and Ike knew it already and didn't like it. And if *Ed* knew —

Zech was aware that lads just older than himself often kept the elders from knowing of their mischief — at least for awhile. Without an older brother who got mixed up with such matters, he did not always know what went on, though sometimes Dan or Jonathan Welles told him of goings-on if their brothers were *not* involved. Az and the Barnard boys often were downright defiant of authority. He recalled hearing of late that Jonathan Marsh and Az were not worth their salt these days, but he had not realized such statements were passwords, folks hinting to each other of what was going on.

When he began to breathe regularly, so that there was no pounding in his ears, he could hear the sound of horses far out in the meadows. He hastened along the trail. The horsemen must be in John Marsh's field — racing. Pastor and the elders would be there, shortly, too —

Before Zech reached the edge of Marsh's meadow, Pastor's posse overtook him. He crouched in a hedgerow and watched the riders sweep past, armed with horsewhips: Pastor, Deacon Dick,

Aaron Cook, and Will Markham, all neighbors, all taut in their saddles, so close at hand in the bright light that he could glimpse their savage anticipation. He panted along in their wake, trying not to be left too far behind. The attackers did not linger at the hedgerow gateway. The racers must have ridden directly into their shocking reception. Zech arrived to the loud and angry cries of surprise and alarm and the pain of men and horses shrieking above the sound of thundering hooves. John Markham and Deacon Dick had circled beyond the riders. Zech winced, seeing them brandish their horsewhips at riders trying to escape the oncoming elders.

Zech listened, shaken, while the elders reconnoitered near him, breathless, and hardly less angry than when they arrived.

"Az — of course," they agreed, and muttered the names of the others: Jonathan Marsh, Tom Welles, Joe Barnard, Rich Fellowes of Hatfield, and "trash" from Springfield: rootless ne'er-do-well youths without families, past their indentures, often hauled into court for gross and lascivious carriage as well as for minor offenses.

Zech let the elders get well ahead of him before he started back toward the common. The village was totally quiet, serene, when he arrived at the common gate. He could scarcely believe that he had not dreamed all that he had witnessed.

The next day, he heard no word of the night's escapade. He went by the Welles' house, and the Barnards', and Marshes', but he caught a glimpse of none of the culprits. At Ike's, he found Ike grim and morose, and John Marsh, and Frank Barnard, and Tom and Young Nathaniel Dickinson only a little less distracted; he heard not a hint of what he knew had transpired. He felt certain that his father did not know of the night-riding.

On the Sabbath, the Widow Fellowes and Rich did not appear at meeting, and neither did Old Nathaniel and his wife and Az. Zech noticed how carefully those who usually would mark their absence chose to make no comment. On Wednesday, Ursula Fellowes and Old Nathaniel sent word that henceforth they no longer would risk life and limb crossing the river for any purpose. Instantly, word of the night riders spread through the lecture gathering. Their neighbors were indignant: a likely punishment for defiance of the law was not a worthy cause for withdrawing from meeting. Discussion of petitioning further for a Hatfield meetinghouse was put off for another season, in order not to appear to condone old

Nathaniel's and the Widow Fellowes' blind indulgence of their wayward sons.

On the next Sabbath, Rich Fellowes and Az appeared among the first to arrive at meeting. They strolled past wary neighbors so bent on their discussion they gave not a single nod of greeting, and showed not a sign of guilt or regret for all the mischief they had sparked; they had the look of tomcats about them: pretending disinterest, but ready to pounce, victors by surprise.

It seemed to Zech that the waiting silence as the two conspirators entered the meetinghouse might explode like a shedful of drying, damp hay — suddenly a terrible conflagration. Obediah Dickinson, Old Nathaniel's second son, more burly and combative than his elder brother, Samuel, had entered the meetinghouse early and moved forward to his father's place of honor at the front. He sat cross-armed, immovable. Az hesitated hardly a trice, seeing Obediah ahead of him; he scarcely jarred the rhythm of his pacing as he stopped by Obediah's old pew, half-way down the aisle, and sat down. Rich Fellowes dropped into the pew beside him. Everyone pretended to be unaware that Obediah had thwarted Az by taking their father's place. Az would have gloried in confounding the elders by usurping that honor even for one morning; for surely Samuel would be assigned his father's pew if Old Nathaniel never returned, as he claimed he would not.

Zech caught back a sigh of relief. Most villagers had not known of the night-riding before Wednesday. If it had not been for the Old Strangers, would anything have been done about it, if no accidents took place? Had so much come to pass because random riders, abroad in the night, could be a threat to their safe-keeping?

CHAPTER XI

The next Wednesday that lecture met in Hadley, Zech attached himself for safety's sake to a family returning to Northampton. He arrived back at the river at the end of the ferrying. As he disembarked, he remarked casually enough to Joe: "Last time I ferried with you was a lecture day, too, Joe. The day I saw Old John in his new wig and thought he was a stranger about town."

Joe gave him a quick, hard look, and his lean face eased. He grinned, relieved. "That wig's been nothing but trouble — but Old John likes that, o' course." He shook his head and sighed in mock exasperation.

Carefully, Zech muttered: "There's no strangers about, anyway, so's I do not know why I would think anything so foolish."

Joe nodded. He glanced around, looking for Young Joe who was taking the stairs to the common two at a time. "Give me a hand here!" he directed Zech, annoyed.

Zech waded into the water. "Whenever anyone comes to town, 'tis to see someone he knows — even the French traders," he reminded as he and Joe ran the canoe up onto the beach. "Aye," Joe answered absently, and nodded.

"How did you chance to come to Hadley, Joe?" Zech asked with flattering interest.

Joe paused: "Oh — I had come to Boston, and Captain Leverett — he wa'n't gov'nor, then — had been here surveyin'. He told me that Hadley was lookin' for a weaver. He was my commandin' officer in Col. Rainborough's regiment, ye know. In some o' the earliest encounters of the Great Rebellion."

Zech did not want Joe to wander off and get lost in accounts of his war experiences. Artfully, he probed: "You know — when I did not know who Old John was — and Pastor preached that Sabbath that we might entertain angels unaware — for a while I thought — then — but, anyway — we could not — without breaking the law —"

Joe looked watchful. Zech continued guardedly, pretending to be offhand: "Laws! Laws! Laws!" he scoffed. "Pastor is always preaching 'bout laws. The Bible's laws — and our own — and how we must obey 'em. How? I'd like to know that!"

"Don't git mixed up with them as are always around questioning things and making for misunderstanding," Joe admonished, troubled. "Follow your father's direction. He's a good man."

"Oh, aye," Zech agreed, getting nervous. "I do not challenge — what I am saying is that, when Pastor preaches that we might entertain angels unaware — he is advising us to break the law, is he not?"

Joe collected his paddles and did not answer. Zech tried one more approach. "When I thought Old John was a stranger — why — were — you — why was it — you —"

Joe's face darkened. His mouth set stubbornly. Zech shrugged, as if he did not care whether Joe answered or not. Suddenly, Joe leaned on his paddles and said, as if to himself: "I guess my experiences make me a bit wary. I have seen much that those who came after, those who have never lived elsewhere — like you — cannot imagine; being told only in words, you know, you cannot git the same feeling as bein' there. And much is forgot — left unrecorded. If I had not been in Boston when I was — but I have seen how some do well for themselves, playin' cozy with the king's commissioners, like John Westcarr would do. Anything to make trouble for us, you know! The king's gov'ment is always free enough with grants for informers, you know."

Zech scowled. "Informers?" he repeated, confounded. "Informers?" he probed. He shrugged. "All I can say is, everyone seems so well accounted for, from town to town — I do not see how there could be a stranger about — or what there is to — inform — about —"

Joe half-shrugged, half-nodded. "Well, there's naught to worry about any more — anyway — I do believe —"

"Was there a time when there were strangers about that should be reported?" Zech pressed, genuinely interested.

"Not *should* be, Zech," Joe corrected warmly. "Not if you are right-thinking, that is." He drew a deep breath. "You know of course, 'bout the Judges who was here in the colonies — the two major generals o' Parliament's army who served as Judges when the first King Charles was on trial for misrulin' his subjects? Well, when those Judges fled to the colonies — when the Stuarts was restored to the throne — a proclamation was sent over against 'em. That's when laws about harboring strangers was put into force. Now, if a friend or relative — even — comes to visit, they must be reported. Here in Hadley 'tis told to me."

Zech nodded, well aware of that.

Joe smiled thoughtfully. "I was in Boston when the judges arrived. They was well received, believe me. General Whalley was father-in-law to General Goffe, you know. You know, too, how he protected the king from bein' murdered when he was the general's prisoner of war. Why, some accused General Whalley of helpin' the king escape, 'cause of the letter the king wrote him after his escape, thanking him for his care —

"You see, Zech, that's the way men are — If the General had let the king be murdered, 'twould o' been thought no particular fault o' his — but 'twas another matter when the king was brought to trial. Never before in the History of Man had such tyranny been put to law. Parliament brought the king to trial when he tried to put an end to it. Those parliament men was strivin' t' make him attend to the laws o' the land. But King Charles would have none o' that. He would not listen. He believed in Divine Right. *His word* was *the Law:* the Judges were his subjects. He showed only contempt for those who questioned his actions. 'Twas treason, Zech, for him to disregard laws over four hundred years in the makin'. He betrayed the trust of his subjects! Nor would he pardon those who brought him to trial. He never had kept his word before, anyway. So, those who opposed him — who tried him within the law, had no choice but to sentence him to death — as he did them. They did not want to do it, Zech. He was their king! Parliament wanted Law *and* the king. If only he had promised to honor the Law — No man is more important than the Law — So, the king's Judges became hunted men."

Troubled by his memories, Joe inhaled deeply. "O' course, there was turmoil," he went on. "And in the end, those who had power to begin with, knew how to git it back. They brought back

Prince Charles, and from what we hear now, 'tis to the everlastin' sorrow of those who condemned us most —"

Joe sighed. "For all his lack o' understandin', King Charles was a righteous man, but not his prince. Look at how he's made dukes and duchesses o' more than a dozen high-livin' bastard sons and daughters o' harlots! Livin' off the fat o' the land, they are, at the poor subject's expense. That's *his* way. He put a price on the Judges' heads, and that £100 was all that was needed to keep some men seekin' 'em 'til they was dead."

Zech nodded. His first day at school, Peter Tilton had called and read a letter telling of the Judges' deaths in Switzerland. Peter and the master had discussed for the students' benefit the exciting and interesting things the Judges had done. He had not understood, then, the debt men owed the Judges, but he remembered how impressed the older boys had been, and in time he learned why.

"Zech, I knew those Judges! I saw 'em often in Boston while they was stayin' in Cambridge —" Suddenly Joe started to chuckle. He shook his head and burst into a rollicking laugh. "They gave that pair a time!" he practically shouted, his mirth carrying his voice out of control.

He shook his head. "You know how the Judges fled from the Bay to Connecticut, when the proclamation came for their arrest!"

Zech grinned and nodded. Everyone knew how the colonists had duped the king's officers while they tried to hunt down the Judges. "— Gov'nor Leete — all of 'em in Connecticut — always seemed t' be aidin' the royal agents, but somehow word always got ahead of 'em! Everywhere those ferrets went, the Judges had only been!" Joe grinned, savoring satisfaction, before he lowered his voice and reminded Zech: "Their friends who stayed in England, even those who did not sign the death warrant — like our own Gov'nor Vane o' Massachusetts Bay, you know —" He shook his head as if now, half-a-generation later, he could not believe what had taken place. "Gov'nor Vane went into Parliament when he returned home from Boston. He *was* one of the king's Judges, Zech, but he *refused* to sign the death warrant. He did not sign it, Zech! Yet he was beheaded! There has been such a taste for blood rather than justice —"

Zech nodded. Treachery, too, he thought. Every schoolboy in New England scorned the memory of George Downing, nephew of Governor Winthrop. He had studied at Harvard when Pastor Russell did, and had sailed abroad with the shipload of New England volunteers who served in the struggle to preserve Parliament. He and his Winthrop cousin had been among those who tarried and served the Commonwealth government with honor at the close of England's Civil War. He had been in charge of England's navy, and an agent of Parliament in Holland. There, he betrayed three old friends — Judges of King Charles I — who had fled abroad when the Royalists returned triumphant. His victims had been executed with barbarous cruelty. Joe interrupted Zech's thoughts: "Everyone guessed without much trouble who mought be aidin' the Judges in New Haven, o' course. General Whalley's brother-in-law was the first pastor there, and Dr. Davenport, the new pastor, was an old friend from the early days in the struggle. And Mr. Jones was a likely one, too. His father was one of those so infamously slain through that traitor, Downing." Joe spit contemptuously. "Mr. Jones returned to the colonies on the ship that the Judges come on. So, when the royal agents got too close, and the Judges feared their protectors was bein' endangered, they appeared at meeting in New Haven — t' give themselves up — t' save their friends from the gallows — t' be sent back t' England in chains, themselves. But their friends would have none o' that! Well — they was last seen ridin' off toward New York. From there, 'twas, they made their way abroad."

Zech nodded. He had heard all that Joe had recounted a good many times.

"Ye know, Zech," Joe went on, caught up by his own excitement, "The Protector was General Whalley's cousin, and so was John Hampden, the Great Patriot. Why, General Whalley had twenty relatives at once in Parliament. For a while, those judges helped rule all England: each in charge o' several counties — Lincoln, Nottingham, Hants, Berks, Sussex, such like. Some cities in their charge had most as many folk as there is in this colony right now —

"Why! They grew up concerned 'bout good gov'ment. Sir Francis Barrington, the knight o' my shire, was General Whalley's uncle. He was a courageous upholder o' the law — a stalwart leader — And that fretted the king. Just 'fore I was born, King Charles tried to prevent Sir Francis bein' sent back to Parliament as knight of the shire. He sent a high constable into Essex with an order from the High Court that required freeholders not to vote at Sir Francis' seat, but at Chelmsford. Why, Zech, that's a day's journey afoot! 'Twas the belief o' the king and his minions that the distance and its inconvenience would thwart Sir Francis bein' chosen. My father was a freeholder, and he and 'bout every man in the country towns — not jest those from Sir Francis' own hundred — marched themselves t' Chelmsford! There 'twas discovered that the high constable had ready the names o' two men decided upon beforehand by the king and his council. One was to be chosen in Sir Francis' stead! Mind you, Zech, that day fifteen *thousand* men gathered together at Chelmsford! Twelve thousand was free-holders — and scarce a hand went up for the men the king had chosen! My father used t' love t' tell 'bout it — 'bout how the cheers that went up for Sir Francis was enough t' deafen a man!''

Joe and Zech moved toward the stairway, their steps paced by the rhythm of Joe's recollections.

"O' course, the king's men cried foul, but Sir Francis was chosen by the rules o' the king's own devisin'. That did not make the election go down any better, either, I tell you.'' Joe's face glowed as he recalled his father's recitations.

His expression sobered. "Sir Francis advised his freemen that they need not pay unlawful taxes not voted by parliament: ship money subsidies they was called, and Privy Seal Loans — fancy names the king's councillors made up for ways t' steal the subject's goods and lands from 'im, for no return.'' Joe caught his breath and stared off into space, overcome by a multitude of passions. His tone became grim. "My mother's brother was one who re-fused t' pay. The king's men marched him 'n' a dozen more small-time citizens clear t' Portsmouth! Hundreds o' miles! They was t' be pressed into navy service in one of Buckingham's great follies. Zech, that was contrary t' all the laws o' the land! In the end, they dared not go that far. 'Twas too much a breach o' English law — and believe me, word o' the outrage was abroad in the land! Townsmen protested all along their way, so they was set free down there — so far from home. They would've had a time findin' their way back, if they had gone on their own, but they was heroes, Zech! Countrymen conducted 'em from town t' town — like the victors they was!''

Joe caught his breath. For a moment his expression was triumphant, full of satisfaction. "So, then, the king had Sir Francis arrested.'' His voice faltered, his words slowed. "Sir Francis and his son-in-law, Lord Masham, was thrown into jail for their advice t' their freeholders,'' Joe sighed. 'Twas an illegal imprisonment, and Sir Francis died of it —'' Joe stood silent, thoughtful.

" 'Twas then the families in our shire began t' talk about gittin' away. Without Sir Francis t' champion their cause, life would only git more 'n' more oppressive: squandering courtiers bent on ignoring all the laws o' the land. Our families wanted no longer t' live under a gov'ment that would grind 'em t' dust as was happenin' everywhere else. Why, Zech, the first meeting o' Squire Winthrop and his friends was at General Goffe's brother's house in London. He served as president of the council that planned their comin'; he provided more 'n' one ship for the Great Migration. But he did not come himself, so Squire Winthrop was elected president o' the company in his stead."

Joe inhaled deeply. He sighed. "That's why we come here, Zech, t' this wild land. 'Cause we believe that Man is made in God's image, and we do have Rights! Englishmen had enjoyed 'em for four hundred years! Rights life ain't worth livin' without. The Stuarts wa'n't willin' t' let men think for themselves. Life ain't worth livin', Zech, if you can't act and think for yourself."

"Aye," Zech agreed solemnly. "Aye!" he repeated. "Aye —"

Joe sighed, again. "Seems now sometimes as if some have forgot what's gone before. Some jest don't want t' let others think for themselves. Make a law! they cry out. Stop every man from doin' what *I* don't want t' do!" His tone sharpened with indignation. He pressed his lips together in a grim line.

Hoping to mollify Joe before he took his leave, Zech ventured: "I have heard men tell how, because of the Judges, New Haven lost its charter." Hastily, he added: "They do not blame the Judges — but the King's Commissioners."

Joe's head bobbed appreciatively. "Aye! New Haven had its own compact gov'ment, 'n' every man a signer. Hartford was separate, then. But after New Haven sheltered the Judges for that spell before they left, the king's ministers drew up a new charter, and lumped New Haven under the rest o' Connecticut — under Hartford. New Haven fought it, o' course, but it did no good."

Joe leaned on his gate. "You know 'bout the fast days we had here when the commissioners was sent t' demand the surrender o' the Bay Company's charter," he reminded.

Zech nodded. Every schoolboy was taught that stirring bit of History.

"Three King's Commissioners, in four ships, with over three hundred soldiers aboard! But I was in Hadley by then —" Joe's voice trailed off, full of regret. "We knew, here, though, what was goin' on, and don't you forgit it! The General Court warned those commissioners not to set a foot on our land! Every town in the colony held three solemn fast days that season — 'cause of it. And drew up petitions signed by *every* male — not jest the freemen. Every male over twenty-one! The Court stalled the commissioners with letters 'n' conferences 'til the petitions got in from all the towns; then, when the King's Commissioners ordered all the males in the colony t' assemble in Boston on election day — t' hear the colony cited as defendant — Well! — Then things happened! Why! We'd-a been from town a fortnight, goin' 'n' comin'. And who'd tend our farms, and protect our womenfolk? 'Twas the story o' Sir Francis Barrington all over again! Imagine them tryin' t' manage us here — by inconvenience 'n' numbers! We had a gov'ment o' our own! We wa'n't about t' let 'em do such a thing! No Sirreee, Bob! Ha! Right here — right there on the common —'' Joe pointed toward the meetinghouse. "At a time appointed by *our council* in Boston — and at the same time in every town in the colony! — our trumpeters — Deacon Smith did the honor here — blew the trumpet 'n' Pastor read in the king's name — that by the *authority* of our charter, everyone was forbid t' attend any meetin' that would be disruptive t' our gov'ment. In Boston, not one Royalist dared step up and accept the citation! That was the end for the King's Commissioners! They knew when they was beat —''

Zech relished such recitals as Joe had shared with him. They made life in the past so exciting, so much more appealing than the ordinary life he lived, with never anything more than chores and supper waiting. Before he hurried away from Joe's gate, he said: "It pleases me that the Judges escaped the king's men."

"Aye, 'twas the Lord's doin'," Joe agreed. "And it could not have been easy for them, either. 'Twould not be hard for some to drop out o' sight. Those as look so much like the common lot o' men. Some — even in costly garments — have the look o' ploughmen in borrowed finery. That's one o' the attractions o' wigs, I s'pose." He and Zech grinned at each other, thinking of Old John. "But those Judges, now, they was generals, too, and they looked the part. No one ever mistook their importance. My, they was distinguished lookin'! 'Twas in their bearin'. They could not hide their worth — their station. They was too tall *not* to be noticed, too. Both of 'em. Bigger than Pastor, they was. Head 'n' shoulders above other men they stood. Lordly men, no mistakin' that, from their trim goatees to their fine leather boots, there was no mistakin' 'em, Zech! Men like them could not hide no more nor Adam —''

Joe was carried away, remembering. Too much so to notice that Zech appeared close to fainting.

CHAPTER XII

Zech all but fell into his father's yard. Aunt gasped at the sight of him. "Are you sick, Zech?" she cried, anguished.

Zech crumbled onto the bench by the shed, genuinely spent.

He was sick. He never had been so sick in his life, before.

Aunt turned toward her gaping children. "Go 'way!" she ordered in a panicked squeal. "Go away! Go to Aunt Bets! — Now! Quick! Go!" She dreaded smallpox, or one of the fevers or agues that sometimes struck destructively and without warning.

Zech tried to hold up his hand, to assure her she need not fear for his health. He could only lift his eyes and stare at her blankly. Aunt hovered halfway across the yard, clutching her apron with one hand; she pressed the other to her mouth. Her image began to waver.

Zech leaned his head back against the shed and closed his eyes. The sun-warmed boards felt comforting. Solid. So did the knowledge that Aunt would not desert him. Her thoughts were of the others, but she did not plan to leave him all the same. He opened his eyes again, and the darkness that had begun to overtake him ebbed away. Aunt looked firmly placed, not waxing and waning as she had.

"Zech!" From across the yard, his father's hollow tone echoed Aunt's horror. In two strides he reached Zech's side. He dropped to his knees beside Zech and cried out: "Zech! Zech!"

Zech reached for his father's hand. It closed over his, and its huge size and roughness, and warmth, felt good. Zech let his fingers go limp in his father's grasp. He could feel his strength oozing back; his father was a wellspring of life. He closed his eyes again. He tried to sit more erect. Aunt edged forward. Finally, Zech whispered: "It must have been something I ate —"

"What?" his father and Aunt demanded to know, wanting to guard against anything so noxious.

Zech let his head loll, and tried to smile. "I ate so many things — today —" he told them in all truth.

"Aye — noonings have been the death of some!" Aunt muttered distressed, still anxious and not a little relieved.

Zech began to wonder how he could live with his new knowledge. One wrong word on his part could doom to destruction or flight — to what place? — the refugee Judges and the decent people, the good people, the kind people who sheltered them. He tried to assure himself that New England men would not follow through on the king's proclamation and surrender anyone to certain execution. The colonies would defy the king's agents as they had the king's commission in Boston. But Zech knew that that had been another matter.

At the next waxing of the moon, at a safe interval after the watch called the hour, he returned to the manse. At this season he and the boys slept on pallets near the fireplace. Biscuit, asleep at his feet, roused concerned when Zech began to pull on his trousers. His tail began to thump against the worn floorboards. He became watchfully silent when Zech assured him with cautioning gestures that he could go, too. The steady, even breathing from the bedroom did not change as Zech slipped out into the night.

The leaves were gone from the trees, now. Zech inhaled the still, crisp air, conditioning himself against the cold of night. This time he moved full of a dread he had not known when he had not been aware who the Strangers were. The moon's cold, white light transformed the village from the confusion of daylight to an appearance of ordered serenity; everything looked to be in place, frozen and motionless, as if all were right with the world.

Zech tied Biscuit to a tree beyond the common fence, above where the school lot pasture joined John Hubbard's. He warned Biscuit to stay quiet. Biscuit, sensing that Zech planned to venture into the preserve of the mortal enemy of all Hadley dogs, the mastiff at the manse, whimpered a protest as Zech left him, then settled down, grateful to have been brought as far as he had.

With the leaves gone, Zech could not hide in the tree where he had taken refuge the first time he had visited the manse at night. He climbed into a hemlock that hung above the Middle Highway: it would provide all the view he needed; when the men rode out — if they did — they would go almost directly under him. He could hear the mastiff inside the manse, sounding an alarm of his skulking. He told himself that those inside did not know whether he was a possum or a dog that had slipped its tether, and wondered how often he would have to come before he saw the night riders again. How would he survive if he had to come often? Of course, once snow fell and left a record of every passage, he would not be able to be about, and for the most part, neither would the Judges.

A moving shadow in the barnyard congealed his blood. He stared, telling himself it must be a trick of his imagination. But as he peered, he knew the shadow had substance. Had someone been watching him? He clung to the rough branch, hardly daring to breathe. Inside the manse, Nero's deep baying began. The shadow in the gloom near the house did not move. A click of the door latch nearly squeezed Zech's heart dry. Someone was coming out! Zech held tight to his perch. It seemed as if the door would never open. His fascinated gaze darted back toward the lurking figure. Ike! Ike squeezing awkwardly through the common fence! Nero's alarm reached a point of frenzy; Zech groaned, watching Ike drag himself along the common as fast as his misshapen leg would permit. He reached the Highway-to-the-Woods before the mastiff bounded into the yard. Nero, well-trained, stopped at the fence and bellowed his contempt after the fleeing refugee. No doubt he had been held back long enough to allow Ike to make good his escape. So Pastor must know of Ike's visits! Did Lydia? How could people be so cruel?

From his station, Biscuit, forgetting himself, barked excitedly for a moment before he subsided to a low moaning howl that died away into doleful silence. Other dogs along the common picked up Nero's and Biscuit's alarms and passed their messages the full length and breadth of the village before quieting down. Zech hardly breathed as he watched the mastiff make a round of the barnyard. Finally, he trotted to the deep shadows beside the barn door. He began to wag his tail happily. Someone in the shadows was petting him!

The stable door swung open and Pastor emerged leading his two chestnut geldings. He and the same tall rider — General Goffe?

— crossed the barnyard to the Middle Highway. Again, they led the horses slowly. When Zech was certain the horsemen had mounted and were riding into the wilderness, he slipped down from his perch and took Biscuit home.

At meeting, Zech took special notice of Ike and Lydia. He noticed that others watched them, too, secretly, trying not to be noticed themselves. Ike, his jaws taut, did not once glance in Lydia's direction, and she kept her eyes downcast, so she did not know. Perhaps Lydia was aware of the watching eyes, the curious glances; perhaps she was just very lonely, cut off as she was. Toward the end of the nooning, she looked to Zech as if she were weeping quietly; he was certain of it when Mistress Russell reached over and patted her hands gently — as if *she* understood!

Before the moon waxed again, snow began to fall. It came early this year. Zech did not return to watch the manse.

The first heavy snow came silently during the night, a soft, beguiling blanket-cover. Warr had foretold its coming. He had brought in a twelve-point buck, telling Ham it should hold him for fresh meat until he could go for more. The sky had begun to grow dull the day before, and looked close enough to touch; the wind became still, the air clear and cold, but not sharp. Later, winds might come with the snow, as if to try to whip the settlements into submission, but not this time.

At times of heavy snow, the Indians hibernated like bears, whole families snug in fur suits, drowsing the days away in their wigwams under piles of fur or deerskin coverlets. The colonists wondered that no one suffocated from the smoke that lifted lazily from the butt end of a log that smoldered in the center of the wigwam, edged in by squaws as fire consumed it away. The overworked squaws and the young children would not appear much during the winter, but the braves would be about as the spirit moved them, traveling swiftly on their cleverly webbed snowshoes. They had taught the settlers to walk in them, too. Without them, Hadley and Hatfield families could not have gotten about in winter. They could not depend on dug pathways for such long distances as they had to travel, even from neighbor to neighbor. That was one disadvantage of Hadley's spacious planning.

Zech — the whole village — perhaps every settlement in every colony — savored the first gentle letdown when winter set in.

Families gathered about the fire, unhurried, munching apples still crisp from their own trees. In those first days they did not fret about how long supplies would last. Strings of sliced, dried fruit would be empty before the trees blossomed again, but Faith assured them that spring would not be so late or so wet that they would approach a state of near-starvation. Friends like Warr brought them game; they had barrels of pickled eel, and salmon, and shad to dip into; and great piles of dried fish of every variety with which to make hearty stews. Tow sacks of dried peas and beans hung near the fireplace, and in sand-strewn cellar bins quantities of potatoes, carrots, cabbage and squash provided a sense of security. For a spell, everyone could rest a bit. In the spring, as their stocks dwindled, they would dig parsnips. The settlers had taught the Indians about parsnips. They marveled at such a strange vegetable, one that thrived by staying in the ground all winter.

As soon as the snow stopped, Tim Nash appeared with his woolly-coated ox hitched to a huge log. The ox dragged a makeshift snowplow along the edge of the drift by the common fence, breaking a broad path for the neighbors. At every household, Tim would stop in for a draft of hot, mulled cider and dispense the news he'd picked up along the way. Where young ones the ages of Ham's family dwelled, all possible paths in the yards were cleared at play; more than needed. The children's paths started with a snowball; it rolled up the snow as it grew larger and larger. Boys — and girls, too, while they were young — built forts, and snowmen, and hills for little ones to slide down on pieces of lumber or hard, discarded hides. Bigger boys gathered down by Joe Kellogg's and raced downhill into the meadow. Every lad had his own homemade sled for that sport. Almost every lad, anyway.

Throughout the years, Joe and his sons had built up and dug out a ridgeway below the edge of the steep hill directly behind his house. It curved diagonally across the hillside toward the river and stopped just short of the stairs to the common. It was a convenience for driving animals up to the village, and in winter, when covered with snow, pure joy. Even older men like Frank Barnard, and Rob Hinsdale, and Ed Grannis and Tim Nash tried the run a few times each winter. Sometimes when the snow was crusty, a youthful, careless slider would not navigate properly and would careen off the track and down the steep hillside into the meadow. That only added to the merriment. For the few who went amiss, before a path was broken, it was a bothersome task to flounder from the meadow to the stairway; the ride directly downhill, besides being dangerously steep, was too short for satisfaction.

Once winter set in, school sessions that had come to an end with spring planting met according to convenience: when the weather was not so severe as to consume too much hard-gotten firewood, and traveling not so difficult as to excuse the only half-interested boys from gathering with the master for a few hours a day. It was one way to keep brawny lads occupied.

That winter, before the true January thaw came, a warm day softened the snow, followed by a cold snap that set in during the night. At school the next day, the boys shifted about restlessly during their lessons. They knew the hill behind Joe's would be slick and icy. Even dangerous. They were anxious to get out to slide.

"You hurrying home t' spin with the girls, you little spider?" Jack Waters, a bound boy, taunted John Goodman as John darted ahead of Jack at the schoolyard gate.

"Aw, leave 'im alone!" Jonathan Welles reproached Jack. "He's too young to go sliding with us, anyway. He'd get hurt."

"I would not!" John protested, stopping in his tracks and turning to face the older lads.

"Scat!" Jack ordered, annoyed.

"No! I am going sliding, too!" John decided.

His classmates looked at one another, surprised and dismayed.

"You must let him come, now," Jonathan warned Jack uneasily. "You started this, you know."

"Huh!" Jack scoffed. "He can't go sliding." His voice became a squeaky, irritating little sound: "He has to go home and help his Mum spin! Don't you, Spider-boy?"

"I do not!" John Goodman protested, red-faced. "I am going sliding, too!"

"Where do you keep your sled?" Jack taunted.

"I can use one of Uncle Joe's," John answered defiantly. "He told me I could — any time I should want to."

"Any time you ain't spinnin' like a girl-spider, you mean!" Jack persisted.

"Leave 'im alone, Jack!" Jonathan warned, again.

None of the boys felt comfortable about John Goodman's joining them. John, among the youngest attending classes, was as thin and poor as a June shad, not robust like the other lads, though the whole town knew that he worked as hard as any man. More than that, his classmates knew that Deacon Dick did expect John home to help with the spinning; that it no doubt would go hard with him if he were late getting to his chore. Deacon Dick would berate them for delaying John, too, and he would complain to their fathers because their sons were not made to put all their time to "good use." He was not like other boys' fathers at all; he seemed not to have a loving bone in his body.

A tall, handsome, but dour-faced, rugged old man, Deacon Dick served in many town offices: as fence viewer, hog reever, and keeper of the ordinary. Thus he decided the strength of the grog and how much should be doled out, and to whom. He never refused offices that other men preferred not to accept because they did not like to be in contention with their neighbors. The town meeting never voted to fine Deacon Goodman when he resisted serving as selectman, when his turn came. Everyone said aloud that he gave much time in other offices. Actually, after he had served once as selectman, no one wanted him to serve again: enough of Deacon Dick was enough. Granny Felton had said once to Zech's mother that Richard Goodman never had been young, and at that time, being only eight or nine, he had puzzled over that statement for a long time.

Deacon Dick had been keeper of the jail in Hartford. Men often commented, usually with added wry remarks, about how Deacon Dick and his mother had relished that job. Fortunately, Hadley had no need for a jail right now, and besides, Goody Goodman had died suddenly, just before the trek to Hadley had got under way. So Deacon Dick had married eighteen-year-old Mary Terry; they had come up the river as bride and groom. As a young man, newly arrived at Hartford in the first year of its existence, he had lost his first bride and their newborn son. The experience seemed not to have mellowed him. For his second family, no other man of his means compared as a miserly provider and an unbending taskmaster. Mary Goodman had come from a generous family not given to harsh dealings with others. Squire Terry, her father, had generously consented to his youngest daughter, Abigail, Mary's half-sister, marrying Joe Kellogg when his wife died and left him with a newborn infant girl and five strapping sons, the eldest nearly as old as she; Joe had no estate other than what he provided for himself in Hadley.

Women clucked over the ways in which Mary Goodman had to provide for her ever-increasing family of youngsters. They knew that it was not Mary's wish that her sons should add girls' tasks to theirs, especially since Deacon Dick had stopped taking bound boys. In the past, his bound boys had rebelled, and run away, and caused the whole town much trouble; in his opinion, even the best of them ate too much, anyway.

"You can go with me, John," Zech found himself offering uncertainly, not wanting to thwart Deacon Dick, but wanting John to feel as welcome as any of the other boys.

"I can have a sled of my own," John told him. "Uncle Joe said so, himself."

But Young Joe intercepted the sliding party outside his father's weaving shop; he had just thrown ashes down the sled-run as far as they would reach; that would prevent the bolder lads ignoring advice meant for their own good.

The boys congregated, long-faced, at the top of the hill. Even knowing that chancing the long, slippery track would have been a reckless undertaking, they protested being denied the pleasure of half-killing themselves; many declared in half-doubtful, half-snarling tones that they could have managed a few hours' pleasure.

Jack Waters, standing at the head of the company, turned back first. His glance fell on John Goodman, puny and uninitiated, standing at the edge of the troop. Perhaps Jack detected a glimpse of relief on John's face. In a fit of bad temper, he pushed John roughly, exclaiming: " 'Suppose this suits you jest fine!"

John, caught unaware, lost his balance. He cried out; his mittened fingers clutched Zech's sleeve edge as he fell backward down the hard-frozen, steep embankment. He dragged Zech down with him. Zech felt his face crack against the rock-like hillside, and the first smarting sensation as he and John skidded swiftly along the sheer, grainy, cold crust. They crashed into a thorny shrub that halted their descent before their momentum tore them loose and sent them spinning off at a tangent, John's skinny bulk cushioning the impact for Zech. They came to rest precariously on a small knoll near the bottom of the hill, completely surrounded by an unnavigable glaze of ice.

Zech stared up at his schoolmates gathered aghast at the top of the hill. He moved cautiously, not wanting to slide farther. Blood colored the snow for the last several feet he and John had slid. He did not know it was his own; the rough ice had scaled the skin from his right cheek. He dug his toes into the crusted snow and backed off John, and onto his knees. John Goodman lay unconscious beneath him.

Zech looked from John's white, drained face to his companions and wailed: "He's dead —"

"No! — No!" voices piped in protest from above. Young Joe appeared among the hovering lads standing rooted, staring helplessly down at the mishap. Almost instantly, he reappeared with a rope. He tied it securely about a tree and let himself down the glazed hillside. "He's all right, Zech," Joe quickly assured Zech, perhaps before he was certain himself. He stamped out a place for Zech to stand, and helped him to his feet. He picked up John as if he were a rag doll. He held him gently and close and judged he could do better crossing the hill to the ferry stairs than trying to climb back as he had come.

Jack had fled the scene of his disgrace before Zech and John came to a halt. The other boys waited uncertainly. They dared not follow Young Joe to Deacon Dick's; they waited, clustered about Joe's gate and watched Young Joe carry John home across the common. Each unhappy lad told himself that he would rather he had been the injured one. They re-echoed the sentiment aloud when they learned that John's arm had been broken.

Zech counted his painful injury a blessing. If *he* had broken *his* arm, Dr. Westcarr would have had him at his mercy — During grace at meals, and evening prayers, he gave fervent thanks for his delivery and pleaded with the loving God that he prayed to, to show more loving-kindness to John Goodman.

CHAPTER XIII

Tom Welles provided diversion that winter by taking off for Windsor to be wed. He had known Hepzibah Buell since childhood and they had rediscovered each other in the spring at a Wednesday lecture in Springfield. Beginning in early summer, whenever rain slowed the work pace, Tom took off for a day or two in Windsor. Many in the village contributed verses to Ben Wait's merry jingles about the sodden swain of the Valley Main. Tom enjoyed the notoriety. In the fall, as soon as harvest was done, he and his father and brothers started to haul logs from the woods for a cottage for Tom and "Bobby," Tom's name for Hepzibah. Some logs were left at Mr. Goodwin's sawmill to be rived, but the Welles men split and hewed a growing pile themselves. In the spring, Hepzibah's father would come up the river and supervise a house-raising. Peter Buell was a prosperous carpenter able to afford to take time from working for others to do for his own family.

Heavy weather put an end to logging early in the winter, and Tom could not abide confinement. He and his oldest sister had made their home with their Grandmother Coleman for several seasons, doing chores the old folks no longer could manage; Tom persuaded his parents that he should go down to Windsor and dwell at Bobby's, and learn some carpentering from her father, which would always stand him in good stead. There were seven younger brothers and sisters to draw on to live with the old folks, and their mother was expecting again. The family would be less crowded with one or two more gone to their grandparents' aid. When Tom arrived at Windsor to stay, Peter Buell saw no need for the betrothed couple to postpone reading their bans. Three weeks later they were wed.

The village buzzed about Tom's capricious ways until Sam Moody's dwelling burned to the ground and provided another interest.

As spring approached, Zech began to be full of dread at the thought of another trip to Hartford. He knew that he could not allow himself to move out of sight of friends — not that he would hang to his father's shirttails, but he no longer could wander alone about town or the wharves, or linger at the trading post or tavern while his father went about his business. He feared that, regardless of whatever care he might exercise, one as crafty as Dr. Westcarr would outsmart him. Next time, he knew, a stranger with a grievance might not arrive to interrupt and spare him.

Mountains of ice piled up along the Connecticut between the late winter's thawings and freezings; early in March, they began to dissolve into cold black water that swept up over the sandy beaches until the river spread to twice its usual width. For a few days, the river churned down the Valley, its current impassably swift, swirling ice floes in mad patterns; the noise of the rushing tumult assaulted the common for days, so that even men with deep voices had to shout to be heard. Again, Hatfieldfolk, not able to breast the treacherous maelstrom, petitioned the General Court, in vain, pleading for permission to build a meetinghouse of their own.

Ham carried on much trade by barter. Coins were in short supply in the Valley, and wampum of little worth. In the early years, a single black shell, or a string of six white ones, bought a penny's worth of goods; but Captain Pynchon had transported so many bushels of shells from Long Island's beaches to be strung as wampum that twenty-four shells no longer bought a penny's worth of anything. Ham preferred handling goods to being responsible for someone else's coins, anyway. He was not unhappy that Deacon Dick, and Small Pockets and but few others wanted silver or gold.

Barter served craftsmen very well, so that when Hepzibah Welles arrived in Hadley as a bride, just before the first fish migrations began in the spring, she brought a dowery such as many of Hadley's oldest women had enjoyed in Old England: bountiful compared to those of late years. She brought a chestful of linen sheets, and bolsters, and blankets and, in addition, a length of fabric for Tom's mother and one for each of his sisters. She owned several gowns herself, and had a selection of aprons and caps. It did not seem possible that a few miles of river could make so much difference in the ways of village life. Many in Hadley were beginning to know such prosperity as Windsor enjoyed; it seemed as if the time had come to follow its example.

Early in the spring, Warrwarrankshan began to fashion a second long canoe; he patiently, expertly, burned and chipped out the heart of a mighty chestnut log until it reached just the proper degree of buoyancy; he shaped the ends deftly, so they plowed through water as sure and swift as a mallard.

Ham had grown increasingly uneasy as spring came on. In the past, he had brought back staples: salt for potables and cattle, knives, hafts, canvas, rope, hourglasses, brimstone, paper, pins, nails, stockings, hats, iron for blacksmithing, and occasionally coarse duffel cloth. The only finery had been of no consequence, being but an effort by some lass to refurbish a home-loomed or inherited garment. Now, suddenly, however, young girls did not cherish homespun linsey-woolsey, especially if the garment was second- or third-hand. They wanted dornix and dimities; and lace and ribbons for their caps, too. Many women, more knowledgeable than their daughters, asked him about silk stuff and tiffany for scarves and hood linings. Mary Dickinson and Pru Cowles talked of going down to Hartford to visit Esther Bull and Sarah Goodwin. That bothered many who claimed they really were going to shop around at first-hand for themselves. Such an advantage bred resentment. Ham feared that bringing Hannah's gold buttons to town had sparked a fire of worldliness that might consume them all.

While Ham brooded over the women's rebellion, Zech tried to discover Dr. Westcarr's whereabouts. No one had seen him of late; since anyone he could approach did not care at all about John Westcarr, and thought the village well rid of him at any time he was not about, Zech worried lest the errant physician was in Hartford waiting for him, again.

Suddenly a haunting disaster made Zech anxious to put Hadley behind him, regardless of the consequence he might encounter. He wanted to get away from town, away from the recollection of the afternoon when he, and Sammy Smith, and Dan Crow, all in fun, caused so much sorrow.

He and Sammy and Dan, returning from hoeing in the meadow, found themselves behind Jonathan Welles, delivering an ox cart load of fish that his uncle had smoked and stored for his neighbors. Dan nudged Zech and prompted: "Let's get 'im!"

Without needing any more urging, Zech took off with his companions. They dodged around a couple of tethered calves and poked Jon in the ribs with their hoe handles.

Instantly, Jon turned and scaled a trencher-sized piece of shad at Dan; it caught him in the shoulder and sent him staggering backward. "I can match your jousting skills any day!" Jon proclaimed gleefully, and grabbed up a shaft of salmon about three feet tall that protruded above the cart boards like a fence picket. He stood atop his unwieldy load, king of all he surveyed, as the stolid ox inched along the hummocky track, unperturbed by the activity behind him. "I can out-match you dainty weed-pluckers any time — you — with your lady-like poles!" he taunted, and swung his odoriferous club in a wide arc that came within easy, offensive distance of his assailants' noses.

Zech fended off Jon's first feints, and the second time around, lunged forward. He caught him a jab in the ribs, just as Dan caught him behind the right knee, and the cart lurched into a fault. Jon lost his balance. He fell sideways, shrieking with terror as he clutched at a length of shad that fell with him; he screamed with pain as his leg caught between the axle and the wagon; his right arm clutched the moving wheel. The boys yelled their fright and horror. They plunged toward Jon. The ox plodded on; the cart-wheel carried Jon to the ground. It rolled over his shoulder; with his leg caught between the axle and the cart, the turning wheel tore Jon's hip asunder.

Screaming futile protest, enraged and helpless, the boys finally stopped the steadily plodding ox by the manse gate. Zech's horrified glance, flying from Jonathan's crumbled body in vain search for help, stopped aghast at the upper window of the manse. For an instant he stared appalled at a stranger there transfixed by the disaster below. In the next instant, in the turmoil of assistance, he forgot the shadowy figure. Ever afterward, though, whenever he could not keep from remembering that awful day, he pondered the special emptiness the Judges must have known — not able to rush to aid the injured or comfort and sympathize with Tom and Mary Welles, or tongue-lash lads who, with more high spirits than good sense, had blighted a young life.

Zech suffered agonies of self-reproach and remorse that no one but Dan and Sam could begin to understand. He welcomed the prospect of getting away from all these latest haunting memories for a few days.

In spite of his grief, Zech felt a swell of pride as the whole family gathered below the falls to celebrate the maiden voyage of their second long canoe. Their little flotilla passed Springfield before Zech began to suspect that arrangements for a second canoe had not been prompted entirely by their growing trade. He and his father had not discussed his assault at Hartford, but a wordless glance between his father and Warr when a pair of Dr. Westcarr's Pocumtuck friends skimmed between them as they slid down the river, told him that his father and Warr knew more than he had realized. He wondered if Warr had picked up information and had warned his father, or if *that* evil look of Dr. Westcarr's that Aunt had witnessed outside the meetinghouse the day of Lydia's first public appearance had alerted his family.

He knew, instantly, at Hartford, that his suspicions were based on fact. Benji lingered close-by and nothing was going to move him away. Warr seemed not to pay any mind, either, but he tarried about. Zech felt relieved, but annoyed. When he and his retinue dropped in on Jack at the stable, Zech warned Jack under his breath that his friends were paying more attention than appeared likely. Jack was both impressed and puzzled. He had saved up many details that he had expected would impress the country lad from up the river. In spite of himself, Zech could not pretend interest in the accounts Jack had gathered since his last visit. Jack was visibly disappointed.

At the tavern, the innkeeper presented Ham with a package to deliver to Annie Grannis, at Hadley. Her brother-in-law, a prospering New Haven merchant, in town on a court case, had asked that the package be entrusted to someone going up the river. John Westcarr was about now and then, but the innkeeper thought he was not the sort of messenger Mr. Wakefield had in mind. The package was small and soft, the outside wrapping a worn cloth, soiled along the edges by its travels. Ham tucked it into one of his pouches with the silk scarf he had bought for Joe Kellogg — a surprise for Gail, Joe's young wife, just delivered of her third baby. No doubt Joe's warmhearted impulse inspired Ham. He bought a length of bobbin lace for Aunt, and a ribbon for Thanky's fine, fair hair.

Aunt's surprise and appreciation of Ham's thoughtfulness seemed boundless. Several of her friends consulted with her about how to use the trimming to best advantage. They planned to order lace for themselves, too, now that they knew it was available and they could afford it. Finally, Aunt stitched the lace in a double row down the front of her ancient Sabbathday frock. The finery made a beautiful sight and gave the whole family pleasure. Aunt had not had a new Sabbathday gown since Thanky was born, back in Wethersfield. She had renewed its green color by redying it with tansy every autumn, and as she had had time and yarn to loom more fabric, she had replaced the sleeves and sections of the bodice as they wore out; only the skirt remained of the original garment, and it was artfully mended in spots where flying sparks or sharp twigs had had their way. She said that the lace gave her the feeling her gown was entirely new. Thanky's ribbon, of a rosy hue, Aunt plaited along with her hair so that no streamers would fly about and give killjoys like Deacon Goodman a chance to accuse Ham or Aunt of allowing their child to flaunt her finery.

At meeting, the sense of outrage that stiffened the faces of many members of the congregation took Zech by surprise. The sight of Hadley's suddenly acquired finery, gathered together in one place at the same time, slight as it was, did not impress many with the town's growing prosperity so much as rouse an indignation that Zech thought better suited to commandment-breakers like thieves, and cheats and murderers. He could hardly believe his eyes when Widow Bacon accosted Annie Grannis. She snatched at the ties of the hood Annie wore — the contents of the package Ham had relayed from Hartford. "How do you come to wear a hood of such quality?" the cranky old lady sputtered, outraged, knowing full-well where the hood had come from and how it had arrived in Hadley.

Annie drew back, crushed. Ed flew at the ancient widow. " 'Tis my duty to provide for my wife," he snarled. "There are those who will go barefoot it they do not know she may wear whatever is rightfully hers, wherever she wants to!"

At the nooning, Ham's embarrassed uneasiness because of Aunt's pride in her suddenly more-spritely appearance offended Zech. Why should they not be able to reflect publicly the pleasure they all had known at home as a result of his father's generosity? He appreciated, of course, that some blamed his father for transporting the finery to town in the first place, and that his father, as a quiet, conforming man, did not like to cross men of authority; and that annoyed him, too.

Ham looked preoccupied as he sat down by his lunch hamper.

"Don't mind!" Aunt admonished him quietly. She pressed her lips into a thin line that showed she was provoked and did mind. The next minute, in spite of herself, she all but cried out defensively: "There's no good reason for all this ill-feeling! None of the goods here today was purchased at sacrifice of a more worthy requirement!" She examined her lace thoughtfully, then smiled at Ham; for a moment she did not look at all like an aging woman, but so pleased she looked young, indeed. She picked thoughtfully at a stewed partridge before she went on. She spoke slowly, but not so softly as to deny her point of view to those nearby, straining to hear: "My mother spoke often of Old Essex. Her father employed a dozen men at his looms, you know. She had fine clothes there, and a house as large and comfortable as any here in New England; and it did not turn her family's heart from God — They would not have considered coming to this wilderness in the first place if such were so. Life need not continue so spare as it has been. It should become pleasant again — here — for our offspring — in — time —"

Gaining confidence, she asked, "What is the harm of something beautiful, when — for all our generation, in fact — we have had to do with so much that is hard and makeshift? Why! Scripture finds no such faults! Think of the garments folks were told to wear to temple! Why, Solomon —"

"Aye — Aye — Aye —" Ham agreed, and motioned for her to say no more.

CHAPTER XIV

Ham did not tell Aunt Esther that later in the week Deacon Goodman hailed him as he and Zech passed up the common together. "You'd best run on," Ham advised Zech.

"I want to stay with you," Zech told him.

The deacon's glance ordered Zech away, but when Ham did not order Zech to leave, he went right to the point: "You know the Sumptuary Laws regarding the wearing of finery —" he began. His cold green eyes stared unblinking into Ham's, as if to cast a spell on him, as if Ham were not a man at all, but a darkness in which he did not expect to catch a glimpse of light.

Ham shook his head slowly from side to side. "I have seen no such laws posted," he answered evenly. He had heard reference to such ordinances in the past though, posted years ago, before he had come up the river.

" 'Twas posted on the meetinghouse door in Northampton!" Deacon Goodman growled, his voice so full of emotion he almost choked.

"I have not seen it — nor heard of its being posted — in my time —" Ham repeated. He spoke carefully.

"There's those who need guidance or their substance will be wasted — such truck as you are bringing up the river is only a cause of confusion," the deacon warned testily.

Ham's brows shot up. He waited for the deacon to go on. When he advised Ham: "You should use better judgement than those who have none!" Ham shook his head, as if dismissing such an opinion.

100

Outraged that Ham would resist his instructions, Deacon Goodman rebuked him: "You should not be so willing to sell your soul for a mess of pottage!"

Ham's mouth dropped open; his purposefully blank expression turned to controlled fury, hot blood colored his weathered face and the pulse in his throat and forehead throbbed. He stared at Deacon Goodman in disbelief. "Sire —!" he finally sputtered, his tone making the word sound distasteful, "I recall that the advice of The Master is to judge not, that ye be not judged!"

He grasped Zech's elbow firmly, then, and spun him about, facing homeward.

Ham was too distraught to go directly home. He did not want to discuss the incident with his already resentful wife, but he had to talk to someone his own age. He turned back to Ike's trading room.

"Seen the deacon, have ye?" Ike asked as soon as he saw Ham.

Ham nodded slowly.

"I was looking right at him at meeting when Gail Kellogg showed up sporting that new silk scarf of hers," Ike explained.

Ham groaned. He smiled indulgently, remembering. "She wears it with such pride —" he agreed sorrowfully. "They all do, don't they? Nice things give pleasure — and we have had so little — of nice things — here —"

"Aye. And you know that scarf of Gail's is a challenge to Skinflint Dick!" Ike snorted. He banged his fists together.

"Aye — Ham agreed, pained. "Mary should have at least a scarf —"

"And believe me, she would like as good as what Gail has! She should not need to begrudge Gail anything. She should have a scarf — *and* hood — *and* a new frock — silk or velvet — Instead —" his voice trailed off, muttering. Full of wondering exasperation, he went on: "There's no young ones in town so mended and put together as the Goodmans."

"They are well cared for!" Ham defended.

"I am not saying they are not," Ike replied defensively. "I am but saying what we all know. They should be better provided for. And that means Mary, too!"

Ham sighed. He had heard two wives and Granny Felton remark aplenty about Richard Goodman's stingy, penny-pinching ways and marvel at his young wife's ingenuity. "He told me the law regarding finery was posted in Northampton —" Ham said pointedly and as if he could not believe what he was saying. The men looked at each other and began to shake their heads. They began to laugh from weakness.

"Why — that ordinance was posted there 'fore we came up the river," Ike snorted. "Twenty years ago! Pa says, when men and women on this side of the water were scratching to keep alive. Most families was lucky to have tow, then, much less anything fancier. What they'd brought with 'em was worn out, and their substance spent. And nothing to do with, either. That law was to halt new ones coming over from flaunting their possessions when the colonizers had nothing left."

He sighed. "I will tell you something that did not help this matter at all," he exhorted: "Old John and that wig! The old law warned against men wearing wigs and long hair, 'cause that was a way of life our fathers were fleeing. Only men of means had wigs in Old England. Now, that wig of John's was like a camel's nose in a tent. In this town, what one does, others think they have the right to do, too, and not without reason. When Hannah bought those buttons — and that dress of hers — and Sally's! Why — they really got the snowball to rolling!" He shook his head. "The younger ones, now, just married, or thinking about it, and those who remember back — Well, 'tis human nature to want the best for those we care for. Not one Jack Man in the village is about to bow the knee to the like of Richard Goodman in this matter — or Pastor Russell, either, if he goes along with Dick on this."

"I doubt Dick's going to leave well enough alone," Ham murmured unhappily. "Nor is he alone in his thinking, you know."

"Ha! Not alone, to be sure. But a prime mover!" Ike responded angrily. He cried out, vexed: "They caught us asleep! We should have suspected something sooner. For years, Dick begged off bein' selectman because there was no fee in it for him, and nobody wanted him tending their business anyway, so his excuses were always accepted without fines for not taking his turn. Then he decided he wanted his turn — and everyone goes along with him. I s'pose he could not be refused, but not a one of us sluggards gave one second thought to his intentions. Not one! And then he gets himself elected *chairman,* to boot. And still nobody gives a thought to what he might be up to! We will see more of this trouble before we see less, let me tell you!"

"What *does* the law state?" Ham asked cautiously.

Ike gave him a piercing look, as if to discover if he were being cowardly. "So far as I can recall," he answered stiffly, "there must be an estate of £200 'fore folks can wear finery."

"Most families in town can claim that much, now —"

"Aye. And some started with naught but their hands and backs, too. But even if there should be quibbling about substance — and the amount raised — the law now states: £200 — or *educated*!"

"Educated?" Ham echoed as if caught unaware. He whistled involuntarily. He and Ike exchanged a knowing look.

"Ed - u - cate - ed!" Ike repeated.

"HHhhmmmmm," Ham muttered.

"Aye!" Ike agreed. "Of course, they meant University men, twenty years ago. Some of them, being younger sons, were not men of wealth, but they were gentlemen. Now, here, with Madame Hopkins' Trust providing schooling for *every* Hadley lad, there is no distinction. And that's all to the good, I say. Forget what we put on our backs! Our fathers and grandfathers believed that schooling gave men better understanding, so they could have a better life. The more learning a man has, the less he has to take from anybody. Providing, of course, he uses it. 'Twas not unlettered men saved Parliament, and no one mistook any of them for beggars, either."

Ham's head bobbed agreement.

"Now, you think about education in Springfield, Hamblin Gillette! You know why there's no school there, in spite of all the orders from Boston to get crackin'. Without schooling, John Pynchon keeps everything as he wants it. He is not interested in having more than a few choice lads instructed. Just such as is necessary to his convenience! At the same time, men are losing sight of the problems that brought so many here to begin with. Some men, hired on, never did understand or care. But there's no excuse for not keeping schools. Without 'em, the oppressions our fathers turned away from will catch us all. Those same problems are right here, now. We got King Richard Goodman and his Buckingham — Pastor Russell — or perhaps 'tis the other way 'round. They are all for deciding what we shall do, and how, and when — and trying to make us swallow what they tell us, telling us 'tis good for our souls!"

Ham inhaled, and the prolonged sound seemed to rise from the soles of his feet; he sighed, and the long-drawn-out sound that escaped his lips was almost a groan. He threw out his hands in a gesture of despair and turned toward home. Zech followed in his wake and tried to digest all the ways of men that he had been exposed to that afternoon.

Zech's befriending of John Goodman complicated his life from time to time, afterward. John returned to school after his sliding accident, while walking was yet hazardous to one with his arm in a sling. He was no help at home in his crippled condition, and his father believed the pain John suffered moving about would add to his punishment for disobeying his command and not returning home immediately after school.

Zech's skinned face smarted for days before it began to heal. His right cheek became a solid, hard scab that kept him from smiling or laughing. As soon as his friends discovered that, they made every effort to make him do both, until sometimes they all fell down laughing and holding their sides. When Dan tried to carry the sport into the classroom, the schoolmaster cracked him sharply alongside his head with his heavy oak ruler. John supposed that Zech received the same cold treatment at home that he received; since his father constantly reminded him that it was his fault Zech got hurt, he tried to make it up to him. Once, he prompted Zech as he stumbled through a Latin conjugation in his usual inept way, and received a scathing denunciation from the master as well as a sharp knuckle rapping, too. Fewer lads were brighter than John, yet he lacked understanding to a degree that baffled his schoolmates.

The last day classes met, as spring chores began to increase, John appeared lugging three well-cured beaver skins nearly as long as he was tall. All the boys sank their grubby fingers into the soft, thick pelt and knew real luxury for a passing moment. They all supposed that John was bringing the pelts to Zech for some debt Deacon Dick owed Ham; otherwise the pelts would have been delivered directly to Ike Dickinson.

"Let me carry one, too," Dan offered, as Zech reached for one of the skins at the end of classes; both lads expected to share any part of a companion's burden.

"No! — They are mine — I will carry them all!" John insisted stubbornly, and Zech and Dan stood back, puzzled. John had no idea how to enjoy the company of other boys. He threw the pelts over his shoulder and started across the common ahead of Zech and Dan. By the time Dan turned down his homeward path, their classmates had disappeared from sight; the afternoon's walk had been without the usual idle observations and skirmishing play familiar to Zech and Dan: just John leading the way, trudging along, glancing back to be sure the pelts were not dragging on the uneven ground, and Dan and Zech following solemnly in his wake.

At Ham's corner post, John stopped and draped the furs over the middle fencerail. "These skins are mine, Zech!" he announced as he caught his breath.

"Oh?" Zech answered, confused, wondering what might come next.

"Wappawy gave them to me. He calls me 'Brother,' you know. — I want your father — you and your father — should take them to Hartford for me —"

Zech caught his breath and glanced away from the intense blue eyes staring at him, studying him, ready to be offended and not wanting to be hurt. With a rush of words, John cried out: "I want you to take these and get something pretty for my mother."

Zech gasped.

John's eyes filled with tears. His voice almost too husky to be understood, he lashed out: "She can not help it that we are so poor, Zech!"

"*Poor?*" Ham echoed, when Zech gave him the pelts and told him what John had said. "*Poor!*" he repeated. "We should all be so poor!"

"Poor in *spirit*!" Aunt shrilled angrily. "Blessed are the poor in spirit, heh?" she muttered between gritted teeth. She clenched her fist. "Why — that should make King Richard the Flinthearted the most righteous man in town — the county — the valley — the colony — *the whole world!*" By the time she reached the word *world* her voice had risen to an explosive shriek.

"Esther! — Esther!" Ham admonished gently, and grinned, amused, in complete agreement with her words.

"What are you going to do, Ham?" Aunt asked as she got herself under control; she made a face in the same way her boys did at the thought of taking medicine.

Ham stared at the fire. Finally, he murmured: "So Wappawy gave those skins to John!"

"What a mischief-maker!" Aunt snarled.

"Aye! He's a sly one. He knows what he's doing," Ham said, as much to himself as in answer to Aunt.

Warr had little use for Wappawy, who was half Pocumtuck, a surly strain. Wappawy's mother, a Nonotuck, had attached herself to Mary Goodman when Mary had come to town a bride, one of the first settlers. Fair-skinned blondes in particular attracted the swarthy Indians' attention, and the Terrys, tall, angular blondes with square jaws and steady blue eyes had a noble look about them. From the first, Mary had needed help, and Wappawy's recently widowed mother, her sannup carried off by smallpox, had welcomed the opportunity to provide for herself and her three young children. Everyone in the Valley had known that Deacon Dick would do less providing than Squaw Mechekan. Deacon Goodman planned to bring up the sturdy, eight-year-old Wappawy as a well-trained farmhand, but Wappawy's Indian heritage withstood Deacon Dick's attempts and made them mortal enemies. The hostility of the two men had not affected the relationship of the women, however. Mary Goodman's family had come up the river only recently; until last winter, when Mechekan died of old age, she had been like a mother to Mary, and no children in the Valley had had a more attentive grandmother than the Goodman children had in Mechekan. Wappawy resented the Goodman children. He did not go near their home in his mother's last illness, through which Mary and her children nursed Mechekan with loving care. Now he was playing games with the old deacon; with everyone in the Valley, really.

Zech helped to resolve John's problem the next week when lecture met at Hatfield. At the nooning, Ham and Aunt carried Philip Russell and his wife, Betsey, Mary Goodman's half sister, to one side to talk while they lunched. Zech lingered nearby. He expected the elders to banish him from their discussion, but when they did not, he hovered about, attentive but silent.

Betsey Russell's face shadowed as Ham related the details of John's request. Philip Russell looked downhearted, too. He was Pastor's half brother, a generation younger; though no one was likely to mistake they were brothers, the two men were very unlike. Philip professed no scholarly interests and spoke seldom, not always answering when addressed. Ben Wait often sang a song to the effect that Philip, being Pastor's brother, never had an opportunity to learn to talk.

"Mary could use something pretty," Betsey mused, when Ham finished talking. She hesitated, and added grimly: "Mary could use *anything!*" The adults sat in silence and finally started to eat.

At length, Philip said thoughtfully, "Mary could have a very fine dress length for those skins."

"Aye," Ham agreed, and sighed.

The women's eyes met, each looking to the other for a way to manage the purchase. Zech made the proposal, then, that finally resolved the situation: "Could not Papa pretend to trade the skins to Goody Russell? Wappawy will brag that he gave three fine beaver skins to the Goodmans so that Deacon Dick's wife could have a new garment. Of course, he does not expect that to happen. But if Deacon Dick thinks that the skins were given to Goody Russell, and she took them to spite Wappawy because he was trying to make mischief, and she has Papa get her sister a dress length because she knows that Squaw Mechekan would have liked her to have the skins to trade — and she *was* so good to her, and all — then Deacon Dick will think that he is getting the best of Wappawy, this time — and he won't know about John —"

He stopped, out of breath.

The adults blinked, trying to follow his explanation. Finally, Philip murmured, "You have made several good points, Lad." He did not know Zech's name. He added, drily: "Dick would take special pleasure from a trade that he thought was intended for someone else."

The others nodded in uneasy agreement.

After a pause, Ham swallowed and said: "Ah — Goody Russell — " he grinned and blushed as deep a red as any cranberry in the bogs. "That's a mighty fine-looking apple tart you have there —"

Betsey Russell glanced at him quickly, perplexed for a moment, not realizing instantly that Ham was starting to bargain for the beaver skins. The second she understood, she answered in a rush: "Oh — Aye. Thank you, Sire. 'Tis tasty, indeed, my husband tells me."

"Oh, there's none better," Philip prompted, catching on immediately. His warmth and amusement surprised Zech.

"Well," Ham ruminated, the way he did when trading at Hartford; he was savoring the fun: "Wouldst take a well-cured beaver skin for it?"

Betsey made a wry face. She looked reproachful. "Three, Sire!" she parried, and they all laughed.

Betsey held up the tart and regarded it appreciatively, as if she were not sure she wanted to part with it. She looked at her husband for approval, her expression for all the world one of pleading for permission to make the trade.

Philip pretended to consider all the conditions for a full minute before he threw out his hands in a gesture of surrender. "For *three* — if you insist!" he consented, finally.

Ham took the tart from Betsey's outstretched hand. "Don't ever tell what a poor bargainer I am, at times —" he warned, half-choked with relief that made him laugh. "I'll — I'll — lose all my trade, if you do!"

They all laughed, then, their anxiety spent. Neighbors looked to see what provoked so much merriment, wanting to share in it.

"What about John, though?" Aunt asked soberly when their thoughts returned to the problem at hand.

"Aye — *John* —" the others mumbled, baffled, again.

"I will speak to John," Betsey offered, finally, dabbing at her eyes. A few little spasms of laughter interrupted her words. "And I will tell Mary, too — enough — she should know her debt to him." She added unhappily: "She is harder on John than is her nature — she — well —" She did not go on; she had no need to speak more of details with which they all were so well-acquainted.

On their next trip to Hartford, Ham's lading for the return trip doubled. Besides a staggering amount of what some considered to be fripperies, he carried a bundle from Goody Buell at Windsor to Bobby Welles and a bolt of sober grey worsted to Mary Goodman. Mary's grey cloth had a rosy cast to it. Ham presented it to her himself. He made certain that Deacon Dick was at home when he stopped by with the package; this time, he sent Zech home ahead of him. Later, he related how he had quite shamelessly played on the Deacon's vanity. Deacon Dick had stood by Mary's side, looking for all the world like an insulted mastiff, ready to erupt with a torrent of loud, baying objections and condemnations; but they had frittered away as he came to believe Wappawy had been cozened.

Mary had been quite overcome by the gift. She had turned and looked at John when Ham put the package in her hands: Betsey Russell had done well explaining as little as needed to be told to either mother or son. John had bolted out the door when his mother began to weep. Ham supposed that her husband thought that she wept, remembering Mechekan; but John had known why she wept. Ham believed that John had rushed someplace to hide and weep, too.

CHAPTER XV

Before the Sabbath, a notice in Deacon Dick's crabbed hand-writing appeared on the meetinghouse door: his version of the Sumptuary Law of 1651:

> Liable to action at Law, and of utter detestation and dis-like that men or women of less than £200 estate and of mean condition, education and callings, should wear long hair or take upon them the garbe of gentlemen by the wearing of gold or silver lace, or buttons, or points at their knees, or walk in greate boots; or women of the same ranke to weare silke or tiffany hoods or scarves, which though allowable to persons of greater estates or more liberal education, yet it cannot but be judged intolerable in persons of such like condition to wear silke in a flaunting manner, and long hair and other extrav-agances contrary to honest and sober order and demeanor not becoming a wilderness state, at least the profession of christianity and religion.

His incensed fellow selectmen — Timothy Nash, John and Tom Dickinson, and Frank Barnard — had refused to sign their names to the copy of the ancient order, but Pastor Russell's signature appeared below that of his deacon's. To emphasize their stand, at the Sabbath morning service, Pastor preached sternly that the thoughts of men now turned too much from godliness, not a new text by any means; in his chill monotone, he exhorted his congregation to watch their ways and warned grimly of the snares of pleasure.

Feeling ran high throughout the entire upper Valley. Many sternly tucked in their lips and with glazed eyes nodded agree-ment, but most townsmen took offense. Men and women of all conditions pondered the matter, annoyed and confused.

" 'Tis only a threat — liable to action at law —" Young Tom Welles challenged whenever men met. He liked to remind everyone that in Old England his family had been lawyers; he liked to quibble over fine points in disputes at town meetings; but this time he was straightforward. "We must have action at law over this," he declared. "Every Man Jack of us should be able to spend our substance as we please without needing to put up with all this haggling, and sniffing and snuffling about."

Peter Tilton agreed. He urged that the matter be taken to law and settled once and for all. He claimed that Squire Goodwin had spoken in like manner. But Squire Goodwin had died suddenly while on a trip to Hartford and Deacon Dick had posted his notice immediately. Squire Goodwin, a leader of power and wealth, had been a University man; Hartford men called him the Cato of the Connecticut Valley. The villagers agreed as one that if Squire Goodwin were alive Deacon Dick would not have felt so bold. Ham felt reassured, hearing of Squire Goodwin's opinion.

"Since our last rate set most families above £200, how will the court decide who is a gentleman and who is not?" Ed Grannis demanded to know. Due to his stubborn set of mind he alone was not a property owner among those incensed by the warning. Hadley's selectmen, needing a shoemaker, had petitioned Ed to come to town; he rented a cottage for a nominal fee. He would have had a land grant of his own by now but, though he attended meeting each Sabbath as required, he clung to the Church of England and refused to become a member of Hadley's congregation. According to the covenant drawn up by Hadley's engagers, only church members could become freemen; not being a freeman, he could not have a grant of land or a dwelling of his own.

"Who needs a court to decide who is a gentleman?" Az Dickinson scoffed. "Gentlemen don't get their hands dirty — that's all."

"Well, then," Ben Wait reminded, "that puts Unwillin' Will ahead of all us others —"

Everyone grunted amused agreement.

"Aye — most of us were freeholders in England," Ed reminded. "But not one of us lived only by other men's labor. But take some who did: Stephen Terry, now — As much as Mr. Goodwin, he was born to gentry. An Oxford man — with one uncle Bishop of Salisbury, and John White his uncle, too. Squire White refused to purchase a title, and spent a fortune transporting the Dorchester congregation to the colonies. But Squire Terry's offspring here are neither gentlemen nor educated. Not a one of his sons in Connecticut, nor his sons-in-law here, has as much schooling as every

Hadley lad is exposed to."

"Captain Pynchon, himself, has less schooling than any lad here, if it comes to that," Experience Hinsdale reminded. "What reading and writing he learned, he learned at home, or from Mr. Moxon who was the preacher down there when he was growing up."

"Who that you know of in the Valley — besides Pastor — is planning to send sons off to college, anyway?" Experience pressed in a scoffing tone.

"I am!" Frank Barnard barked defensively.

"And so am I!" Ike declared.

The men avoided looking at each other. They swallowed, nonplussed by Ike's statement. Ike, twenty-eight, and not able-bodied, had yet to wed, much less decide how he would educate his sons. None of his companions had great expectations for Ike's plans for the future; they would not have believed that his first-born son would found and be first president of a college in the wilderness of New Jersey that would become a university equal to Harvard, and Oxford, and Cambridge. None had the gift of prophecy to foretell that a descendant of Deacon Smith would found the first college for women in the shadow of Mount Holyoke, or that a Smith family, descendants of both Deacon Smith and Ben Wait, would found an eminent college for women across the river in Northampton, and a renowned agricultural school and singular, never-ending charities. If they were inclined to prophesy at all, they might have thought rightly enough that Frank's descendants would become leaders of great universities, and, of course, champion education for women.

"Good for you, Ike!" Ed Grannis cheered as soon as he found his voice; he went on as if there had been no interruption: " 'Tis Pastor's duty to tell us how to preserve our souls. How many times in doing that has he warned us that love of money is the root of all evil? Well, as I see it, I am sharing what I gain with my family, trying to make life pleasant for them. The good Lord knows life is hard! We are not tucking away what we earn where moths consume it, or rust corrupts it — which is what the Bible warns against. And that's what King Richard does best, too!"

Three weeks before the March County Court was scheduled to meet in Northampton, Henry Clarke, Hadley's magistrate, nailed a summons to the meetinghouse door. It called to account those who continued to willfully disregard Selectman Goodman's stern warning: Hannah Westcarr; her sister, Sally Barnard; Hepzibah Welles; Annie Grannis; Gail Kellogg; and Mary Broughton, a half-orphaned lass of Northampton, now living with the family of John Ingram, who had come to town indentured.

The names of those summoned left the town reeling from shock.

Mistress Terry, when she heard of the insult to her daughter, Gail, rushed up the common to Deacon Goodman's. She found the door barred against her.

"Afraid to listen to an old woman's counsel!" she wept next door in Small Pockets' kitchen, where she retreated to collect her thoughts and pour out her anguish.

"Poor Gail!" she cried out to Hannah Crow, who had been a firm friend of all her daughters since childhood. "How can Mary let him do this to us?"

"Mistress Terry," Hannah consoled, later repeating the harrowing scene for the benefit of equally-distressed neighbors: " 'Tis not Mary's doing, you know that."

"They can not charge Gail!" Mistress Terry protested between sobs. "Joe is not of a mean condition. He has been a selectman! 'Tis all false that he does not have an estate of £200 value. If he did not have before Mr. Terry died, he does now. What is mine is his. I would not have it any other way! He is not of a mean condition at all!"

Her clouded glance swept from Hannah to Sam and Small Pockets standing inside the doorway. They had been waiting and watching anxiously, wondering what action would follow when word of the summons spread through town. They had not expected that Richard Goodman would go so far as to lock himself in.

"Stephen knew! He knew what Richard Goodman was!" Mistress Terry cried out to Small Pockets.

The old man looked troubled. One of his sons in the Connecticut Colony, being of a grasping nature, had caused him much pain in a similar manner.

"When Stephen knew his time was coming — he told me that Gail must marry someone who would protect Gail and me — that he could not die 'til he had us safe from Richard's greedy ways."

No one spoke. "He did not know anyone could be like Richard. Not at first. 'Twas not his nature, and he did not see that Richard was like his mother. Stephen thought that he was arranging a good

112

marriage for Mary. Richard needed a wife — with his mother gone — Stephen could not believe that a man not of mean condition would not provide willingly for his family. There were those who tried to warn him! But he could not believe — 'twas not his way! He did not know! He did not know!'' She repeated the whole statement several times until she could speak no more.

Hannah put a cup of warmed posset before Mistress Terry and patted her shoulder, trying to console her.

'' 'Twas the hand of Providence provided us with Joe Kellogg when we needed him. One who would protect us — take care of us as he does —'' the spent voice quavered.

"Aye —'' Hannah agreed, happy that Providence had not blessed her with a ready-made family of six, at nineteen years of age, as he had Gail.

Most townsfolk agreed that there may have been justification for calling-up Sally Barnard and Mary Broughton. Sally delighted in sharing Hannah Westcarr's ever-increasing stock of finery, most of it brought to town by Doctor Westcarr, more to confound his neighbors, everyone agreed, than to indulge his wife. With no children of her own, Hannah doted on Sally; Sally's preening provoked many women who championed the Westcarrs' right to expend their substance as they pleased. Mary Broughton was of another stripe entirely. The daughter of a Northampton widow, she would have been ill-clothed, indeed, were it not for a cousin of her father's, a man of great estate at The Bay. He served in the General Court with Peter Tilton and often sent a store of fine clothes to his unfortunate relatives by Peter. Mary's mother unselfishly gave many garments away to others, but she did permit Mary more than one Sabbath gown, and over a period of time Mary had acquired a tiffany hood and a silk scarf. The quality of Mary's clothing equalled that of any lass north of New Haven. She vied with Sally. Between them, they made many girls their age — and their mothers — very unhappy.

Ham was relieved that it was Peter and not he who had brought Mary's controversial finery to town. He held himself to blame, in part, for Annie Grannis' being made an example.

Notices posted in Springfield, Westfield and Northampton summoned thirty women altogether to appear in Northampton to face the consequences of their misplaced pride.

The day of the trial, the families of the accused and their sympathizing neighbors converged at Northampton, bound for the quarter court scheduled to meet at Mr. Woodward's tavern. Most of those who agreed with the charges chose not to attend. For the most part they were older folk who claimed to disdain their neighbors' weaknesses, their being taken in by Beelzebub. Many men cared not at all about the matter one way or another. They remained at home attending to their chores and their youngsters; few women stayed away. Ham Gillette went, grim and not reluctant. Serv and Gracie, good paddlers, now, helped ferry their family across the river. Zech helped Dan with his.

Dan shared none of Zech's secret anxieties regarding the trial. He did not have much interest in it. No one would question the right of any women in his family to wear whatever they chose, and his father had not had anything to do with the cause of the furor, either, though that vain old man had helped stir up the witches' cauldron with his wig. To Dan, the trial was an outing, a fun-kind of mid-week lecture: a milling throng and shared collations without the requirement to attend a crowded session of older men talk — talk — talking. Recently, however, lectures had begun to be more interesting: many young blades brought to town as youngsters had grown to the age where they did not always listen patiently and agree with their elders. Some said that Tom Welles liked the sound of his own voice, but so did some of the oldsters; and sometimes Tom's challenges posed questions the elders were hard put to reply to without the heat of uncertainty. There would be arguments aplenty at the trial today, Dan knew, but he would not be among those permitted to squeeze into the small courtroom. So he carried a dozen rope quoits with him to pass the time away. He wore them like bracelets on his thin, birch-strong arms. They interfered with his paddling, and ever-anxious Mary Church complained to his parents that such a practice was a danger to their safety, but she roused no interest on their part at all.

Richard Goodman arrived with Pastor and Mistress Russell. They looked to neither right nor left and did not speak to each other; they appeared indifferent to the uneasy sociability of the occasion. For once, Mistress Russell seemed not to be ailing; she moved right along, keeping up with the men's brisk pace. Hannah Crow, carefully controlling the tone of her voice, inquired of Deacon Dick regarding Mary's absence. He answered that Mary was expecting again and was home sick, and the older children attending to the young ones. He spoke quite civilly, as if, for once, he were concerned.

Dan and Zech paced off a length of highway beyond where those coming from the river turned in at the Woodward gate. By the time they had stakes driven into the ground, more players had gathered than could be included in a single contest; teams were drawn by lots and turns assigned.

Zech played a poor game in the first playoff. Dr. Westcarr was lounging on the Woodwards' fence, watching him; his presence and all the other excitement that held significance for him kept Zech from enjoying himself or performing well. When his team gave over to the next in turn, he wandered into the crowded dooryard. By then, Dr. Westcarr had accompanied the Barnard family inside.

Only a few of the defendants' relatives could manage to edge into the courtroom. The more knowledgeable overflow already had accommodated themselves as close to the courtroom door as possible, the remainder milled about in the fresh spring air, finding what shelter they could in the yard and shed.

Henry Woodward, a tall, unbelievably thin man with an abundance of nervous energy and black hair with scarcely a show of white, had come to the colonies a surgeon. In an accident soon after arriving at Dorchester, he had mangled his right arm. No longer able to bleed patients, or set bones properly, yet a proper, intelligent citizen, the General Court recommended he be granted the license to sell liquors and keep an ordinary where court could meet north of Springfield, in Hampshire county. Three of the four officers of the court meeting with him were elderly men of his generation: Hadley's dour, childless widower, Henry Clarke; his cousin, William Clarke of Northampton; and corpulant Elizur Holyoke of Springfield. Captain John Pynchon was a generation younger. His father had been the original grantee in the valley to whom the other magistrates all had been beholden in some way at the beginning of the colony. Slight of build, a diminutive, swarthy man of obvious importance, he perched on a thick, hard cushion in order to appear as commanding as his fellow judges.

It seemed to Zech that most women present were as well-garbed as those on trial, if not more so. He moved about outside the house, wanting to find a vantage spot where he could hear the session within, if possible. Wiser citizens than he, and older, had come early; they occupied all places that might serve that purpose. He wandered back to the front yard, seeking a place in the sun. The best spaces there were taken, too. He began to seek out a nook sheltered from the brisk spring breeze.

"Hey, Zech!" Dan hailed him, his voice bubbling with excitement. "Look what we've got for you!"

Zech turned and craned to see what Dan had. He sagged with dismay. Dan and Joey Grannis flanked Biddy, one of Elder Strong's younger daughters. They had managed to separate her from an intrigued gaggle of Northampton girls, sisters and friends, who watched his reaction, their expressions fierce with doubt; they stood ready to rescue Biddy and flail the boys good and proper if they were just making sport. Dan and Joey, two of the cleverest fakers in the world, beamed at Zech as if they were doing him the greatest favor possible. Not that Zech had no interest in Biddy. He did. Perhaps more than in any other maiden he knew. In a moment of weakness, he had confided to Dan that he thought her the prettiest, sweetest girl he knew. Her soft, wavy brown hair and big green eyes and impish ways appealed to him. But she was deaf and dumb. Her affliction distressed him. As much as he admired her appearance — and he had heard much of her remarkable home skills with the distaff and needle, and cooking and baking, too — her family of fourteen brothers and sisters, quicker and more capable than most of their neighbors, had lavished every attention on Biddy's training — the unpleasant sounds of her occasional outbursts when excited hurt his feelings, though they seemed not to affect Biddy at all. Zech suddenly realized how often he had managed to be within sight of Biddy — but he had entertained no real expectation of closer acquaintance.

Biddy did not look completely taken-in. Just hopeful. Her half-smile was uneasy, unhappy, as if she expected she might need to retreat to the unwelcome comfort of her friends.

Zech's annoyance with his comrades and his understanding of the injury to the lass prompted him to act without further thought. He masked his first shock and embarrassment and caught his breath. He did not flee, as his first reaction prompted. Instead, he moved toward the waiting group. Biddy's expression changed to uncertain pleasure. Her companions beamed, relieved and pleased. Dan and Joey shoved Biddy in Zech's direction and romped back toward the quoit players, hooting like a couple of beset owls. Biddy's friends yelled: "Fraidy cats!" after them

116

derisively. By then, everyone in the crowded yard was watching for want of anything better to do.

Zech caught the pained regret that for an instant shadowed his parents' look of surprised interest. He took a deep breath and ushered Biddy toward a makeshift bench where Tom Cooper, Springfield's carpenter, made room for them between him and Ben Wait's grinning brother-in-law. A host of Springfield folk had swarmed up the river together.

Zech had no idea how to proceed with Biddy. They could not make small talk like other folk. Someone behind him patted him on the shoulder in a way that said, "Good Lad!" and he breathed an involuntary sigh, longer and more eloquent than he meant any confession to be. Biddy turned and smiled at him shyly. Her sparkling green eyes told him that she understood all that had transpired and she was grateful for his kindness. Her smile set everything right. Zech straightened his shoulders and smiled back, suddenly pleased by the unexpected turn of events.

A stranger to Zech greeted Goodman Cooper and wedged himself between Tom and Zech. "I should not have thought the day would come when any of Squire Terry's kin would be considered folk of a mean condition," the stranger remarked, shaking his head as he settled down.

"They are not, of course, you know!" Goodman Cooper replied grimly.

The stranger shook his head again and sighed. "Mr. Terry learned to his sorrow that 'tis not the amount of a man's estate that makes him a good provider."

"Aye!" Tom Cooper agreed quietly.

"I knew the Terry girls when they was young," the stranger went on. "When I come to Connecticut to build for Sir Richard Saltonstall. Remember? 'Fore I went over Guilford way. I'm of Westfield, now. My niece is one called up from there."

Jack Leonard leaned around Tom and crowed to the stranger: "Squire Terry would not allow his daughters to marry young men of their own generation who came bound — Those older men had a lot to learn!"

Zech groaned to himself. At least Biddy's affliction spared her the embarrassment he suffered just now. The stranger had not recognized Betsey Russell, one of Squire Terry's daughters, as a grownup. She sat just behind Tom, out of his sight, quietly trotting her youngest on her knee. She had walked to town with the

Hatfield delegation and had left her older children at home with their father. Philip Russell would have nothing to do with a fray such as this.

"Well," the stranger went on, his tone bitter: "I say covetousness is the sin that should be guarded against — if 'twere possible to change men's hearts by law —"

"I say amen to that!" Tom agreed. " 'Tis not estate and mean condition that is, in fact, on trial here, my friend."

"Aye —" the stranger replied thoughtfully, and said no more.

Zech glanced about at the vexed expressions of those sitting and waiting, out of touch with the proceedings that meant so much. They knew how the trial *should* go. They were worried, though, that right might not prevail. If there was so much right-thinking going on, would there be a trial at all?

Mistress Terry appeared first in the doorway. Joyfully she raised her arms and crowed triumphantly: " 'Tis done!" She tried to appear bleak and forbidding in imitation of Squire Clarke reading the complaint to the justices as she announced that neither Gail nor Hannah had been called to the bench. No case could be made against them. Relishing her relief and satisfaction and distaste, she mimicked the judges' examination of the castoffs that brought humiliation to Annie Grannis and Mary Broughton. In scathing tones she mocked the lecture that addressed the error of the ways of those who did not bear in mind that they lived in a wilderness where all must be of sober mind, ever mindful of the wickedness of the world and of their station in life, and never — never — not for a trice — should expect that God would provide bountifully for them!

Bobby Welles dabbed at her eyes as Mistress Terry recounted the Judges' admonition to her for misleading thoughtless young ones into ways of self-indulgence. It took a while for the hushed audience to realize that only Sally Barnard and two other lasses, one from Springfield, one from Westfield, had been fined — twelve shillings, sixpence each.

Sally Barnard's vanity was only momentarily wounded. Once she emerged into the milling courtyard she became a center of attention. She dried her tears, a heroine. Relieved Valley folk murmured and muttered their gratification and displeasure to one another as they disbanded. There was no jubilation: just unhappiness at thought of the dreary business that had brought the trial to pass in the first place.

118

The fathers of the girls who were fined appealed their daughters' cases at the next quarter court, protesting that their estates and condition permitted them to provide for their families as they pleased without being subject to anyone's unseemly guidance. The court agreed and remitted their fines.

CHAPTER XVI

Though the court sessions were not the last frays in a battle that Deacon Goodman and Pastor Russell already had lost, the Valley began to turn its attention from trifles to more sobering matters.

By the time Zech reached sixteen, he had been out of school two years and had acquired a brother and sister of his own. At first, he had worried about Aunt's condition. He feared losing her — or the infant. That happened often, especially with older women. Their lives would be dreary without Aunt. But she gave rise to no alarm, and she asked Zech to name his brother. He called the baby Timothy. A year later, Aunt delivered another daughter. Thanky very importantly decided that Mindwell would be a good name for the little mite. Mindy was a collicky baby. She fretted everyone for six months. Zech hoped that she would be the last of his father's offspring; even as much pride as he took in a family of his own, there were times when young ones brought little pleasure.

At sixteen, he began to drill with the militia. He marched up and down the common with all males able to bear arms and learned the twenty charges required to fire green powder: . . . open pan . . . clear . . . prime . . . shut . . . cast off corns . . . charge powder . . . draw . . . scour . . . turn . . . shorten . . . and on . . . and on . . . He also watched Az Dickinson, and the Marsh boys, and the Barnards who attracted all the giggly interest beyond the fence; he hoped that somehow he could take on their confident ways. Following the trial, he had scarce been able to contain himself at thought of lecture in Northampton and the opportunity to be with

120

Biddy Strong, again. He had caught sight of her as he arrived, and she smiled at him across the milling crowd. Dutifully, he stayed with his family until the nooning, trying to get his feelings under control. Then he ambled away to join Biddy. As he got to her side, she turned her attention to a hulking bucko that he mistook for one of her older brothers. He patiently awaited her notice, not expecting a new suitor to turn and order him away with a contemptuous "What-are-you-tarrying-about-for-Little-One?" glare. His face grew red and hot, remembering. He had stared at Biddy, unbelieving. She had not seemed aware of his presence. There were advantages to being deaf! Next time a girl showed an interest in him, he did not intend to be cut out.

As he paraded, he knew that General Whalley and General Goffe watched from behind the draperies of the upper chamber. He wondered if they ever picked him out from the others and discussed the day of his discovery.

Since he had stumbled onto the Old Stranger, many changes had come about in Hadley. Twice in recent years, Hatfield had petitioned the General Court for permission to become a separate township with a congregation of its own. On both occasions, Thomas Meekins, representing his neighbors, carried to Boston petitions signed by all Hatfield families. The composers of the petition borrowed heavily from Scripture, and made reference to laws of Exodus and Leviticus that forbid on pain of death such activities as Hatfieldfolk engaged in on the Sabbath in order to attend divine service. Composed in lyric language, Hatfield's petition left no room to doubt the hardships involved for those devout folks who

". . . . at the appointed seasons . . . could not durst to pass over the river, the passing being very difficult and dangerous, both in summer and winter . . . in rainy weather . . . we are forced to . . . empty our canoes that are half full of water, and before we can get to the meetinghouse are wet to the skin . . . In winter season, we are forced to cut and work them out of the ice till our shirts be wet upon our backs. At other times, the winds are high and the water rough, the current strong and the waves ready to swallow us — our vessels tossed up and down so that our women and children do screech, and are so affrighted that they are made unfit for ordinances and cannot . . . profit from them by reason of their anguish of spirit;

and when they return, some of them are more fit for their beds than for family duties and God's services, which they ought to attend . . . That none hitherto hath . . . lost their lives is to be attributed to the care and mercy of God . . .

The Court continued to reject all consideration of separation until a renegade Indian burned a Hatfield house to the ground on a Sabbath, while Hatfieldfolk were at meeting. Families began to watch and ward, then, and rotated guard duty. Their plight finally moved the General Court to grant their petition. Immediately, Hatfield men threw up a meetinghouse and engaged a pastor. At the same time, restless braves, including Wappawy, joined wandering malcontents who camped on the crest of a high, picturesque bluff below Hatfield, across from Hadley's Great Meadow. Through David Wilton, townsmen delivered their minds in the matter: separation did not grant a license to their Indian friends to ignore their neighbors' laws; braves would not be allowed to drink themselves drunk, nor should men banished from Valley towns he permitted to powwow in their midst; nor should they play host to marauders such as Callowan, Wurtow, and Pacquellunt who had murdered fellow tribesmen when liquor fevered their brains.

The older Valley men knew from experience, however, that understandings and treaties with the Indians depended upon the will of the sachems involved. In early years, Uncas, a Connecticut chieftain, had embroiled the settlers in tribal warfare. When Hartford and Windsor men had tried to mediate settlements between Uncas and his enemies, Uncas had agreed to treaties as a matter of convenience: he had ignored them at will.

With Hatfield a town unto itself, and many of the Nonotucks departed from the common, traffic about Hadley slackened to an astonishing degree. Hadley's unaccustomed repose comforted no one, though. Rumors already had begun to fly about that surly Pocumtucks of the territory north of the villages had begun to powwow with their powerful ancestral enemies, the Mohawks. More and more they harassed outlying cottages. When a company of rogues — two Dutchmen, an Irishman, and a Frenchman — stole seven mares and other cattle from John Webb's Northampton farm, they drove the contraband to Pocumtuck country. Wonopequen, the Pocumtuck sachem, advised Goodman Webb that he could ransom his stock for fifty shillings each. Yet, when John and a company of neighbors arrived above Deerfield to meet the ransom demands and drive back the herd, Wonopequen demanded more wampum, plus coats, shirts, liquor, and a list of sundries. He claimed rightly that the stock would bring £20 in other colonies. Only David Wilton's skill concluded the matter, though it seemed to be to no one's satisfaction.

After a roving band of Mohawks murdered a Nonotuck lad crossing a meadow on horseback, and boldly raided local farms of livestock, the General Court in Boston made formal complaint to the government in Albany that held the Mohawks in fee. Mohawk messengers delivered leather worth £20 to the aggrieved towns to redress the wrongs. But trafficking strangers increased. They were blamed for much mischief. Hadleymen worried more about Wappawy and his friends in their new village than they had fretted about them when they dwelled in their midst. They watched in consternation as, with unexpected and stunning industry, young bucks began to erect a semicircle of peeled logs and fortify the land-approach to their campground.

In the spring, the squaws did not plant corn as in the past. Always, before, when budding maple leaves swelled to the size of a squirrel's ear, the squaws had bargained for a corner of plowed land in exchange for planting a tract. Later, some helped with hoeing and husking, too, depending on their friendship with the family. When pressed to tell why they did not plant, the squaws gave uneasy excuses. Old settlers pondered the unaccustomed behaviour; abashed, they realized that they should have observed more closely how the squaws had proceeded so that they could grow corn as thick and lusty as the squaws had. Suddenly, almost too late, the squaws set to work; they planted as if nothing untoward had delayed them.

When Ham's company arrived home from their next trip to Hartford, they found the remaining Nonotucks on the common had plucked up their wigwams and were gone. Their hearts skipped a beat, hearing it. That boded ill. At Hartford they had heard much discussion of a Christian Indian at the Bay who had been murdered for warning his English friends that Philip, the chief of the Wampanoags, the overlord tribe at the Bay, was making plans to go on the warpath.

Philip was the son of Plymouth's good friend, Massasoit.

Following the death of Massasoit, a dozen years before, his sons Metacomet and Wamsutta, had presented themselves at Plymouth Colony to treat with the colonists. They asked for English names, and Governor Bradford chose Philip and Alexander, names of other great heathen leaders of men. After days of feasting and dancing, they set out to return to their camps. Along the way, Alexander became ill. He died a few days later. Philip claimed that Plymouth men had poisoned his brother. Since then, settlers often heard of Philip's sounding-out neighboring tribes, trying to incite an uprising that would drive the English out of the country forever. Until now, though Philip's campaigning made the Valley uneasy, men had believed their friendship with sachems such as Warr assured them of peace.

Tom Dickinson, waiting at the falls with Naseby and a wagon, told of the departing Nonotucks and demanded that Warr explain what was going on. Why had his tribesmen left the village so suddenly?

Reluctantly, Warr told his dismayed friends that the Nipmucks who had been about the village lately had come at Philip's direction. Furthermore, Philip had appointed the troublesome Pocumtucks to overlord the Valley. He had said nothing before because most Nonotucks liked life as they lived it and resented interference. But just before he had left on this trip, one of his 'cousins' had come to him and threatened that certain English families would be captured and tortured if Philip's orders were not followed. From the pain that shadowed the old Indian's eyes, it was plain that Ham and his family had been among the hostages threatened.

When Ham's shocked entourage reached the common, Warr and Benji took their leave silently, striding off toward wherever the Nonotucks were keeping their canoes to ferry over to the new fort. Their friends watched them depart with sinking hearts.

Warr returned with fish and game and tried in his silent ways to reassure his family, but they hardly felt less uneasy than their neighbors: news from the East was of plunder and bloodshed.

The moon waxed and waned through days and nights of speculation. Everyone waited for the next move. Some claimed that the steadfastness of the valleyfolk had thwarted Philip's grand design, that life soon would return to its old ways.

July faded into August, and on the first night of the month, in the cool of evening, after chores were finished and the villagers resting and discussing their plight, a blast as of ordinance shook the three river-bend towns. The thunderous sound reverberated into silence. Everyone froze where he was, listening, confounded. An explosion — at the fort! Spine-chilling war whoops followed.

They echoed through the evening stillness: war whoop, after war whoop, after war whoop. Those with presence of mind counted eleven bloodthirsty bellows.

The next morning, Normanville, a French trader passing along the Mohawks' Trail to Albany, told Ike of an attack on Mendon in the East. Philip's men had set fire to the houses and had slain many settlers. He related that four Indians who told him of Mendon's attack had lived on Hadley's common at times; he described them well-enough so that Ike knew who they were. Normanville claimed that they bragged to him that the English were afraid of them, now. He warned that the warriors had offered him any house in Hadley as a gift from them, and one told of a Hadley maid he planned to knock in the head. But he would not say who the lass was, if he knew.

The next afternoon, as Zech and Serv returned from the meadow, Zech caught sight of Thanky on the west side of the common, dragging Timmie who struggled to keep up with her hasty steps. Zech guessed that she was looking for him and Serv. When she recognized them, she quickened her pace until her pigtails thumped her shoulders. As soon as she was close enough to be heard, she called out anxiously: "Zech, did ye hear what just happened at Abbey's?" Usually Zech threw Timmy into the air by way of greeting, but this afternoon Timmy, who ordinarily would have wriggled in his arms to let him know he wanted to be tossed about, sensed the anxiety. He snuggled close and clung to Zech. Zech's arms tightened about Timmie as he shook his head in response to Thanky's breathless question. "Remember that saucy Nipmuck that lingered around Montagues' so much?" Thanky prompted while she tried to get her breath.

"Aye — I remember him —" Zech answered slowly. He did not like that one at all. Carefully, he swung Tim around to his shoulder.

"He stopped by Big Abbey's just now, Zech. I was there, waitin' for our bread to come out of the oven. Right in front of us all, he told Little Abbey that he was going away — but that he would be back — and that — when he — came — again — she would bake just for him! And Zech — this time he was not just teasing! When he was gone, Abbey fainted dead away."

Zech's skin crawled. He cried to himself that Warr would not let any harm come to them. Warr would not let anything happen to them! But he knew that other Indians counted, too. King Philip and his warriors. Could Warr know or do anything about Dr. Westcarr's drunken Indian friends and what they might be up to? And they had not seen Warr for days! His father said that he thought it was a good sign; Warr wanted to know what was going on; for that he had to stay at the fort. But Zech took no comfort from Warr's absence. Sometimes, suddenly, he feared for Warr's life.

The following afternoon, Zech found Mr. Tilton's chestnut gelding in the yard when he returned home from chores. Thanky, perched forlornly on the edge of the doorstep, shrugged her thin shoulders when he looked to her for an explanation. "When he came — he sent me out here," she told him, unhappily.

Zech scowled and chewed uneasily on his lip.

Before long, Mr. Tilton and Ham emerged from the house, both pale and long-faced, both as sober as death. As soon as Peter left, Ham motioned Zech into the barn. He told Zech: "Sarah told Peter that more of Philip's men have come to the fort — and the young bucks are preparing to go on the warpath." He folded his hands together, and clenched them until his knuckles turned white. "Warr let Sarah know —" Ham's voice dropped to a whisper that Zech could hardly hear, he murmured the unnecessary precaution that had been echoing through Zech's memory for four years: "Never speak of this to any one!"

Zech's throat tightened 'til he could hardly breathe.

"Warr is going to stay there — to know what's going on," Ham went on. "Sarah warned Peter that Warr says the families below 'Hamp should move into the village."

Zech thought that his heart must have stopped beating. When he became aware of its pounding, he began to tremble helplessly.

"Peter's goin' over to Hamp now, himself, with the message."

Zech wondered at the old man's courage . . . he would not want to cross Old Rainbow Meadow right now — alone. He wandered out of the barn and dropped down onto the stone doorstep next to Thanky. In a minute she began to whimper. Zech put his arm around her as he never had done before; as she dissolved into sobs she could not control, he kept trying to assure her: "Everything will be all right, Thanky. Everything is going to be all right —" But he really did not believe what he said.

Two hours later, naked but for a doeskin breechclout and a woven wampum belt from which hung a tomahawk, Wappawy appeared abruptly at Deacon Goodman's ordinary door while the family sat at supper, a silent and disturbing menace silhouetted against the setting sun. Streaks of vermillion stained his high cheek bones, and a painted yellow beaver gleamed across his broad, oil-polished chest; a band of woven wampum lay across his forehead; he had braided wampum into the single plait of black hair that hung over his left shoulder. Richard Goodman rose in his place; John, and Richie, and Stephen rose too; two of the smaller children slid from their stools and slipped closer to their mother. Wappawy surveyed the scene disdainfully. He did not speak, but stood arrogantly, his arms folded across his chest while his squaw went to the shed and hoisted onto her back a bundle of goods that another squaw had left in Mary Goodman's care. When she halted at the common gate to wait for him, Wappawy announced curtly: "I no fight my cousins!"

"No one wants you to!" Deacon Goodman sputtered helplessly in reply.

"Nipmucks, my cousins," Wappawy told the deacon loftily, and added with a meaningful pat on the tomahawk hanging at his side, "Many heads chopped off before snow."

Deacon Dick gasped. The setting sun stained the bronzed buck with an unholy light; it illuminated half his face as he looked from the Deacon to Mary Goodman, clutching the cradle beside her. Wappawy's lips curled mirthlessly; he returned his gaze meaningfully to her elderly husband. Then slowly — deliberately — he surveyed the square, low-ceilinged, smoke-darkened room. His glance slid past the fieldstone fireplace, his lips compressed as he studied the cupboard beside it, with its row of pewter tankards; he leered at the trap door to the cellar where the Deacon stored his liquors. No one could misread his thoughts when he turned and looked back at the Deacon. He weighed his tomahawk in his hand. "When me come back," he announced in measured tones: "Me drink. Me drink what *me* want! *You* no say *no* — to me!"

He looked again at the trap door, then at Mary Goodman, before he returned his gaze to the Deacon. "You not be here!" he promised. With a raucous laugh, Wappawy swaggered away across the common, his unhappy squaw trailing in his wake.

With the last rays of light, musket shots rang across the Valley; a boy in Northampton was shot at; and the Hatfield miller passing homeward through the meadow beyond the Indians' fort; and a Hatfield farmer in the meadow; and in the night, the watch at Hadley going his rounds.

Suddenly, with their corn just beginning to tassle, Hadley's Indians abandoned their crops as well as a way of life to which they had become accustomed in the last generation.

CHAPTER XVII

Two days later, Nat Warner, a husky young blade who rode post from Brookfield, forty miles to the East, rode into town with a dispatch from the Council of the United Colonies. He had word of a treaty with the Narragansetts, the most influential of the Eastern tribes. They denounced the Mendon attack. Sachems of other Eastern tribes also had crowded into Boston to protest that they wanted no part of a war; they wanted nothing more than to hunt and fish along their trails, and to die in peace, too. To prove their good faith, they left hostages and promised that they would give over to the colonists any of Philip's inciters who came within their councils. As a reward, the colonists promised a coat, or two yards of trucking cloth for the headskin of every buck who could not be brought in alive; for every live captive, two coats; for Philip's head, twenty coats; and if Philip were delivered-up alive, forty coats.

Hadleymen took small comfort from the Eastern assurances. Few braves at the fort wanted to make trouble in the valley; it was the villainous Nipmucks who held control there. A dozen warriors in a surprise attack could leave a town in ashes and all the settlers slain. In the new Indian camp, fires glowed in the night like taunting eyes that watched the villagers' every move; through the day, wisps of smoke unwaveringly straight and spectral lifted lazily from the banked fires, constantly reminding the villages of the warriors; like the smoke they, too, seemed able to fade mysteriously into the clear summer air.

129

On the oppressively hot August evening when Zech and his father and the older boys went to their section of the meadow to pull and lay their flax, it was with an urgency they had not known other years. In all the years of Zech's generation, no one had worked evenings trying to keep ahead of the dusk as it edged out of the low places of earth. Since permanent homes and crops had been established, everyone had rested through the long summer twilights. Older folk gathered on the common and in barnyards to reminisce, and philosophize and gossip, while the young ones played amongst themselves, the girls at housekeeping and the boys with balls and quoits, or they wrestled, Indian fashion. Now no one rested. Without saying much about it, the villages had begun to prepare for a long siege. No one ventured beyond the village bounds, now, or turned dry cattle loose in the woods to graze; groups of women no longer took their young ones berrying on day-long outings; now they depended entirely on friendly squaws who brought baskets of berries to those who had befriended them in the past. Friends like Warrwarrankshan continued to supply venison and small game, and fowl, and fish. Warr had been especially faithful. The Gillettes had venison on hand, and fish salted in good supply for the winter; Aunt had been able to make pies and puddings as in former years; in addition, she had dried bushels of berries in the blazing sun. In the winter, her puddings would be colored and flavored with reminders of these watchful, waiting summer days.

This was a fragrant time of year indoors, the air heavy with the aromas of drying fruit and vegetables. Soon the door could not be left ajar for a long-enough spell to clear the air of the odors of stewing vegetables and spitted meats, the smoke of firewood and tobacco, and the pungency of seldom-washed bodies packed close together in their single set of everyday clothes. Often, especially after rain or snow added their peculiar, unpleasant dampnesses to stifling indoor air, breathing became a problem. To disguise mingling stale odors, meetinghouse clothes were tucked away in a clothespress redolent of lavender and coriander and camphor; and sweet flag and lady's bedstraw seemed to help freshen the air. They were pleasant when freshly-cut and newly-crushed underfoot, but as they grew musty, if not removed in time, provided nesting places for fleas.

In the fields, the August evening that Zech's family pulled their flax, other families collected bundles of rye, or meslin, or provender — wheat and meslin sown together where wheat alone no longer would grow without blasting. A few families, far behind schedule because they had too few lads of their own or indentured, mowed barley, past its prime. Their neighbors would help them, later. While Zech pulled up flax plants and shook their roots free of sod, and spread them on the ground to rot in the next month's dews and dampnesses, he tried to ignore the repeated, despairing trills of a nearby thrush, pouring out its muted liquid evensong. Its short, sad, persistent query haunted him, made him feel insecure. He wondered what story of creation could explain the damnation that bird's melodic query seemed always to be warning of: he asked himself what experiences of mankind warranted such a heart-rendingly sad song. He stopped to rest, to ask his father, and musket shots split the air.

He froze where he stood. Everyone in the meadow swung toward the Indian fort. Figures appeared suddenly at the bluff's edge, peering toward Hadley. Quickly, the harvesters came to their senses: the shots had been fired in Hadley! Three shots, fired simultaneously. An Alarm! A wild, wild booming — the drum — calling the militia to assemble! Zech grabbed up Timmie and swung him across his shoulders. He could not catch up with Serv and Gracie; he halted at the meadow gate and waited for his father while he watched the villagers swarm toward Peter Tilton's.

Those at Peter's called to their neighbors: ". . . Brookfield . . . burned . . . eight . . . eighteen . . . killed . . . ambushed . . . fire . . . Indians . . . hundreds . . . two nights . . . relief . . . *no stopping* . . . now . . ." Their earnest, weathered faces reflected concern, fright, horror, anger, speculation. Peter stood in the yard, his face drawn, a haunted look in his eyes. Behind him, townsmen rubbed down three spent horses. Nat Warner, the post rider, and two strangers slumped on the door-side bench. Nat's bravado had annoyed Zech in the past; now he looked defeated. His stubble-darkened jaw drooped against his heaving chest; his black, wiry hair bushed out about his sagging shoulders; but for his sporadic breathing, he appeared drained of all life. His companions, older, slighter of build, looked more careworn. Someone whispered that one of the older men was Nat's father; no one seemed to know the other rider, but a few years Nat's senior.

A youngster at the front of the crowd piped: "TWO DAYS?" and a gasp of revulsion swept through the crowd. Nat raised his head and tried to speak; as if he wanted to agree: "YES — two days." Words would not come. His head dropped again. He sighed, a long, quavering sigh. The crowd groaned, aching with sympathy. Someone muttered: "Leave 'im be. Let 'em rest!" Mary Tilton moved to Nat's side. She took him by the arm and led him toward the house as if he were a child. Many who watched shook their heads meaningfully, full of foreboding. Peter turned back to his neighbors and announced officially: "The Nipmucks attacked Brookfield, Monday." A gasp swept through the stunned crowd. "The United Council had sent Captain Hutchinson of Watertown with twenty militiamen and ten praying Indians to powwow with the Wampanoags near Brookfield. They were ambushed. Eight men murdered. Some got to John Ayre's — in the village. They were besieged two days — until travelers to Hartford saw the smoke and hastened back to Boston for help. I know no more. We must wait for our messengers to recover —"

The villagers huddled in shocked, little knots, speaking in low tones; they drifted from one group to another. Zech wandered aimlessly . . . listening . . . weighing . . .

"Peter's sent to Connecticut for help, already —"

"They'll be more — from the seaboard, for sure."

"They are standin' ready — 600, I heard tell."

"Major Pynchon's mill burnt — at Brookfield — d'ya s'pose?"

"E'erythin' but Ayer's — I heard that much myself."

"Y' know the Hutchinson they talk of?"

"Aye. A big plantation near Watertown. Did a heap o' tradin' with the Wampanoags."

"He related to that Baptist, Anne?"

"Hmmm. Her son. She was massacred by Ind'ans, you know —"

"Aye — a proper judgment — I say —"

"Aye. Thirty years agone, now —"

"One of his sisters was carried off, you know. Down Long Island way. Did not want to come back to civilization —"

"Scared to — scared to —"

"I hear he's one leaves well enough alone."

"Did you hear how many was kilt, all t'gether?"

"Sixteen —"

"There was a dozen families at Brookfield."

"Sixteen when I came through in the spring."

Heads shook; whispering continued.

132

"We should palisado! That's what they understand!"

Eyes swept the length and breadth of the mile-long common. It could not be done!

"Them at the fort —"

The men turned and stared in dismay at the Indians' fort across the river. How had all this come to pass?

CHAPTER XVIII

At dusk Thursday, Eastern militiamen and friendly Indians from the East and Connecticut began to pour into Hadley. They continued to straggle into town until after dark. A Connecticut militiaman, a cousin of Ham's, stopped in to visit, but would not stay. He was en route to his brother-in-law's family, newly settled at Hatfield last year. Joe Kellogg, sergeant-in-charge, assigned four new arrivals to Ham's barn. They had eaten stewed venison prepared at a commissary set up near the manse and accepted only a drink of cool water before climbing into the loft. They wanted nothing more than to be able to lie down and sleep in a safe place.

In the morning, Zech stayed on his pallet in the loft and watched three of the men in their restless slumber. One had departed already. When Serv and Gracie awoke, Zech slid down into the yard with them and stared at the strangers strewn about the common.

"How many do you think there is?" Serv asked.

"I have heard tell two or three hundred were coming," Zech told him.

"Will ours waken soon?" Gracie asked hopefully.

Serv and Zech nodded knowingly. The cornmeal, boiling over on the nearby tripod, popped thick gruel to the outside of the kettle and into the fire. The odors of scorched cornmeal and crackling pine, together with the unaccustomed sound of so much activity, would soon reach even the most weary dragoon.

Ham joined the boys at the gate. "Our hay must be comfortable —" His words trailed off. A slight, ferret-faced dragoon was bearing down on him. He threw Ham a jaunty salute of recognition and with a calculating glance dismissed the boys as of no account. Ham tensed and waited.

The advancing militiaman bowed confidently as he swept the gate open. "Mungo Crawford — Newbury Militia, here," he announced importantly in a hardly-understandable, thick burr. "I slept here last night." His bravado suggested his quarters were less than he would have liked; that a flourish of drums, with troops at attention, would be more appropriate to his station. Mistaking Ham's confusion for awe, Mungo eyed Serv and Gracie, again. He settled into a stance of command; he thrust his right arm behind him and his chin up; he jerked his fawn-colored head toward the horses tethered at the barn door. "Git some hay here for our mounts, lads," he ordered imperiously. "On the double, now! Step!"

Everyone stared, dumbfounded.

Mungo swelled visibly. "Come! Come!" he urged. Serv and Gracie remained rooted where they stood.

Mungo's brows shot together under his low-hanging thatch. He sucked in one corner of his wide, thin-lipped mouth, and glared at his subjects. When his disapproving scowl did not move them, and Ham did not prompt them to act, he glanced at Ham. Ham's hostile glare checked him. Mungo tried to salvage his air of command. He tossed his head toward the barn. "S'pose the others are in there still."

"Aye. They are *still* —" Ham remarked dryly.

Mungo's bravado did not waver. "Soft!" he chuckled, shifting course. "Soft! Soft! Soft! Why, I bin 'round for hours."

Aunt emerged from the house lugging her nocake kettle. Mungo demanded: "Goin' t' be able to feed everybody?"

Aunt stopped short and stared.

Mungo laughed, delighted. "Not you alone, Mam!" he crowed, relishing the astonishment he provoked. "But this ain't a big town — you know. And there is a deal of us —"

Aunt's face took on a rare closed look that would have warned one a bit wiser. "Why, Mam —"

Aunt thrust her kettle at Ham and whirled about and disappeared into the house. Ham moved deliberately. He scraped through the ashes to the red coals at one side of the fire. Carefully, he set the kettle in place. He stepped back, viewed his handiwork with approval, brushed his hands, and turned and followed Aunt into the house as if there had been no interruption in the daily routine. As if Mungo did not exist.

Mungo gaped open-mouthed. He snorted his disdain. "Some welcome!" he snarled. "Some welcome!" He turned on the boys: "You get some hay here and quick!" he ordered, and tossed his head about and sneered: "Country folk! Backwoods! Never even have seen the sea!"

"Never even 'ave seen the sea!" another voice mocked from the barn doorway. A tousled young giant but a little older than Zech loomed there, sleep still half-closing his eyes. He yawned and stretched. His worn blouse clung to his huge frame as if it pleaded not to be rent asunder by the strain he put it to. He ran his fingers into his mop of blond hair, and with both hands shook his head to awaken himself. Then he hunched toward Gracie and told him with mock seriousness: "If you 'ave never seen the sea, you do not miss the tang o' the sea air, but if you want to know what the sea looks like —" he pointed toward hills rising beyond Northampton. "When the wind stirs those chestnut trees yonder, when they are white with blossoms in the spring, 'tis the way of the ocean — 'eavin' so —" He stretched his arms before him and made a tossing, rolling, rhythmic motion that almost made the boys feel as if they were rocking.

He looked from the boys to Mungo, and hitched at his breeches. He grinned devilishly. Mungo bristled. He shifted uneasily. "Everything to your likin', Mung'?" the newcomer asked innocently.

Mungo spit. "Better git those others to movin', too!" he barked, trying to preserve an appearance of command; but his voice had lost its first ring of authority.

The young giant laughed him down. "No one can do naught today but 'ope the Ind'ans is as weary as us. They may's well sleep awhile."

He yawned and stretched again, and the younger boys caught their breath, expecting his shirt to split. He noticed and slumped at ease, and grinned. He rubbed the thick stubble along his jaw. Fully awake now, his voice boomed when he spoke: "If those Hamalakites struck us today, 'twould take the women and childrun to save us, for a fact!"

The boys gasped. Thanky's eyes swelled bursting-wide. Aunt appeared in the doorway, her face a worried mask. The newcomer swallowed and scuffed his feet uneasily. " 'Mornin', Mam," he greeted awkwardly. With a nearly formal bow, he introduced himself: " 'enry Bodwell, 'ere, Mam. Apprenticed blacksmith to Jedidiah Smith, Medfield." Apologetically, but with an undertone of amusement, he soothed: "I do not mean to scare you, Mam. If those 'eathen should come 'round, we would take care of 'em, don't you worry."

He comforted no one.

" 'Tis the truth, Mam, that they do not know 'ow weary we are," he coaxed. And there is no way they kin know 'fore t'morrow, either. By that time we won't be, you know." With a gleam in his eye, and an attempt to keep his mouth firm, he diverted attention by nodding from Mungo to the horses. "Git 'em fed, there, Boy! Put your spirits t' good works!"

Mungo flushed. His eyes bulged, his jaw worked, but no words came. He remained as stubbornly planted as Serv and Gracie had.

"Kin ye spare us some o' your oats and hay, Mam?" Henry asked politely. "Mung' don't seem in condition t' fetch from afar off."

"Of course," Aunt answered, her mood suddenly nearly matching Henry's. "Our samp will be ready soon," she added.

"Thank you, Mam. That's kind of you —"

"We fed your horses last night, ye know," Gracie broke in.

Henry nodded his appreciation and asked: "Is there a safe place t' water 'em?"

Gracie nodded. He glanced out toward the meetinghouse pond. Henry asked, as if he were conferring a great honor: "D'you want to water 'em?" Gracie rolled his eyes in assent. Henry had been measuring Zech out of the corner of his eye. Now he turned and said to him, with a nod toward the barn, "There's a 'eavy crop ye 'ad earlier, eh?"

"A good thing, too, if we are going to have a hundred extra horses to feed," Zech answered too quickly. Realizing his brusqueness, he blushed painfully, and added lamely: "With the drought we got now, I mean."

Henry, offended at first, relaxed. He nodded agreement. "It showed everyplace, comin' up." He added, "I 'ope this won't take us too long."

Everyone fell silent; the sound of mounting activity on the common moved into their thoughts. Distracted, they watched the visiting militiamen milling about — youths not yet family men, and older men whose family ties were broken. They were tending campfires and horses, and taking stock of their gear, fatigue slowing every movement.

"Those are not *all* Connecticut Ind'ans," Gracie remarked, motioning toward a group of Springfield Indians among those nearby.

"No," Henry admitted, "A dozen or so came from Springfield to Brookfield with Captain Watts of Hartford. Those others not from Connecticut is Pastor Elliott's Prayin' Ind'ans. They came with us." He admonished levelly, "They ain't all 'eathen, you know."

Gracie took his measure with a steady eye. "We know," he countered evenly. Abashed, Henry murmured, "There's good Ind'ans, just like they's bad English —"

Across the common, Zech glimpsed Mary Tilton and Sarah weaving their way toward Sam Porter's with baskets of herbs for some of the wounded who had been carted from Brookfield. Sam was unofficially town doctor now. A considerable spell had passed since anyone had seen Dr. Westcarr; Sam was good at setting bones, and Sarah and Mary Tilton kept him supplied with the herbs each knew of according to the lore passed down by her own people, from generation to generation.

Zech tapped Serv and Gracie and motioned for them to follow him into the barn for hay. They grinned at the loud snoring from the loft. During their second trip, another young dragoon slid down from the loft, but the snoring there continued, more sonorous than before. The latest arrival was as poorly clad as the others, and as gaunt as Mungo. He pushed stringy, dun-colored hair back from a high forehead, and darted a look at Zech with dark eyes so deep-set and close to his blade-like nose they looked crossed at first glance.

"Rest any?" Zech asked by way of greeting.

The new lad nodded. He grinned wryly. He jerked his head toward the snoring in the loft. The foursome listened, fascinated, to the strangling sounds followed by exploding gasps that subsided with a sigh, then started again.

"You from Newbury, too?" Zech asked.

"No. Med - field. Jon - a - than Plymp - ton, I am. Call me Jon." His voice had a decided twang and he spoke each syllable separately and distinctly, but not with difficulty, though Zech thought so at first. "We are all from Es - sex coun - ty. I was bound in Med - field." Hesitantly, he added: "My fa - ther moved up to Deer - field two years back. When it was

138

laid out. May - be ye have heard a' him. Some call him Old Sarg —''

Zech's heart sank. He did not know the Old Sergeant, but he did know that Deerfield and Northfield, the new, settlements up the river, were in worse danger than Hadley and the other nearby towns. "Has he got family there with him?" Zech asked, hardly breathing.

"My moth - er an' four young 'uns. Us old - er uns stayed East — in - den - ture - d, you know." Jonathan tried to add hurriedly: "They ain't *real* small." He went on defensively: "Jest big e - nough t' be help - ful t' a man as wants t' git a new star - t on his own. Pa al - ways was hired, be - fore." Then, as if to change the subject, he asked: "You bound to a trade? Or farm at home?"

"Both, I am learn - in' glaz - in'." Zech found to his horror that he was stretching his words out in the same manner as Jon.

Jon didn't notice. His eyes rounded, impressed by Zech's statement. He whistled appreciatively, "Glazin' — That's a *good* trade."

" 'Tis an old man I am with," Zech explained. "We have not done much lately — with things as they are. He does no farmin' any more. Rents out his land. So I live at home and help. Here and on the river, too. My father's a boatman."

"And ye'll be the gla - zer?" Jon marvelled softly.

Zech shrugged in an attempt to make his admission offhand. Inside, he glowed, pleased with his guest. Jon leaned over to gather up an armload of hay. He held himself suspended. "I never rid much, be - fore," he explained, "or walk - ed so much, eith - er! I kin hard - ly move!"

"Either of the horses yours?" Serv asked.

Jon shook his head before he jerked it towards the loft. "One is his, the oth - er was pres - sed."

"Ye spelled each other?" Gracie asked.

Jon nodded and grimaced.

"No luck scoutin', either, heh?" Zech asked, knowing the answer.

"No. Ye know how them Ind - 'ans is. We could be a pike's len - 'th from 'em an' not spot 'em in the swamps. And we was nois - y!" That offended him.

"That does no good," Zech agreed.

139

"Seems like 'twas more our mind t' let 'em know we was 'round than t' find 'em."

Zech shook his head.

"Ye know how they car - ry their musk - ets," Jon reminded. His eyes took on a glassy look as he demonstrated with an imaginary musket laid across his chest and upper arm. "They shoot run - nin'!" he exclaimed, his voice wild with excitement. "Think o' them stop - pin' t' use mus - ket rests!"

Recollection of long years of training overwhelmed Zech, of Indians lounging along the common fence, watching impassively as the militia marched and practiced their twenty commands. He snorted angrily, and Jon blinked at him, not knowing what had caused his disgust. He drew away with an armload of hay. At the barn door he looked back. Zech was close behind him. "They showed us where they am-bushed the Brook-field men," he told Zech. "I have seen where they got oth - ers — East. 'Tis al - ways bog - gey, you know. They kin run ov - er bog that we would sink in - to up to our knees."

"They know woods ways, for a fact."

"Aye. There is a preach - er — Mist - er El - i - ot — among - st 'em. Claims they are child - like!" Jon's tone flatly denied that.

Zech told him evenly: "We know Indians as trustworthy as a man can be." He did not like to think about John Warner's recital of the Brookfield attack, of the burning buildings, that the Nipmucks caught a lad trying to creep out for help and cut off his head and kicked it about as a football in full view of the town's defenders. "Many are like foxes —" he cried out. "Foxes — no animal — is worse — than a warrior on the warpath —"

From the house, Aunt called: "Come!"

CHAPTER XIX

Mungo had disappeared while the others were after hay. Henry gobbled up a trencherful of samp, before he explained that he and Mungo were both bound to the same master. "Mungo ain't a bad sort, once you git to know 'im," he explained. "But Marster Smith, now, 'e could not git anything much outta 'im. Sending 'im 'ere, 'e won't 'afta feed 'im for a spell, and 'e might do some good. 'e is rare good with animals."

"Do you have a family in the East?" Aunt asked Henry.

"No, Mam," Henry answered slowly. "I have got two sisters — in London — last I knew —" He measured his words, as if to control himself. He added: "My father was a wool stapler in London. Of St. Martin's Outwick parish." His expression darkened. He looked at Aunt with a pleading look that asked her not to doubt him. "My grandfather was high sheriff o' County Carnarvon. We 'ad a fine 'ouse in London. A fine 'ouse." No one could mistake the pain in his voice. Aunt nodded, full of understanding of the way things had been. "Everything my father 'ad, 'e lost in the Great Fire," Henry concluded.

After a pause, when no one spoke, he said quietly: "My father died — soon after the fire, of a broken 'eart, if ever a man did: and my mother, soon after that — I 'ad two sisters, older, married and with families, as bad off. I was ten years old. I was lucky when our congregation pledged my passage to New England. I am

141

grateful for that.'' When no one could think of a comforting response, Henry went on: "I ain't never worked for anyone but Marster, 'e was a Middlesex man. Come over when Prince Charles — King Charles, now — come back. I will come of age 'fore I git back to the Bay. Then I will work for wages, and get a forge o' my own, some day.'' He flexed his brawny arms without intending to brag. "Should stand me in good stead, making my way in some new town that will be opening up,'' he prophesied matter-of-factly. Everyone eyed the solid arm and nodded in agreement.

"Don't soldiers get pay?'' Serv asked, to be part of the conversation.

Ham and Aunt looked pained; Zech shot Henry a quick glance. He would understand the burden to the town to try to provision *and* pay its garrison.

"We are s'posed to get six shillings a week,'' Henry told Serv, trying to sound offhand. "Ours goes to our master 'til we are of age.'' Without rancor, he added lightly: "A good reason for sparin' us, ye know.''

Ham grunted. "The only way Hadley will be able to meet its debt will be country pay. And if the dry season continues, we won't have provisions with which to feed you proper, anyway. So — eat hearty — while we've got it.'' He pushed Mungo's untouched trencher in Henry's direction.

"Pleases me,'' Henry boomed. "Better still, if I am here 'til I come of age, pay me in seed corn.'' Lowering his voice, after a moment's hesitation, he asked: "How long d'ye think we will be out?''

Ham looked wary in the way all men did now when pressed on the subject. He pondered the question as he refilled his trencher with samp. He watched a thread of amber apple molasses mingle with the fragrant steam. Before he settled down to eat, he said to the waiting bowl, "If we knew how many of them was of a mind to fight, we could say better. They are not all against us — just like they are not all for us.'' He paused before he lamented: " 'Tis the things we *do not* know —''

Jonathan stopped eating and studied Ham. Zech knew his father did not realize Jon was thinking about Deerfield and his family. He floundered for words to prevent his father's worrying Jonathan. Before he could speak, Jon asked: "What about the fam - il - ies up the riv - er?''

142

Ham heaved an eloquent sigh; he shook his head. "The Pocumtucks are not 'good' Indians like our Nonotucks. Men have been fool-hearty to try new lands in such times as these." He glanced at Jon, expecting him to agree. Too late, he realized Jon had a special interest in Deerfield. Nonplussed, he pushed himself back from the table and muttered gruffly, "They'll be calling muster in no time, now." To Zech he said, "Better get the other one up and about."

Jon turned an alarmed look toward Henry who quickly volunteered, "I'll git him!" He asked Gracie, "Will ye git me a mug of old ale? I'll take it up." In response to Ham's questioning look, he added hastily, "Andy's — shy like — " 'e won't 'ave time to eat, now, and 'e'd go 'ungry 'fore 'e'd come in and eat with strangers."

"A lit - tle ale 'd help 'im some t' hold bod - y and soul to - geth - er," Jon agreed, nodding emphatically.

As Henry and Jon disappeared into the barn with a tankard of ale, the first warning roll of drums began, Ben Wait's distinctive summons to assembly.

"That means us!" Zech exclaimed, and he and his father reached for their snaphances on the rack beside the door. Their family watched them take down the jingling, cumbersome bandoliers and ease them over their left shoulders.

"There's powder in all your boxes!" Gracie assured Ham proudly as Ham's practiced fingers began to run down the dozen dangling time-darkened copper cylinders that held the charges for his firearm. "As soon as that *Mungo* went away, I looked to be certain!"

Ham chuckled. His calloused fingers deftly explored his doe-skin bullet bag and the priming wire tied at the bottom of the band. Expertly, he weighed the attached length of match cord; he cocked his head expectantly as he flipped open the priming box and checked its contents. Satisfied, he snapped the box shut again.

"Will you be trainin'?" Aunt asked dubiously.

Ham looked doubtful. "There's no need to," he told her uncertainly. His tone said he would rather not — with the Easterners and the men from Connecticut to witness.

"Will *they*?" Aunt asked with a nod toward the common.

"They are spent, already," Ham reminded.

"Why do ye have to take *that*?" Thanky asked squeamishly as Zech took his sword down and buckled it to his belt.

" 'Cause the law says I must," Zech answered, trying hard not to sound as if he felt important, hoping he did not betray how nervous he felt.

"You do not use it much," Thanky remarked, her tone half admiration, half skepticism.

"No —," Zech admitted. He made a wry face and added, "If I should have to start runnin' — *after* — or *away* — you can be sure I will leave it behind 'fore it has a chance to trip me up."

" 'Tis for takin' headskins," Gracie informed Thanky with fiendish relish, and Aunt and Ham and Zech flinched. Unconcerned, Serv mourned, "I got to wait three more years!" He ran loving fingers along the edge of the blade, and the way his fingers closed around the butt betrayed his intention not to be excluded that long.

His mother's look of guilty relief at his last words turned to concern. She looked up at Ham and gave her head a quick shake. Ham shook his head ruefully in reply.

Zech moved thoughtfully across the dooryard, his usually springy step restrained by the weight and awkwardness of his gear. The younger ones followed respectfully in his wake.

Henry and Jon and their companion were passing through the gate. They did not look around, but moved along, trying to appear in step with their companion. Both men usually moved in the same manner in which they spoke, Henry with an easy stride, Jon with quick, short steps, stiff and deliberate. They could not disguise the fact that they were supporting their companion whose gait was uncertain, if he could manage at all. The three dragoons lurched through the gate and turned in the direction of their station near the South Highway to the Meadow. Serv turned from viewing their exhibition and exclaimed, half unbelieving: "He's still half-asleep!"

His mother humphed loudly. "He's drunk! It beats all how some manage!" she muttered angrily. "He must have carried that stuff with him all this way!" Ham followed the trio with his eyes, his lips a grim line of disapproval.

Zech looked out at the throng milling about the common and for the first time in days thought of the Old Strangers. Where could they be, with headquarters at the manse? All of their old friends were billeting militiamen, save the Goodwins, and they did not have room to hide anyone; many of the Crow young ones dwelled with them, now. Their mother was gravely ill.

Zech's self-consciousness before the seaboard men, lounging

144

about the fences, watching their host-militia, took his mind off the Judges. Everyone knew that their drilling and most of their inherited weapons were of no value except to be melted down for shot. How could they prove themselves to their more experienced visitors?

Zech took pride in the sight of the smartly bedecked local officers. No one could gainsay the impressive appearance of Hampshire's militia officers in full regalia on their blooded mounts. Their lieutenants, melancholy Deacon Sam Smith, erect and gimlet-eyed and nearly eighty, scanned the scene before him like the patriarch he was; beside him, burly, rosy-cheeked, tow-headed Aaron Cook, Jr., who had been granted his father's rank since hostilities began, looked anxious to justify his appointment ahead of more seasoned troopers. He had difficulty maintaining his dignity, though. His three-year-old son struggling to be free of an older sister so that he could run out to his father, squealed loudly for his father to come to his rescue. "That's my papa! PaPa. PAPA! *Overrrrr herrrrrrrre!!* Let me go! Let me go! Paaaa! Paaaa! Paaa! Paaaaaaaa!''

With a feigned black look and a flourish of his halbert, Joe Kellogg wheeled the mare that had been Stephen Terry's toward the shrieking youngster. Everyone grinned broadly as the three-year-old fell back, abashed.

All eyes then swung toward greying, goateed John Pynchon, recently advanced from Captain to Major. He nodded to Ben Wait. Ben's mighty trumpet blast brought the assembly promptly to attention. Ensign Wilton of Northampton, astride one of Pastor's chestnuts, hauled in the regiment's proud banner and leaned against the staff. He bowed his hoary head and lowered a noble face, deeply seamed by years of intermittent physical agony. Lieutenant Smith's thin voice rose in a long, detailed prayer that enumerated other girdings-on of swords in opposition to other Amalakite assailants. After the Lieutenant finished admonishing God to guide and protect His children, Joe Kellogg stretched out the company's vellum roll. He waited importantly a moment, before he sang out:

"Jo-seph Bald-win, Jun-i-or —"

From his place in line Joseph Baldwin, Junior, crisply snapped out: "Joseph Baldwin, Junior, here!"

"James Bee-bee —"

"James Beebee, here!"

"— AZ-ah-ri-ah Dick-in-son —"

"Az-ah-ri-ah Dick-in-son, he-re!"

"— Ed-ward Gran-nis —"

"Edward Grannis, here!"

"— Nich-o-las Worth-in'-ton —"

"Nicholas Worth-ING-ton, here!"

Four-and-a-half minutes after he had begun, Joe announced to the officers: "— Company all present and accounted for, Sirs." He withdrew, and returned the roll to its leather case.

John Pynchon reviewed the men before he spoke. "We have had word that the Indians at the fort are not anxious to be at war with us. Like the Connecticut Indians, and the Natick friends of Pastor Elliot who are among the Eastern bands, some have offered to join us rather than be our enemies." A murmured wave of interest rippled along the lines as each Hadley man muttered his conviction to his companions. The Major scowled at the unsoldierly response and waited for it to subside. He continued: "On Monday morning, after the Eastern bands have rested, we will scour the woods with such of you as have your crops sufficiently 'tended to — until the camps of those who sacked Brookfield are found!"

A murmur swept through the watching crowds. Some heads bobbed approval.

"More Connecticut militiamen will arrive this afternoon. With a company of Indian friends. You who have Nonotuck friends to go with you, will please report to the manse. We have powder, and flint, and saltpeter for match in good supply." He concluded: "Tim Nash will melt down musket rests and make shot of 'em, today and tomorrow." Then he raised his hand and silenced the growing restlessness. Every head bowed and Lieutenant Smith pronounced a benediction. The assembly was at an end. The men broke ranks and fell into groups or wandered toward home with their families.

"Our crops are pretty well in," Zech remarked to his father as they waited for Aunt to join them.

"Aye," Ham answered absently.

"Do you plan to ask Warr to go with — *us*?" Zech ventured.

Ham did not answer, and Zech stole a glance at him. His father's trapped expression did not surprise him. Aunt joined them, trailing the young ones. Zech asked, "Shall I take our musket rests down to Tim's?"

"Us, too?" Serv asked eagerly, grabbing Gracie by the arm.

146

Ham shook his head at the younger boys. His tone rasped unexpectedly. "There won't be room — or time — just for watchin', now!" More reasonably, he explained, "Only yesterday, Joe Baldwin asked for your loan — to help get his provender in." He tried to ease their disappointment. "He's got only one boy, you know. Younger than either of you."

"And a whole houseful of womenfolk," Aunt reminded.

Importantly, Thanky echoed the remark she had heard her mother make at some time: "And not very hardy ones, either."

The boys sighed their disgust; they kicked loose stones from the path. Their steps began to lag.

"Get your peahooks, now, and your baskets, too," Ham ordered brusquely. His tone did not suggest the possibility of bargaining. "You don't need to wait 'til Joe can go with you. You know which field is his. There'll be others nearby. It will be safe — enough —" His voice trailed off. He wanted to call back the last words. He had put into words a possibility he never had had to give thought to, before.

The boys dawdled a few more steps before they suddenly gave in and loped ahead to get their equipment.

The Gillettes found Henry and Jon waiting in the yard, offering to be of service.

"My grain crops are in and my flax spread," Ham told them. "But we have corn to husk, aplenty."

"— And I'll need more water," Aunt decided. "I had better brew again, today. We all must brew extra, now."

Worried that their billets might think they were imposing, Zech explained hurriedly: "Our rye bran's holding out, though Pa says we may be using birch twigs 'fore the pumpkins are ready for brewing this fall."

"What's wrong with birch beer?" Henry asked heartily. "We each have a jug with us, if that will help any."

"We saw!" Ham remarked pointedly, disapprovingly. Jon and Henry reddened, uncomfortably aware that they had failed to mislead their hosts regarding his fourth billet's condition.

CHAPTER XX

When they got the husking well under way, Ham asked Henry: "Where do you s'pose your friend Mungo is?"

"No place much, now. But there will be a time when 'e'll be 'alfway to Albany — or Maine — when 'e's been outta sight this long."

His hosts looked taken aback. Jon kept husking, unconcerned.

"Do you think he would desert?" Ham asked with child-like disbelief.

"I am sure 'e plans to light out," Henry assured him. " 'e does not say so, o' course, but 'e don't plan to risk 'is scalp for anything — or *any* body."

"He'll risk it aplenty — 'tween here and Albany," Ham remarked aghast.

" 'e'll find a way —"

In the silence that followed, the only sound was the tearing of the sheaves being stripped from the corn, and the dull thud of the ears landing in the crib. Finally, Jon turned toward Henry as if he were nudging him. After a second look from Jon, Henry asked self-consciously: "Did ye notice Mung's 'and?"

Ham and Zech shook their heads slowly, and Zech recalled the peculiar way Mungo had motioned for the boys to bring hay, awkwardly, with his left thumb toward the right, with his right hand tucked behind him, into his breeches top.

" 'e ain't got most of his right 'and," Henry told them, his whole face drawn together with distaste.

Zech knew from the way his father faltered in his husking that Ham understood something that escaped him.

Henry glanced at Ham, then at Zech, and seeing Zech's bewilderment, explained tersely: " 'e got it chopped off!"

When no one spoke, he snarled defensively, "And they did not do a good job!"

Zech gasped.

"They —?" he repeated, suddenly recalling oft-told tales. He felt sick. " 'Twas a punishment?" he asked faintly.

"Aye!" Henry barked, disgusted. He started to husk and throw corn with incredible speed and force. Then he stopped altogether. " 'e was but a lad. 'is mother taken off in the plague and 'is father in debtor's prison. I tell you — for a while things like that did not go on! But they started up all over again." He worked fiercely a full minute before he glanced up. He warmed to Zech's wide-eyed wonder.

"You see, the way 'twas over there . . . the magistry did not — *care*. Mung' got caught stealin' — to eat — and t' punish 'im, 'is fingers was cut off, 'fore 'e was put in the workhouse. 'e were sent over 'ere with a boat load a' prisoners — by the King's gov'ment."

He waited for Zech to recover and digest what he had said. Zech stared at him blankly. The grandfather of Preserved Clapp in 'Hamp had been the most mutilated he had heard of: his ears cut off, his nose slit, his hand . . . for his Independent beliefs. But that had been two generations ago. Before . . . and a *child*! As from a distance, he heard Henry explaining, "Mung' ain't good for much, I grant. But I know of no one'd be any different with sech 'elp."

He fell to working like a demon before he stopped a second time. "In London, when I was a lad, I oft saw men 'anging from gibbets and London Bridge — 'til the flesh dropped off, or was picked away by birds. Nor for uncommon crimes, either."

"Hush!" Ham interrupted gruffly. Henry shot him a black look that wavered at the sight of Ham's distress; he husked slowly for a minute before he said, apologetically: "That is why we are 'ere, o' course. T' live otherwise." When no one spoke, he went on: "Marster says —" He stared thoughtfully into space a moment and shifted uneasily. " 'e is not 'appy with what 'as gone on 'ere, either. If mistress did not 'ave family nearby — 'e 'as told me often — 'e would go to Long Island or New Jersey. But 'e's too

149

old now — and 'as no sons —'' He glanced at Ham uncertainly; with an uncomfortable smile, he explained lamely, but persistently: "Men like you and Marster are so busy takin' care o' those dependent on ye that when other men begin to make decisions not to your likin' — you do not — you only talk about what troubles you — and then not to those as can do anything —''

Ham looked offended.

Henry hastily added, "Marster's a real good man — same's you, but 'e's always tellin' *me* that men now are gittin' t' confuse righteousness with what they want for themselves. There's a meanness of spirit that troubles him. 'e says men are forgettin' too much, too soon. Those that remember — many — are movin' on —''

Ham scowled. He did not like those about him to speak of dissatisfaction with authority. That worried him.

"They do not mutilate 'ere,'' Henry went on. "And there's no debtor's prison. But Marster thinks affairs 'ere should be as — as men tried to make 'em be during the Commonwealth. 'e 'as told me much o' what went on then. O' 'ow some tried to make things be right. Now, take General Whalley, who was a gove'ment leader then. Marster were 'is neighbor in Middlesex, 'fore General Whalley moved to Whitehall Palace. All New England knows o' the General, o' course.''

General Whalley's name hit Zech an unexpected blow. He caught his breath and fought to keep from pitching off balance. He stole a quick glance at his father. His astonished alarm told Zech all he needed to know. Henry noticed nothing amiss. He was rambling on, talking of General Whalley, telling the tales everyone knew. Zech had no idea how much he had missed before he got himself under control.

"— My mistress' family all come to once, when King Charles come in. They all tell how there was no rogues left free to prey on the country during the Commonwealth — as we 'ear they are doing now, again.'' He clucked his tongue and shook his head. "Some of the villains they shipped out are right 'ere on the common, you know. General Whalley shipped 'em out rather than put 'em in jail, to be a charge to good folks. 'e saw to it that weights was judged honest, too, the same for buyer as for seller — as they are 'ere. So we are not all bad 'ere, now are we?'' He laughed a short, nervous laugh. When no one spoke, he went on: "Marster tells that in Old England, where they do their selling in markets, that,

150

'fore General Whalley's time, the opening bell was rung at four in the afternoon — a ruling of the devil, so to speak. The late hour gave farmers little time to sell their produce 'fore dark — they was robbed either way.'' He sighed. ''Marster says that 'fore the Commonwealth, a man might's well be a robber as honest — 'e 'ad naught to lose but 'is life — either way. 'Twere a fact, smart robbers was far safer in some shires than the good folk they preyed on.''

He sighed, again. ''Mung', now, might not 'a been a thief — or 'ateful as 'e is, sometimes, if 'ed knowed anything different than 'e did. But 'tis a fact, there's been more ways devised to make men beggarly than to allow 'em to be decent. But General Whalley, now, Marster tells 'ow 'e did not let dishonest men be magistrates. 'e —''

With the cunning that he'd acquired in the last four years, Zech broke into Henry's discourse. Blood raged through his head as he struggled to pretend innocence and asked: ''Did you know — General Whalley — yourself?''

Pleased, Henry exclaimed: ''Oh, I saw 'im many times, as a lad!'' He glowed, remembering. Zech glanced at his father. He bent all his attention to his husking.

Henry inhaled deeply, planning to discourse at length. Ham cut him short. With a tone that left no doubt Henry's lecture was over, that the subject was not one to be discussed, he said admiringly, but with finality: ''General Whalley was a great man. There never was a finer!''

Henry blinked his surprise. ''Aye,'' he murmured, nonplussed.

''I understand he has gone to his rest,'' Ham added quietly.

''Aye. In Switzerland, we 'eard,'' Henry answered, disspirited.

Zech fell to husking furiously. When he and Henry were alone later, he would get him to talking about General Whalley, again.

For a time, the arrival of about a hundred Connecticut militiamen and their Poquonock friends attracted everyone's attention.

''Are you going to seek-out Warr this afternoon?'' Zech finally asked his father. His father did not answer.

''Do you plan to go over?'' Zech persisted. His father made no sign he heard. In the corner of the yard, Aunt, lifting yeast settlings from the bottom of a beer keg for her next batch of bread, banged her spoon against the keg rim. The angry, whacking noise warned Zech to stop prodding. As if her racket brought Ham to consciousness, he sighed. Zech glanced anxiously toward Henry

151

and Jon. They were watching a pair of horsemen riding across the common. The men seemed to be coming directly toward them: Peter Tilton and a rider bent over his pommel as if he were a captive being taken to judgment. Eastern militiamen all seemed to know Peter's companion. They called to him from all sides. He waved awkwardly to his friends, in passing. Peter led him unswervingly to Ham's gate.

Peter nodded to Ham and with an uncharacteristic twinkle, announced with a flourish: "Ham, meet Captain Richard Beers of Watertown!" His tone crackled with anticipation. Ham stared in complete astonishment; the wizened, grinning little man bobbed his head at Ham a half-dozen times in rapid succession; his little, pox-marked face hardly cleared the collar of his worsted doublet. Ham stepped closer and peered unbelieving at the newcomer, as if to state that the Captain Beers he knew of could not be taking an active part in a gruelling expedition, but would be settled by a fireside reliving dreams of past glory.

The old man cackled: "There's life in me yet, you see!" No one could miss his delight in the role he played.

"Aye! Aye, Sir!" Ham answered, awed. "My father was with you when you faced the Pequots at Mystic! He has been gone for over ten years, now."

Capt. Beers nodded soberly. "There's lots of Connecticut names hereabouts — was there — then, though the men with us are gone." His sober, withered face suddenly crinkled, again. "Most of 'em, at Mystic, did not have the rest I had for years after, you know. I did not wear myself out like them — so — 'tis time I was useful, again."

Ham's gaze slid to Peter, who smiled indulgently. "A real soldier never let's anything keep him out of the action!" Peter exclaimed.

Ham shook his head in speechless admiration.

"You are asking Warrwarrankshan to scout with us, Ham —" Peter directed suddenly, rather than asked. "We are going over to the fort as soon as supper is done, when all the braves will be in. There are about a dozen we feel to be trustworthy."

"I have not seen Warr for several days," Ham answered evenly.

Peter's expression and tone of voice did not change. He went on, as if Ham had not spoken: "We would like you to go as one of a committee, and for you and Warrwarrankshan to go as guides to a militia troop, when we go searching tomorrow."

152

"I have not seen Warr for many days," Ham repeated.

Peter half shrugged, as if to say that did not matter. "Those on the south end are going up in Joe's long canoe." he directed. "Those on this end can use Nat Dick's." As an afterthought, he added: "You could go out with your father as a guide, too, Zech."

Zech turned toward his father. Ham stood rigid and unhappy, his hand resting on the gate post.

"Fine!" Peter decided for Ham. "We will be glad to have you along. We are going to Dan's and Tom's now." He bowed, and Captain Beers raised his hand awkwardly in a farewell salute.

The two men wheeled about, and while yet within earshot, Henry exclaimed heartily: "Ain't that Cap'n Beers a caution, now? Did not wear 'isself out like the others! Why — 'e is too crippled t' walk! They say for eight years after the Pequot War 'e could do naught! 'e 'ad a 'uge estate t' begin with, once — and sold it a bit at a time — t' keep 'imself and 'is family." He added, as the horsemen disappeared from sight among other militiamen on the common: " 'is son Ephr'm is 'ere with 'im. 'e was one of those ambushed at Brookfield, ye know.

Zech began to feel nettled that Henry could talk on and on of people and events of which he knew little. "Marster told me, once, that Capt'n Beers' family 'ad been part of a boatload of Baptists migratin' t' Saint Kits when pox broke out aboard ship. The sick was abandoned on a beach on Long Island. 'im an' Eph was the only ones t' survive. 'e shows the pox worse'n 'is father, even. 'e's tough all right. They say 'e was the most injured of any who survived at Mystic. 'Tis sad to see 'im crippled so."

"I wish the - re was a way we could kill 'em all!" Jon exclaimed bitterly, suddenly, to everyone's surprise. For an instant no one realized he meant the Indians. "Then there would be an end to all our troub - les, I say. They hand - dle a flint - lock bet - ter'n most Eng - lish - men —" He drew a deep breath: "I am not — I can not feel easy — fol - low - in' any man again - st 'em, no mat - ter who 'tis — Not after what I have seen and heard."

Henry snorted: "There ain't any Ind'an smarter than the like o' Capt'n Beers — or Capt'n Lothrop — or Capt'n Savage."

"All the same," Jonathan expounded at the top of his voice, " 'til we are rid of ev - ery last one of 'em — there is go - in' t' be troub - ble!" Almost choking, he added: "Mark my word! Mark my word!'' and turned and stalked stiff-legged from the yard.

"Jest cause 'is father's a old soldier, 'e thinks 'e knows all 'bout everything,'' Henry scoffed. " 'is father — Old Sarge — were a sergeant in the Great Rebellion, ye know. At Naseby — 'n' Marston Moor. To 'ear Jon tell it, ye'd think 'e was the one that fought there in company with Col. Whalley, 'n' Col. Goffe, 'n' General Fairfax, and not 'is father, at all.''

Henry's reference to General Whalley caught Zech and Ham unaware a second time. Zech kept from glancing too quickly to check his father's reaction. By the time he looked, there was nothing to see.

Gamely, exultantly, but carefully, Zech grasped at the subject. "Jon told me that his father is a settler up in Deerfield —'' His heart skipped a beat as he saw his father tense. He would stop this conversation, too, as soon as he could.

"Aye — Old Sarge — 'e's called — 'e wears a white piece in 'is 'at all the time. That's the way the New Model Army did, so's they could tell themselves from the king's men when they got mixed up together in battle.''

"Oh — I know who he is, then! I have seen him about at lecture, sometimes,'' Zech exclaimed, remembering a slender stranger who always had what looked like a piece of white kerchief attached to his hat.

"Well, 'e may be a good soldier — but 'e's not one can git on — on 'is own. A man born t' be a soldier, and nothing else, 'e's farming out for someone, now, up the river. For Gov'nor Leverett, I believe.''

Zech started to say that he thought Jon had told him his father had a grant, but he caught himself. After a moment's reflection, hoping he was not showing too much interest, he asked: "How come Jon's father is in Deerfield, anyway?''

Henry looked perplexed. "Why should he not be?''

"What I mean is — Deerfield and Northfield, now, they are being settled by men — families — from here. From Hadley. And Hatfield. And 'Hamp. Families with more sons than land to divide amongst 'em. How come Old Sarg did not go to Billerica — or one of the new settlements in the East, but came here from the seaboard?''

Henry shrugged. "I 'eard a man say that Sarg was goin' t' be workin' a farm — I s'pose he had t' go where 'e was sent —''

154

He looked at Ham, and added for emphasis: " 'Twere Mr. Gookin."

Zech wondered what Mr. Gookin might have to do with General Whalley, and if the farm in Deerfield was General Whalley's and Mr. Gookin his agent.

He persisted: "Men from the East are not settlin' farms here themselves. Men like Governor Bradford and Governor Leverett sell their government grants here to Valleymen." Afraid he might reveal his interest to his father, Zech said uncertainly: "I do not recall ever hearing of any Mr. Gookin —"

" 'Tis no matter that you have not!" Ham cut in sharply. "You do not know him, yourself, so what difference can it make to you?"

His father's sudden belligerence took Zech aback.

"There's other things should occupy your mind than what is none of your affairs," Ham reproved gruffly, with more irritation than Zech had heard for a long time.

Zech pretended to be chastened, but he was secretly pleased. If he were not getting close to some of the answers that had been denied him, his father would not be so disturbed. He planned, while his father went to the fort, to work Henry around to a discussion of his Marster's hero — General Whalley.

155

CHAPTER XXI——

Mungo appeared at suppertime. Not with the flourish with which he had introduced himself in the morning, but not humbly, either. He strolled into the yard and greeted everyone pleasantly, the morning's rejection over and done with. He had returned knowing that he would get more flavorful and perhaps more bountiful fare at Ham's table than at the campfires scattered about the common. Following Ham's grace and amen, Mungo hunched over his bowl and spooned up his food with his left hand, so swiftly and expertly that Zech marveled that he was not naturally left-handed.

Andy, the fourth billet, did not reappear. When Ham asked if he would be coming, Henry shrugged and mumbled something about fireside companions. With ten appetites to take care of, and doubts of Andy's worthiness, Ham said nothing of searching him out, nor of saving a portion for him, either.

After satisfying his first pangs of hunger, Henry tucked a straying chunk of half-chewed stew back into the corner of his mouth with one knuckle, and remarked, "I 'ave not ever been in a Ind'an fort. They do not live so close to us in the East as 'ere. Right on the common, once, I 'eard." He looked at Ham, and after Ham's nod, went on: "In Marlborough, they are buildin' their own village." Almost timidly, remembering Ham's strange reaction to the name before supper, he added: "Mr. Gookin's Christian In'ans, they are, you know."

"The best land they got, too!" Jon put in resentfully. As an afterthought, he added indignantly: "Thous - ands a' acres!"

156

"They was 'ere 'fore we come — or Mr. Gookin!" Henry protested. The young ones pricked up their ears, intrigued by the men's combative tones. Henry noticed, and returned his attention to his supper. But after a moment, he added: "We know not 'ow far this land stretches. West. Nor South. Nor North."

"But we do know 'tis In - dans is help - in' t' keep us from find - in' out," Jon scoffed.

"The likes of the Marlborough Ind'ans is not keeping anyone from tending to 'is own business," Henry answered, trying to sound only conversational and keep a hostile edge out of his voice. "They are Christians, living like Christians."

Jon raised his head and pursed his lips defiantly, primly. "They are jest In - dans. They car - ry the mark of Cain!"

Henry slammed his spoon down. It banged the edge of his trencher. The trencher flipped over and fell upside down across Hope's neglected bowl of bread and milk. Hope leaped back, spewing out a string of surprised, unintelligible sounds that startled the quarreling militiamen to gasping silence. They had not been aware of his tied tongue, that his speech could not be understood.

Hope's injured glance swept from the gaping strangers to his dismayed family. He purposely tumbled backward off his stool and fled out the door.

Mungo spoke first. "That can be helped!" he cried out, as if outraged that Hope's affliction had not been tended to.

"You know so much!" Aunt sobbed, her voice catching in her throat. She swished away from the table and out the door in pursuit of her wretched son. Everyone knew that she would not find Hope right now, that both were beyond comfort.

"It can!" Mungo protested to Ham.

Ham averted his glance, angered and bewildered by his helplessness. His mouth was a grim, distressed line.

"It can!" Mungo persisted. "A lad I growed up with —" Everyone stared at the table. No one spoke. Slowly, Mungo arose and dragged himself toward the doorway, finally admitting to himself that no one wanted him around.

Henry retrieved the contents of his trencher with one swooping motion. "See what your kind of gospel brings about!" he snarled at Jonathan. "What was it your friend Cain asked of Jehovah, anyway, Jon?" he pressed bitterly.

Zech answered to himself: "Am I my brother's keeper?" as Jon hissed distastefully: *"They* are not *my* broth - ers!"

"If the mark o' Cain comes of not being your brother's keeper, Jonnie, then I am going to keep a close watch on you, so's I can see what it is. Then, another time, I will know it — proper — like I should."

Jon looked as if he might explode.

Henry addressed himself to Serv and Gracie: " 'Tis well to bear in mind that the Scriptures admonish us to beware of false prophets!" Then he turned to Ham, as if no unpleasantness had come to pass. "— Like I was saying, I 'ave ne'er been in a fort. The selectmen want the Narragansetts in a fort of their own for now. Guess they think they — the Ind-ans — will be safer that way. And I shouldn't wonder!"

Jon sniffed loudly.

"Do you think — Henry — could go over to the fort with us?" Zech asked his father timidly. He had a host of questions to ask Henry. On the trail tomorrow, with his father along, there would be little opportunity for him to try to lead Henry to what would seem like idle conversation about General Whalley, nor would the Sabbath offer much opportunity to discuss the king's Judges alone. Jon, offended because Zech did not include him in the invitation, rose abruptly and stalked out the door.

"Can you point out some of the men that General What's-his-name sent over here; the rogues you told us of?" Zech prompted as he and Henry set out for the Hatfield ferry after supper.

"Aye —" Henry agreed, pleased. "General Whalley — that's the name o' the General —" he began to glance about the common, searching for certain faces he had seen in the last few days.

Zech coached: "The General did them a favor — sending them here where they could become freemen. Do you suppose they thank him for it? Maybe they did not want to come."

"No doubt they did not," Henry grunted. "They come as enemies, you know, so they would not feel welcome. And they came in bondage, too. More severe than others. The worst was sent to Barbados, o'course. Many that come here lit off to other colonies — or went to sea, some of 'em did."

"How did you come to know the General, yourself?" Zech asked.

"Oh, I did not know 'im," Henry quickly corrected. "But we would see passages o' important men riding along the street, you know. They would have outriders, and some a footman or two.

Some 'ad large parties about 'em, depending on where they was going, and 'ow far, and 'ow safe 'twas — and, o'course, 'oo they was.''

"I suppose General Whalley would have many riders with him.''

"Sometimes 'e did — '' Henry agreed, peering at idling groups they were striding past. '' 'Twas not like 'tis, 'ere, at all —'' He stopped, and drew a deep breath and addressed Zech gravely, his expression one of profound concern. He did not want to offend Zech. "Zech,'' he expounded, "you cannot know how different things are here — no leagues of stone buildings — no stone buildings at all! No cobbled streets — Zech, 'til you 'ave seen something in part — 'ow can you know 'ow a palace looms so high in the sky — when you would hardly believe the size of the cornerstone if I was to tell you. 'ow were they cut? — 'ow did they git there? Where did they come from —''

Zech had no inclination toward offense at the moment. His fear was that Henry would get off the track of conversation he wanted to pursue. "They must be wonderful to behold, Henry,'' he murmured, pretending an interest that he might have felt at some other time. "Whitehall Palace! Imagine —'' That much awe he really experienced, thinking of the men at the manse. "Whitehall Palace. You did say that General Whalley lived at Whitehall, did you not?''

"Aye,'' Henry sighed. "All those in the councils o' government that came from out o' the City and did not 'ave great 'ouses o' their own near Westminster was granted quarters at the palace — if they was important enough. A city itself, it is. 'Tis a long ride beside it, along the Thames. Very fine, it is. Very fine. I have seen within the gates. General Whalley were used t' livin' like that, you know. 'is grandfather — the Golden Knight o' 'inchinbrook — were one o' England's wealthiest men, 'is castle, on the Great North Road, is the greatest in all England. That's up 'untington way, in Marster's territory. Marster 'as told me often o' Queen Elizabeth's bein' entertained there on 'er progresses about the kingdom. 'e recalls 'ow, when 'e were a lad, King James stopped at 'inchinbrook on 'is way from Scotland to London to be crowned King. 'e were royally entertained there — for days — o'course. General Whalley were a lad then, too. 'e would 'ave been there to meet the new king, the Golden Knight bein' 'is grandfather. And all 'is cousins would 'ave been there, too. 'im and 'is cousins! Once there was two dozen of 'em in parliament all t' once.'' His voice was husky with awe. "John 'ampden were one o' 'is cousins, ye know. Ye know of 'im, o'course — The Great Patriot?"

Zech nodded emphatically, pleased that he could assure Henry that he did know something. Everyone in the Valley knew about John Hampden's resistance to the unlawful, unparliamentary taxation that eventually led to England's Great Civil War. At the time he had stumbled onto the Old Stranger, the Massachusetts General Court had proposed a tax on all produce transported to the settlements of the Connecticut Valley. That unfair, shortsighted scheme had roused everyone in the western county and the Connecticut colonies. For a time, everyone had talked of little else but government, and representation, and taxation. They had recounted endless tales of events of the past and the people who shaped them: men like John Hampden, and those who headed the Great Migration to the New World — to a New England whose settlers intended that their new government would preserve representation and proceed with moderation. Most Englishmen had fought on foreign fields and were aware of the lot of men in Europe who had no rights at all by law. Only in the Netherlands and Switzerland did the common lot of men live better than England's serfs had lived in the centuries before Magna Carta. In all other countries subjects existed little better than animals, their labor supporting doting courts living in careless luxury.

"*There* — there is one —" Henry warned Zech under his breath. "That one there with those Connecticut men. The one whittling."

Zech studied the ragtaggled dragoon for a moment before they resumed their march. The rogue looked no different than his companions whose lives no doubt had been less colorful.

At the beaching place at the north end, Old Nathaniel and his look-alike youngest son, Az, waited in a canoe that belonged to their family. Four of Nathaniel's nine sons had settled in Hatfield. Two weeks ago, at the Sabbath service, the first bans had been read for Az's marriage to Dorcas, an orphaned girl come to town from New Haven in the spring. Their bans were posted now on the meetinghouse door. Dorcas had bewitched all the males in town, though the older men tried to pretend otherwise. Annie and Ed Grannis had known her as a child; they said that Dorcas had always created a stir. One of a large family fallen on hard times, she made it a habit to flash a knowing smile and arch her brows in a fashion that entranced the beholder and drew the unwary into a chase. Zech did not think that anyone could deny that she had the most disturbing walk in the Valley. All the other girls tried to imitate her to the dismay of their mothers. Dorcas seemed able to do anything well that she turned her hand to, and that did not please those who disliked her ways. Liza White, her mistress, doted on her, though, and Dorcas took full advantage of that. Only the Dickinsons did not draw sighs of relief when Dorcas finally decided on Az. Most neighbors agreed that Dorcas and Az deserved each other. Hadleyfolk were prepared to sit back and watch the match with keen interest. No doubt it would prove more fascinating than most other marriages. As soon as the sun set this Sabbathday, and took the sanctity of the day with it, Az and Dorcas would hasten to Mr. Tilton's to be wed, and Hadley would draw a sigh of relief on that score, for the time being.

John Gardner, Hadley's ferryman at the north end, remarked to Henry and Zech as they arrived: "I am happy you are going over, Zech. 'Tis good, as long as Warr is one of the best of the lot, that we have our young men take part, too — to show them how our young men are thinking. We should not go in too small numbers, either, I don't think."

Zech forgot General Whalley by the time the flotilla pushed off. He tried to keep his attention from the fort. He stared at the river, dark and forbidding, cold-looking in the long shadows of evening. The sun no longer glanced across its barely-rippling surface. He felt no urge to throw himself into the river to refresh himself, as he generally did at sight of it. The progress of the canoes did not seem to interrupt the evening rituals of flocks of birds along the river's edge. A flock of blue heron, some diving from precarious perches atop pine trees, did not take flight at their passing. It mattered not to them who lived where, or what men did to each other. Of a sudden, to Zech, twilight was not the comforting, quieting time he had perceived it to be. It seemed a fearful time of day: all nature's creatures gorging themselves, preparing for the night in which many would die, prey to nocturnal enemies. So often he heard blood-chilling screams in the night. Screams of protest. Even small prey did not always die quietly. He watched two great hawks wheel about in the busy sky and glide down above Great Meadow. What were they watching? A falcon darted suddenly below them, its pointed-wing flight impatient. In an instant it dived, lost from sight, swiftly gone for its kill.

Everyone had heard of the Wampanoag taunt, relayed by Normanville: "The English are afraid of us, now!" Everyone paddled purposefully, grimly, because of that boast. Each settler assured himself with each dip of his paddle that he was *not* afraid. If he was afraid, would he be making overtures of friendship and trust? Would the braves be invited to go on the morrow if everyone was afraid?

Joe Kellogg's canoes reached the fort's beaching place just ahead of Old Nathaniel's canoe; they joined the Northampton and Hatfield delegates, arrived on foot. Only a pair of older girls and a squaw watched their arrival. Grave and jut-jawed, the settlers filed up the path to the fort in Major Pynchon's wake. No brave or sachem waited at the half-opened gateway.

A seven-foot-high palisado of peeled logs, split in half and set round-side out, formed a circle around the wigwams. Warriors needed only half a tree as a sturdy shield; space between the logs kept nearby enemies in view and prevented fires being set against them unnoticed. Many settlers hesitated and turned from their mission to stare blankly at family and friends watching, across the river. No one made a sign of greeting; everyone appeared transfixed in the beautiful evening serenity.

Inside the propped-open gate, only a handful of older braves and sachems waited in an irregular semi-circle before the wigwam of Sanchumanchu, the chief still respected by the young hot-bloods who disregarded most of their moderate elders. Those who waited on their English neighbors had solemnly donned their ceremonial headdresses; they were not the braves who would give trouble. Zech's gaze moved in despair from one watchful face to another, and rested on Warrwarrankshan who had been watching him as he searched him out. Zech thought that he saw a look of greeting kindle in the old man's black eyes, though his expression revealed nothing.

Sanchumanchu towered above his tribesmen gathered around him; he waited with his sinewy, bronzed arms folded across his unpainted chest, his leathery face unfathomable. Close by, a carcass dripped, abandoned for the moment by squaws banished from the area of the council of government.

"Netop!" Major Pynchon greeted Sanchumanchu, as soon as he got his bearing. He stretched his arm out before him in Indian fashion. Sanchumanchu replied, "Netop!" and bowed his head in the English manner.

162

"We invite your men to scout with us for those who murder," Major Pynchon said, and Sanchumanchu replied, "Braves go with you — second day of week, and held up two fingers.

"Second day of week," the Major repeated mechanically; very plainly, he had not expected the matter to be settled so suddenly and definitely. "Sun one hour high," he added quickly.

Sanchumanchu nodded slightly, then turned to indicate those who would go — older men like Warr, long-time friends of the settlers — and Benji, and another young brave. Not Wappawy, of course, nor any of the other young warriors.

"Netop!" Major Pynchon greeted his now-declared Indian allies. He stepped up to Sanchumanchu and took his outstretched hand solemnly in his; he shook it warmly. Next, he turned to the others and took the right hand of each of those who would go with the militia Monday morning.

Each Valley man followed his example before everyone sat down and passed a peace pipe among them to seal their bargain.

The expedition was back on the river, like blind men in the gathered dusk, silent and feeling alone, before Zech realized there had been no Indian ceremony but the peace pipe. Other times there might have been, when there had been something to celebrate. If the settlers had not gone to the fort at all, the Nonotucks who had agreed to go out with the Valleymen would have gone with them, anyway. No headway had been made against the real problem.

CHAPTER XXII

Sabbath morning, Zech led Henry and Mungo to a nook under an arching elderberry bush beside the common fence. The meeting-house could not seat Hadleyfolk and all its visitors; Zech had decided beforehand where to sit, out of the sun, with a full view of the gathering assembly. He settled between Mungo, who sank into morose silence, and Henry, who started instantly to engage in a murmured, running commentary regarding the gathering throng.

Hadley spared no effort to impress its guests. In spite of the heat many young Hadleymen wore the fine woolen suits they had inherited from their grandfathers. Everywhere, faded or age-darkened shades of purple and blue and saffron mingled with the fresher russet tones of homespun and dyed tow. No one appeared as well turned out as Will Webster in his father's best blue worsted.

Over-all in the growing warmth of day, an overpowering acrid odor of cleanliness prevailed, the visiting militia, too, being as clean as men could make themselves. Before sundown yesterday afternoon, the men had gone down to Fort Brook and washed away the accumulated grime of heat, dust, dirt and animals. They had come back smelling of the soft soap Hadley women made from tried-out fat and lye. Henry, closely shaven for the first time since his arrival, presented such a handsome, respectable appearance that Thanky threw herself at him shamelessly. It shocked Zech to discover that a ten-year-old girl could be so brash. Privately, he blamed Dorcas' influence, but that was small comfort. And Henry

164

did not help, either. He grinned, embarrassed, and assured everyone that Thanky's assault was all right! It pleased him! Zech had known no relief last night until Aunt drove her offending daughter off to bed; this morning, Aunt had contrived to let the men get away without Thanky.

Captain Beers rode past, looking painfully lopsided as he picked his way through the shuffling throng; beside him walked his sergeant son, an old man, too, pox-marked, peering, hard-faced, grey-haired.

Henry pointed with one toe toward an aristocratic-looking militia captain strolling with Peter Tilton. "That is Captain Lothrop —" he whispered. Zech studied the white-thatched, lean, reserved-looking, narrow-faced man; his skin was the golden brown of those who had been fair-skinned before New England's weathering. The Captain's carriage suggested a knight in armour, but his composure suggested the calm reserve of a clergyman. " 'is father preached the New Testament without regard for the Book o' Common Prayer," Henry whispered. " 'is father's whole congregation was arrested. Near 'alf-a-'undred of 'em. Hincarcerated two years, they was. 'e were a young man, then. 'is mother died 'fore they was released — if they'd leave the country. I 'ave 'eard tell 'ow they arrived in early winter — the colony was but two years old. Deprived of all earthly goods, they was. Families 'ere broken by 'ardships 'n' climate —" He turned to Zech. "You 'ave lived 'ere all your life. You are accustomed to the cold. You can not imagine what 'tis like 'ere winters, at first. And then, there was only farmin' and building trades — no commerce but furs and fishin' to engage in, and that by royal grant. They come with nothing to sandy soil 'n' salt grass —"

The Captain did not look like a man who had weathered much . . . Every child had heard of the early days, of course. Granny Felton complained in detail of the nuisance of being crowded into makeshift sheds that first summer in Hadley, while permanent dwellings were being thrown up. But Hadley families had household goods, food and clothing, and healthy livestock and just across the river, civilization and relatives and close friends.

"See that 'un behind Cap'n Lothrop — the freckled one? Joe Chamberlain — he's but twelve years old —"

Zech shrugged and pointed his toe toward a group beyond the overgrown groomsboy. "See that man just there?" he directed, his voice hushed. "That's John Warner of Brookfield." The horrors

165

of the attack marked John's gaunt face. "His daughter has not recovered at all, yet. She's taken refuge in the lilacs behind Deacon Smith's. A body must cough, or scrape, before approaching her, or she rears up in a frenzy."

Henry shook his head sympathetically.

Zech glanced toward Mungo to see if he were interested. Mungo was staring open-mouthed at Sally Cook, skirting past in the wake of her mother and younger sister. All the Cook ladies wore fresh new linen frocks of a soft shade of rose; lace edged their crisp, well-bleached caps and kerchiefs. Sally, her blondeness brightened by excitement and the reflection of the rose tone of her gown, eyed every little knot of militia strewn about outside the meetinghouse, her brows arched in Dorcas' maddening fashion.

Mungo looked quickly toward Zech. His little eyes sparkled, his thin lips parted in an appreciative half-smile. Zech drew in his breath and hissed: "She's Thanky's friend!"

Mungo made a wry face at Zech for the pains he took to deprive him of his simple pleasure, and dropped back on one elbow.

At the close of the afternoon meeting, Az and Dorcas traipsed from the meetinghouse toward Peter Tilton's to be wed. Mungo, watching the noisy crowd of young folk giddily waving them off while wishing them long life and prosperity, protested, unbelieving: "No feastin'? No dancin'? No proper merry-makin'? What kind o' weddin' is that? How can they *feel* wed? They cannot!"

Mungo's bitter complaint nagged at Zech; it was on his mind when he stepped into the yard in the morning and found Warr there waiting. For a moment he stared at Warr mindful of how Indians celebrate with feasting and dancing. Was *that* what Mungo thought proper? Suddenly, Zech realized he had not greeted his old friend, so long absent — and he was so relieved to see him! Embarrassment overwhelmed him. He was relieved that Warr could not read his thoughts for surely everyone should dance for joy! He wanted to right now —

Warr nodded first, his face without expression. From Zech's right, the sweetish odor of fresh blood tugged for attention: a twelve-point buck hanging from the corner tackle. Zech looked quickly from the goodwill offering to the old Indian and shook his head, half in wonder, half in abject thanks. Warr nodded again in his stiff fashion. Zech stepped close to the fire that Warr had fanned to a blaze. He shivered as the warmth of the fire fended off the cool dampness, and looked toward the common where hulking silhouettes were poking campfires to action.

"Where we go?" Warr finally asked.

"Through Hatfield," Zech answered reluctantly. Warr would know which way they *should* go. His serenity assured Zech that no hostile Indians lurked close at hand. "Philip is supposed to have many waiting to harvest the corn at Brookfield — and their own at Winimisette."

Warr corrected: "Not many In'dans."

"They are at Brookfield, then?"

No answer.

"Have they been here? Up the river?"

Ham appeared in the doorway with Aunt close on his heels. Their pleasure at sight of Warr glowed through their quiet greeting and relieved appreciation at sight of the venison.

In less than an hour, men began to stream out of town at both ends of the common and along all roads leading into the wilderness. Jon glared balefully at Warr who waited beside Ham, a few steps beyond the gate.

"You will find no one — English or otherwise — more trustworthy!" Zech warned him.

Jon started to retort, but caught himself. Instead, he muttered loudly enough to be heard at a distance: "I go in - to no swamp - land for no - body!" Ham turned and eyed him coldly, and Jon added: "I will hang for trea - son 'fore a redskin lifts the top off my head the one way I know to pre - vent it!"

Ham and Warr were assigned to the nearer reaches of the Mohawks' trail that followed the Deerfield River toward its source in the craggy Hoosac Range; beyond the mountain it wound to Albany; and beyond Albany through dense wilderness to Canada. Along Hatfield's common, local men joined their company. Children cheered them on and from their dooryards the women-folk watched stoically. At the edge of town, Bobby Welles waved calmly from her doorstep as Tom took his leave. She held her little girl by the hand, and looked as if she might be cradling another before Tom returned. Recollection of Bobby that day stayed with Zech, so that eighteen years later, after Tom moved his family above Deerfield and died there, when word came that Bobby and her three daughters had been scalped by rampaging Indians, he recalled her this day, and felt in his heart that she would recover.

The trail passed through a section of rolling foothills that had not been burned the last two Novembers. Young brush narrowed the way. As the company approached the first marshy area, a few militiamen, mindful of Brookfield's experience, held back. Where the trail led directly toward the swamp and at its edge veered to the left and went up over a pine knoll and down out of sight, the lead men lingered to a halt and did not follow Warr over the ridge. Ham and Zech, bringing up the rear, hurried past the reluctant company. By the time they caught up with Warr, the others had closed ranks behind them. At the woods edge beyond the swamp, they found a fallow patch of meadow where squaws had raised winter vegetables; beyond would be an abandoned village.

Jonathan reminded everyone in a loud voice that orders had been to destroy every village they found. Only three wigwams remained in a village that had been abandoned a long time. Against the sandy bottom of the pond fat bass lay motionless, dark shadows appearing to wait for the return of the spear.

Warr relieved Ham of the necessity of giving directions. As the company clambered to a halt at the clearing's edge, he moved forward and looked into the wigwams, then he nodded to Ham and moved ahead into the silvery-grey beech grove beyond. Above him, grey squirrels darted through the trees, frantically jerking their tails and screaming their protest at the invasion.

A pair of willing and eager militiamen offered to stay behind to burn the derelict wigwams. They needed only a few minutes to gather enough tinder to make a smart blaze; the popple poles of the framework would make crisp kindling. The ancient hides began to crackle before Zech got out of earshot. He looked back and could see the licking flames growing to heavy, dark, streaking clouds of smoke. While the wigwams burned, the men laughed and threw rocks into the pond and chased the bass away. Zech caught up with Warr and his father; back in the clearing, he heard the men cheering and knew that the blazing wigwams had fallen in on themselves.

The trail skirted a trashy beaver pond, the lair of beaver and its water-loving cousins, the mink, the muskrat, and the martin, called by those who knew their ways — *notamagus, squash,* and *oppenachi;* for generations, the November fires had not penetrated beyond this broad stretch of swamp; strangling vines held the dense underbrush in a tangled mass of glowering darkness.

Down a devil's raceway caused by a landslide sometime in the past, Ham's company caught glimpses of other clouds of smoke in the Valley, hanging heavy in the still summer air over burning wigwams.

On their return to Hatfield's beaching place, Warr did not turn toward the trail to the fort as Zech expected he would. Instead, Warr climbed into the canoe with Zech and Ham, ahead of Jon, who could not miss the opportunity to look offended. Zech had hoped that Warr would return with them and stay, that he would never return to the fort, but he had not expected that would come to pass — not on this day, anyway. He looked quickly toward his father. Their eyes met. A look of unexpected relief flashed between them. Zech's spirit soared. In that instant his father's distracted expression brightened. His father had been bracing himself against saying farewell, or seeing their old friend walk away without a word — perhaps forever. Zech steeled himself to control his glee.

His spirits soaring at thought of Warr's staying, eager to be first to tell someone who cared, he flew homeward. He found Timmie watching for him along the straggling line of returning scouts. He tossed his musket against a fence and threw the laughing lad high in the air before he swung him onto his back and galloped back to meet his father and Warr.

Zech halted abruptly. His father stood alone. Abandoned. Warr, an erect, lonely figure, was paddling away, across the river toward the fort. He had crossed the river only to retrieve his canoe.

Zech ran to the beach. His voice caught in his throat: "Warr — Warr — come to - mor - row —" He knew Warr heard. He could only pray that he would return.

Later in the evening, Joe Kellogg sent word to Ham that he would like Zech's help with the ferrying in the morning. Ham told the messenger that for the time being he could spare both Zech and Henry.

CHAPTER XXIII

Zech had not expected that ferrying the militiamen back and forth across the river would lead him to one of the Old Strangers. For the most part, the trips to Northampton were a diversion. For want of anything better to do, the visiting militiamen rode over to Lt. Wilton's trading post and bought tobacco, replaced their stockings, and improved their diet with purchases of cheese, bread, dried peas, boiled meat, beer, and sugar. A few bought knives to whittle away their time. Zech had heard of two enterprising individuals who had bought duffel and trading cloth and red and blue shag, and one who had bought moose skins; in their spare time they sat cross-legged by campfires and in sheds and made coats and moccasins their fellow militiamen would wear in colder weather; some would pay for their new garments in better times.

Two long canoes provided ferry service without charge, now. Zech and Henry paddled one, and Young Joe Kellogg and a Sudbury volunteer the other. They were directed that both canoes were not to tarry on the same side of the river together, but with the August sun beating down unrelieved on the glistening water, late in the afternoon Zech and Henry decided that no harm would come if they did not cross back. A band of Connecticut men assured them that no one else planned to cross over to Northampton before supper; their Mohegan companions nodded solemn agreement: all the passengers would be coming back from the post together and both canoes would be needed on the 'Hamp side at the same time. They would wait.

They joined Young Joe and his companion, stretched out on the damp sand in the shade of the willows lining the west bank. They had hardly drawn a deep breath before a loud voice bellowed across the river: "Ahoy, there! Ahoy, there!"

All four ferrymen sat up instantly and groaned together.

"He should use the scow!" Young Joe whispered.

"Aye — I see — I see — " Zech muttered under his breath, and heaved himself up onto his bare feet. "And notice who is with him!" he directed, and pulled his sturdy tow blouse and trousers free from his sweating body.

"Aye — " the others murmured in sympathetic unison.

"Do you know *him?*" Zech asked Henry, referring to the impatient stranger waiting with Major Pynchon, and Joe Kellogg, and Peter Tilton.

"No - o - o - " Henry admitted reluctantly, and added hastily: " 'e must be from down the river."

Joe Kellogg remained at the head of the stairs and held the reins of the horses he and his companions had ridden from headquarters at the manse; the other three men, deep in conversation, sauntered down the steps. Major Pynchon, at their head and always in a hurry, broke away from the others as soon as the canoe beached. He climbed into the bow behind Zech, his small, dark face fierce with disapproval for the ferrymen's not following directions. The stranger tarried at the foot of the stairs, consulting further with Peter Tilton, his voice pitched too low to be heard. He towered above Peter and in contrast to the neat, white-haired Hadleyman looked like an untidy bear. His thick, coarse black mane bushed out about his head and brushed the shoulders of his blouse that hung open, unbuttoned at his throat, without stock or collar; heavy linen breeches dangled unbuckled at his knees; at his broad waist a brace of silver-mounted pistols glinted in the sun.

"Perhaps he is the Connecticut Councillor," Zech thought to himself.

The whispered conference between the stranger and Peter continued a few seconds before Peter turned and started to climb back up the bluff. The stranger waved farewell to Joe and lumbered to the waiting ferry. He eased himself into the canoe just behind Henry. No one spoke while they shoved off and set the stroke, then the stranger remarked over his shoulder in an offhand way: "Peter tells me that Joe still does not know."

Zech expected Major Pynchon to carry on a discussion in the way of men of affairs, talking over other listeners' heads about subjects beyond their knowledge. Major Pynchon's almost inaudible gasp caught Zech by surprise. "No — No! — " the Major protested more than answered, plainly upset.

Zech caught his breath. He knew something that Joe did not know! Was *that* what the stranger spoke of? Zech forced himself to breathe evenly, and to dip his paddle and push. He dipped and pushed, and dipped and pushed again without a telltale break in the rhythm of the stroke. He prayed that his neck did not burn red and betray him to the Major. The silence could not have lasted more than a trice, though it seemed an eternity. He watched the stranger study the Nonotucks' fort above them at the bend of the river. Evidently the stranger didn't have the Indians in mind, though, nor had he caught the Major's anxiety, because he called idly: "*He* looks well, does he not?"

"Aye!" Major Pynchon agreed quickly, tensely; then, because he willed that the subject under discussion must appear to be Joe, he almost shouted: "Joe does not let anything interfere with his duty! Not anything at all!"

Zech could see the Major's warning affect the stranger. His shoulders stiffened slightly; he half-turned his head as if to intercept some further message from the Major. Zech stifled a sigh of relief as the canoe scraped up on the western shore. He kept his head down, as if preoccupied with the beaching, but he knew that while he did that Major Pynchon nodded purposefully in his direction; when he looked up at his passengers to bid them farewell, the stranger was regarding him curiously, wondering how an insignificant ferryman could be a threat.

Zech smiled at his passengers as disarmingly as he knew how, and nodded genially; otherwise he kept his expression blank, as if his heart were not pounding like the hooves of a runaway colt. He waited unresolved for a moment after the passenger he presumed to be Major Talcott of Connecticut started toward Northampton with Major Pynchon trotting dutifully in the lead, then he moved through the willows to where he could watch them. The last time he had been so interested in anyone's crossing Old Rainbow Meadow it had been Dr. Westcarr, the afternoon that Sam Russell's mad denial had admitted the Old Stranger's existence. It

172

was but one month short of four years since that afternoon! He reminded himself that he must not betray his excitement to Henry, or Young Joe, or the Easterner.

He watched a half-dozen Connecticut Mohegans swarm over the stile at the end of Pudding Lane, en route back to Hadley. Major Pynchon's companion stopped to talk to them, as if they were old acquaintances.

"What's got you?" Henry asked at his elbow, and shaded his eyes to see what Zech found of such interest.

Zech shrugged. "I — you — suppose that might be the Connecticut Councillor — the new man?"

"I would imagine 'tis" Henry remarked without real interest. "Those Ind'ans must 'ave the Old Trader pretty well cleaned out by now."

For the remainder of the afternoon, while he helped to ferry the returning passengers, Zech's mind churned with schemes. He made and weighed and abandoned a dozen approaches that occurred to him, including a bold approach to the Connecticut Councillor, evidently a very direct man. Henry tried to resume his tales of incidents in the East and even farther abroad that had fascinated Zech in the past. He finally gave up, aware that Zech's thoughts lay beyond his reach.

Major Pynchon and his companion did not return by suppertime and Dr. Westcarr did, toward the close of the afternoon. His sudden presence, his menacing, watchful silence, squeezed Zech's heart dry. As Dr. Westcarr leapt by Zech, leaving the canoe, he gripped Zech's shoulder, squeezing him meanly, a friendly-looking gesture that made Zech all but cry out. Zech dreaded returning to the common at the end of the afternoon with Dr. Westcarr there. He delayed overlong at the river until Henry commented on the lateness of the hour and his hollowness. What might Aunt and Thanky be preparing for supper? When Henry grumbled that Aunt would be displeased if they were much later, Zech could hang back no longer; he consented to going home.

Everyone had finished eating by the time they arrived, and the younger boys had started on their chores. While he ate, Zech asked his father: "Is that ragamuffin lookin' man in fact the Connecticut Councillor?"

Ham smiled faintly and nodded. "Major Talcott," he told Zech.

"He rode over with us today, but I guess he's gone back down to Hartford. He did not come back."

"He'll be around a day or two, yet, I believe," Ham answered absently.

Zech kept eating in the same manner in which he had kept paddling that morning, mechanically, to disguise his real interest. "He rode Mr. Tilton's horse down to the river this morning," he told his father. "Must be staying with him."

"Wouldn't wonder," Ham agreed.

"He's pastor's brother-in-law," Aunt reminded Ham, as if that might decide where he stayed.

"He was — . He is not, now," Ham answered without saying more; Zech understood well how much death affected the constantly changing relationships, so he did not need to ask questions. Aunt's remark explained a lot to him, though. Major Talcott might bed in either house.

After supper, while they tended the livestock, Henry regaled Zech with his dream of having a blacksmith shop of his own when he got back to Newbury; with his great strength he would do well, he explained matter-of-factly; he would raise a strapping family, and be as respected a man in the community as Tim Nash here in Hadley.

Zech assured him that he would be. He truly wanted the best in life for Henry, but at this point he had other things on his mind. He hoped that he said all the right things and was properly silent when he should only listen; he could not have repeated any of the conversation that passed between them. He seemed to wander about the busy common while he sought a glimpse of Dr. Westcarr. When at last he saw him conferring with a knot of militia he knew to be gamesters, Zech turned suddenly to Henry and exclaimed: "Look, Henry, I must tend to a matter I fear has been overlooked! — I cannot tell you more, now. Look — do not say anything about this to anyone — *for the sake of us all* — and do not go home without me — Wait for me — no matter how late —" His mind flew from possibility to possibility . . . If he were to meet Henry at the Newbury militia's campfire, one of the boys — or his father — might come seeking them out there. "You know where the shoemaker's shop is? Wait by the company nearest there. And make an excuse for me if you must! But WAIT for me! Do not go home without me! And say nothing, for now — or later — of my not being with you. Nothing! Mind you!"

Henry stared at him, astounded.

"I will tell you of what I am about as soon as I can — " Zech promised, his tone both pleading and determined.

Henry frowned, troubled and offended. "Suppose something may happen to you —"

"I am going to be in town. Do not fret — " Before Henry could consent or protest further, Zech darted away. He went into the woods through the Widow Bedient's garden and crossed the Middle Highway trail out of sight of the common. At the back of the manse, he crept to the spot where he had studied the manse the afternoon he had come upon General Whalley.

The yard was full of horses, including those of Captain Beers' and Captain Lothrop's adjutants, the officers left in charge of those who did not go East to scout. Men passed back and forth into the manse and barn, and in and out of the yard, perhaps trying to make arrangements for the seizure of the guns at the forts.

As he watched, Major Talcott turned in at the gate, alone. Zech hurried back to the Middle Highway and made his way swiftly to the manse gate. He threw himself down by a group of Eastern youths who looked surprised by his intrusion. "I got to wait here for my father to come out — " Zech told them. He arranged himself against the fence so that he would see everyone who left; a lad between him and the gate provided a good shield so that no local man would notice him.

Twilight deepened to dusk before Major Talcott reappeared. He stood in the dooryard and boomed a lengthy discourse at a pair of Connecticut men. The young men nearest Zech turned to watch him as well as to listen, and Zech got up and moved slowly toward the middle of the common, as if he were dawdling along waiting for one of the group in the yard; he planned to move rapidly in whatever direction the major moved. Finally, Major Talcott passed swiftly through the gate and started down the common. Zech guessed that he was headed for Peter Tilton's. He raced as fast as he could to get far ahead of the Major; he circled into Peter's back yard before the Major hove into sight of the house. He murmured a thankful prayer to himself that at least he did not need to bother about Biscuit. Now, the law required that all dogs be kept securely fastened. And with so much commotion their barking meant little.

Zech studied the back of Peter's house. He asked himself, full of disgust, why he had not come and scouted the territory earlier. He lurked in the deep shadows by the shed: when Major Talcott arrived, evidently detained along the way, Zech moved into the shelter of the vast lilac by the opened window of the common room.

In front of him, beyond the fence, quiet had begun to settle on the common. Few figures moved away from their campsites. Zech kept back from the dim light that filtered through the sleazy tacked over the window — to help keep out the insects that found him. From inside, he heard the Major boom his greetings. Madam Tilton and Mary, in reply, began to murmur politely about his day, almost as if they expected their guest would give them short shrift. Major Talcott scarcely replied; almost instantly he announced in his loud, booming voice that he had had a trying day, that he must get some rest; then he lowered his voice discreetly and explained apologetically in a voice so low Zech could scarcely hear, "Please pardon me, Ladies, so that I may visit further with our friend —"

The women murmured again and Major Talcott bid them good-night. He plodded up the stairs. Zech's heart pounded as he looked upward in the darkness. The cottage no doubt had two chambers above stairs. He waited to judge which the Major would enter. When he did not hear the Major again, Zech skirted the back of the house to the far side, away from the unsuspecting common. He pressed against the rough clapboards and waited silently, listening, before he realized that someone was standing in the open window just above his head. Had he been cautious enough? Was the person standing there aware of his closeness? Zech held his breath. Must he wait forever? Finally Major Talcott spoke, his voice pitched low but its timbre carrying his words beyond the window. "Well, another day gone — heh?" he inquired gently.

Zech's heart almost stopped beating when a voice answered quietly: "Aye, but in these times they are not so much the same as I have known them to be." A chill zigzagged down Zech's spine.

That must be HIM! Sitting there inside that room in the dark, listening to life out there on the common! Zech tried not to gasp aloud. Could not everyone in the world hear his pounding heart? He must not breathe so loudly! He must not betray himself —

"Eleven years!" Major Talcott marvelled, and repeated: "Eleven years you have been in Hadley. It does not seem possible!"

" 'Tis possible — " the voice answered quietly. "Sometimes it has seemed like eleven centuries."

"It must! It must!"

The Major scraped a chair close to the window so that he could catch some of the air that stirred beyond the window. Zech found himself straining his eyes, as if seeing could help him hear better. Beyond, on the common, a ruckus arose and broke into yells and laughter and subdued cheering. Within the room — silence — The confusion subsided to the unsettled quiet of scores of men at ease, constant and monotonous, comforting in its way. After an eternity of listening, the Major resumed: "Those who fled to foreign refuges did not fare so well."

"Aye. No. No. 'Tis true —"

"But how would things be for any of us, now, if what you and your Father Whalley fought for had not come to pass — at least for a time?" Zech almost gasped aloud . . . *"Your Father Whalley —"* . . . This, then, must be General Goffe!

General Goffe spoke carefully, as if he were searching for words. "We did not want to live in bondage," he said quietly. "A bit at a time — King James discarded our laws and customs. In his native Scotland parliament was of no account. So he tried to make England's parliament of no account, too." He paused, and his voice, when he spoke again, hinted of amusement and satisfaction: "Your father must have told you of the moonlight pony trains."

"Oh, aye! He did! He did!" Major Talcott chuckled.

"Essex was exciting, then," General Goffe mused. "As a lad, my family visited often at my grandfather's manor — Stanmer Hall. We saw the pony trains passing along the byways loaded with goods brought into the little coves and river landings rather than go through ports to the north. Who could afford the high imposition taxes clapped on goods at the ports? — All to support the king's monstrous, cavorting satyrs at court!"

"Aye. They — the moonlighters — were no secret."

"We were told of their exploits as part of our education. 'Twas defiance — to make the king's thoughtlessness — his greedy councillors — reconsider what they had to lose in proper taxes. They got so avaricious — and their taxes so high — trade at regular ports fell away to naught."

"Well, at least the loss to the treasury forced James to call Commons together, again!"

"Aye. And he said he never would! — As lads, we learned early

177

that Englishmen had rights and privileges before any other country in the world. The Dutch borrowed their ideas of liberty and freedom from our example. They were growing in our old ways, as we were being cozened out of them!''

''Just think, where for generations England had been a haven for Dutch and Flemish escaping the Spanish Inquisition, Holland became a refuge for Englishmen — from their own king!''

''When I was put in charge of Sussex and Hampshire, during the Commonwealth, it came as a shock to me to learn how much had been forgotten, so soon.''

''OOhhh?''

''We were not well-received. Royalists held the estates, and they gave us short shrift. My poor little wife! All her life, she had been among friends, before. She suffered their indignities with good grace. But 'twas a difficult time for her. She was happy to return to Westminster and Whitehall.''

''They are all conformists there, now, in the south?''

''Aye, most — but not when my father was banished for non-conformity!''

''Aye — ''

''In Wales, in Haverfordwest, in Pembroke, where my father was rector of St. Mary's, as many Englishmen dwelled — all refugees like us — as are now in Boston or New Haven. We called it Little-England-Beyond-the-Sea.''

''Did you get to Sussex often, then?''

''Quite. And London. My father was a daring man. He knew full-well whom he could trust, where he could go and not be persecuted. My mother's father and brother sat in parliament, you know. That did not make them popular with King James, but he and his bishops did not awe them one bit!''

With great indignation, Major Talcott declared: ''King James all but sold the country out to Spain —''

''Then France!''

'' 'Tis a wonder men suffered his nonsense for so long.''

''Aye. Even as a lad, I comprehended the wonder — men speaking of how to work things out — wondering what they could do. Parliament men would not accept Divine Right for Kings, and yet — what strength did it have — how could Magna Carta's statutes be enforced when the king appointed the judges, and packed the House of Lords with his own creatures? — Men happy to overrule Commons at his behest whenever the House tried to assert its ancient rights.''

"We did expect that Young Charles would not prove so deaf and blind to English rights. He had no use for his father's profligate ways, you know.''

"True! True! After the death of Prince Henry, we put our hopes in Prince Charles — and for naught. For naught —''

"Aye. He would not rule without Buckingham and all his favorites.''

"*Buckingham!* So willing to dispatch our young men to their deaths on foreign shores! Without supplies — to perish for his vainglory — ''

Both men groaned.

"There always are so many ways devised to make men slaves! Government must be for the good of the subject, or 'tis not government at all, but tyranny and slavery —'' the words trailed off into silence.

After a long pause, Major Talcott soothed: "You hear from your family, still, of course.''

All loneliness and longing and heartbreak sounded in the single "Oh — Aye — '' of the response.

Zech batted his eyes and swallowed, unprepared for sudden exposure to suffering he had not understood, had not suspected. He realized then, too, that General Goffe had spoken of General Whalley as if he no longer were living. His father had known that! Zech stared hard toward the common, trying to turn his attention to anything that would keep him from giving way to nerves pressed almost to the point of explosion.

CHAPTER XXIV

"I suppose, if you had been but a Judge, as John Dixwell was, and not in government afterward — that you might be living now as openly as he does in New Haven."

Another Judge? In New Haven?

"Edward and I could not be so easily lost sight of," General Goffe reminded.

"Why, Dixon lives boldly as James Davids, and no one who does not know suspects him in the least." The Major's wonder grew apace as he spoke.

" 'Tis his good fortune that he can. From what he related to us, when he finally arrived in the colonies, we felt we were fortunate we did not go to the continent as he did. 'Twas no simple matter there. Lucerne became a nightmare."

"Well," Major Talcott grumped, resentful for his companion: "Your friends surely made life easy for him, marrying him to that rich old lady with one foot through death's door as they did."

"John — I do not begrudge him!"

"Could there not have been more benefit — some way — for you?"

General Goffe sighed. He explained slowly, huskily, "As you know, Frances writes to me as if she were my mother. We sign ourselves Goldsmith. At first, friends carried our letters and tended to our business, but now we must take more care: many changes have come about; and those going out from Boston now are not always our friends. Our letters go by post to where Frances is not known. The present representative to His Majesty's government — " his tone changed to light derision, "is not one of us. By the time Frances got our last tender, she was in straitened circumstances, indeed."

"Aye. I heard. 'Tis a difficult situation."

"There should be a letter, soon. They come to Increase Mather, you know. I have not heard, yet, this summer." His voice sounded strained. "In her last letter, Frances wrote that she was moving, but she did not give an address, of course. So, I am expecting to hear some other way." He paused. "Perhaps one of the militiamen from the East will bring something to John or Peter. I had expected Peter would bring a message last time he returned home from Boston, but he had nothing."

"These years cannot have been easy for your wife!"

"No. No. No. It has not been. Our youngest was hardly more than a babe when I saw her last." A tortured silence followed, longer than the others. "My eldest daughter is married, now. I know of my new son's name by its being written openly to another. Now, since the Indian troubles have cut down on our trading, I am able to provide but a pittance to help her establish her new home." He sighed. When he spoke again, his spirits were improved. "I am told the young man is worthy, praise be to God, and fortunately of good estate."

"Well, at least you can have comfort from that."

"Aye." General Goffe spoke carefully: "The year after we left England, that crippling disease struck our little ones, you know. Our two littlest girls were left lame and weakly. The last letter told of the younger one — Betsey — dying — after all these years." His voice broke as he uttered the last words.

Major Talcott sighed loudly, and Zech heard a fist pound into a hand. "To live in such shadows!" Major Talcott protested in a savage whisper, and the General cried out: "Frances writes of how dear I am to her, that if she knew of any way to make me happy she would — to the loss of her life!"

Troubled, the Major asked, quietly, gently: "Could ye not have brought them over — in all this time?"

General Goffe reproved quietly: "We were too well known. Too many knew us. When it has taken so much to hide two, could a whole family be concealed?"

"A family can be part of a community, when a man alone cannot."

" 'Tis no easy matter to leave England, you know. For years it would have been impossible — a family of women — alone —"

"Could they not have gone to Wexford — where your oldest son now dwells — and have come from there?"

General Goffe sighed. "So many schemes have been considered."

Half-apologetically, Major Talcott agreed: "As with all else, 'tis easier to say what someone else should do than be able to do it."

General Goffe began to speak rapidly. "I can take comfort that I have been able to provide well. Dan'l Gookin is my principal manager, yet. He and Dave Wilton have done our Indian trading, and Dan'l supervised my farm as you well know. We were fortunate when Dick and John could take our monies abroad — "

" 'Twas no doubt some of those rogues that you and General Whalley sent over here to rid yourselves of, who reported to the King that Dan'l was managing your farm for you — when the commission was sent to seize what was claimed to be yours, years back."

In despair, General Goffe explained: "We did not want our good people there — they had borne so much already — to need to support beggars and baggage in jail. Yet we could not turn the rascals loose to plunder the countryside further. Nor did we believe in the punishments that had been meted out. So we sent them away. The worst of the lot did not come here, they were shipped to Barbados and the Windwards. You had full knowledge of each man who came — and the area is so unpopulated — " He admonished rather than pleaded: "They have not done you great harm. Though some have not done you much good, many have become respected citizens."

As if to change the subject, Major Talcott said abruptly, "John told me that the lad who ferried us today was the one who came onto Edward behind the manse."

"Aye. He's a good lad. Never said a word, after he approached Sam Russell. My youngest lad's the same age, you know. It must have been a horrifying experience for him. 'Twas for Edward! Just think of the trouble we would have been in if he had been one of Westcarr's Indians! 'Twould have been another kind of story."

"Aye!"

"We learned in Milford that we had to stay clear of Indians. That's why John got Moors. The trouble he's gone to! The Moors do not understand our language, or our ways. Everything is strange to them.''

"That Indian girl, Sarah, must know something—"

"Somewhat. Not all the significance, because of course our ways are beyond her. As long as Mary has told her she must never speak of us — or admit that we live — she will not.''

A chair creaked, and Zech guessed that Major Talcott was leaning toward General Goffe. "John Russell and I were lads together," he stated gruffly. "And he married my sister, bless her departed soul — *I* know how stiff-necked and single-minded he can be!''

General Goffe half-laughed. An apology. "John — is — as he is. He can not be otherwise. If 'twere worth his soul, he could not. And he has risked his life daily for eleven years for me — for us — for our principles. For his.''

"Well, once 'twas your battle cry that opposition to tyranny is obedience to God. I say to you, right here and now, that a pious tyrant is more to be feared than any rascal! What liberty of conscience is there where there can be no difference of opinion?''

Zech could feel the General's despair, before he answered: " 'Tis awesome — the turn affairs can take. Peter and I talk this over at great lengths. We wonder if there ever can be a theocracy that will make the kingdom of God come to earth. 'Twas Edward's conviction that where wisdom is exercised to gain civil liberties, religion will follow. 'Twill follow where it cannot be driven, you know. But you know, high priests by their very positions cannot be tolerant. Edward's strongest convictions were that persecution for the sake of religion is a crime and a blunder." He sighed, again. " 'Twas not till men could read their own tongue for themselves that they began to strive to be free. 'Tis each man able to feel worthy, that is important. But everyone is busy! Some say they are free enough. But they are free at all only because there are men like Peter who uphold their cause as he did the Valley women's. But we wonder who will take his place.''

Trying for lightness, the Councillor remarked: "Well, you do not need to worry for a while, I grant. And, anyway, Connecticut's still breeding true Independents. I thank God for that daily.''

The General answered: "Aye. 'Tis good reason, indeed, to be grateful. We have free-thinking men coming along, too. Young men. Solomon Stoddard, and Joe Hawley —''

A steady plodding of hooves, of someone who had arrived in the yard, caught their attention. Peter had returned home.

Zech slipped away from his hiding place, heading for Ed Grannis' and Henry.

In the morning, Major Pynchon rode up to the house as the men filed out after breakfast. "We are going up to the fort!" he announced to Ham.

"I am not going!" Ham told him flatly. Zech stopped short, amazed by his father's defiance. Ham caught the Major by surprise, too. He eyed Ham uncertainly before he warned angrily: "Every firearm there is a danger to us!"

"They all have arms, but only our friends will give them up," Ham reminded. Speaking his mind did not come easily to Ham; he had to swallow before he could go on. When he spoke again, his voice trembled: "If we take the arms back now — after — if we take the arms of our friends — what good then is our friendship at all?"

The Major's eyes narrowed. He flushed as he barked: "We can not have more losses!"

Ham threw out his hands in a quick, final gesture and repeated: "I am not going!"

The two men glared at each other, and neither stirred. After a long pause, the Major snorted indignantly and yanked at his bridle. As he swung away, Ham cried after him: "Do not bring Warr's arms to me, either!"

The nearest campers, who had been watching with interest, scrambled out of the Major's way as he plunged past. Ham turned away from the staring men. He met Zech's astonished gaze. "Have you naught else to do?" he demanded savagely. Zech and the others fell over each other trying to get through the gate.

Henry and Zech moved down the common in silence. The Connecticut militiamen by the South Gate were assembling their gear. "Goin' 'ome?" Henry asked one, perplexed.

"Aye!" the man barked in answer, and a companion quickly explained, "Our folks are havin' alarms, too."

Henry's brows shot up. A third Connecticut man defended fiercely: "Not from *our* Indians!"

"Mohawks?" Zech asked.

The Connecticut men nodded in unison. Major Talcott on one of Peter Tilton's chestnuts, jogged up behind them. Zech felt self-conscious in the Councillor's presence. He suddenly became all thumbs. Henry scowled, noticing his unexpected clumsiness. Zech knew that Henry was studying him, weighing last night's absence for which he had made no explanation. He feared Henry might make some telling comment that would betray him. He knew no relief until Major Talcott disembarked on the 'Hamp side of the river. The Major strode across the beach and called up to Lt. Wilton, waiting for him there: "They are sending to the fort for arms."

The old Lieutenant straightened as if he'd been struck a blow between the shoulders. Outraged, he squealed: "Are they *non compos?*"

"They found sheepskins with the Northfield brand —"

"That's an old Mohawk trick — everyone knows that!" Lt. Wilton stormed, and Major Talcott protested: "But these times are different."

The old man pounded his fists together and protested: "That's just it! I tell you they will be working no good! I have no faith in that Joshua of yours! Not one bit! I knew his father before him! They are a crafty pair!"

Major Talcott paused, nonplussed, before he tried to reason: "He keeps 'em in line."

Lt. Wilton huffed, exasperated: "I have known Uncas since I came. I have powwowed and traded with the Indians since I came, too. Back in the *very* beginning, Uncas cozened you — all of you! Too much store has always been put in that — *plague* — *and* his son!"

Zech and Henry, at first too impressed by Lt. Wilton's response to pretend not to be aware of it, suddenly realized that they were staring openmouthed at the quarreling officers. Zech felt a stab of dismay as he realized the truth of the old man's claims. While the others stood dumbfounded, Lt. Wilton clambered out of his saddle. Major Talcott pleaded: "They — the Mohegans — are loyal to us!"

The old man waved him off imperiously. "I will not be going with you! If I go over to Hadley — now — I may yet do some good."

Major Talcott stared at him, unbelieving. The two men exchanged stiff, angry nods before the older man threw himself down the bank toward a small canoe. He muttered, for everyone's benefit: "These river Indians were never hard to deal with. Not on terms they understood. — But *this!*" He spit into the river and the little canoe sprang forward as if propelled by a swift kick. "They have supplies, you may be sure!" he sputtered, the last words Zech heard distinctly.

He turned from watching Lt. Wilton's stirring departure to stare at Major Talcott.

The Major looked lost, a strange expression for one of such commanding presence. "Until the troubles here are settled, there is naught to do but palisado," he said to Zech and Henry, as if they were a presiding council and that was the subject under discussion. "We did it in the beginning, when we were settling. When there's confidence, again, fortification can be done without, again. But for now, there is naught else anyone can do. Not one thing —"

Thought of enclosing the mile-long common overwhelmed Zech. Because of the November fires, even from the beginning, timber for dwellings and firewood had had to be dragged long distances from the wilderness.

Zech and Henry never did learn exactly how the situation developed that day. They learned, later, that Lt. Wilton arrived at the manse too late to stop the deputation headed for the fort. Some said the Indians' arms already were collected when Lt. Wilton arrived there in hot pursuit of the council delegates, and that he persuaded the committee to leave them; others said the only guns the deputation found at the fort were in the hands of known friends. At any rate, the committee returned empty-handed.

That afternoon, a worried delegation arrived from Deerfield; another arrived from Northfield immediately afterward. Signs that the surly Pocumtucks were preparing to go on the warpath alarmed the upper river plantation. They needed garrison troops, too.

Henry and Zech first heard of the militiamen's being dispatched up the river when an elderly Newbury man arrived and announced that Henry was one of twenty chosen to march to Northfield that afternoon. The messenger was being transferred from Hadley to Northampton for billeting, but he was to take Henry's place on the ferry. With the Connecticut troops withdrawn, and the Valley towns practically in a state of siege, henceforth there would be ferrying only for good reason.

Zech protested to Henry that his replacement could have been sent in Henry's stead and Henry left in Hadley. Henry demurred, resigned, conciliatory, perhaps flattered a bit, too. " 'e could not stand the gaff!" he reasoned quietly, in a whisper.

The parting of the two who had become so close in six days came as abruptly as their first meeting. One minute they propelled the canoe up to the beach where the ancient messenger awaited them, and the next, the mission explained, Henry was striding away to the common and a more uncertain destiny.

Zech watched Henry go — rangy, lythe and ragtaggle, independence and spirit in every sure stride, the set of his great, steady shoulders sure and proud. Unconsciously, Zech reached out after Henry, as if to restrain him. Henry turned at the foot of the stairs and looked back, his expression solemn and full of wonder. He grinned, pleased to see Zech's outstretched hand. He raised his, too, in communion, saluted, and was gone.

When Zech got home that night, only Mungo and Andy remained billeted in the barn. Jon had been dispatched to garrison Deerfield.

CHAPTER XXV

Monday, Captain Beers and Captain Lothrop and their companies returned from their week's search to the East. They had found only villages that the Indians had laid waste by their own torches; they had seen no natives. They believed that the missing tribesmen had withdrawn to Philip's new stronghold, rumored to be southeast in Pawtucket country.

Major Savage, a new commander, arrived with the returning militia, and with him a chaplain and surgeon who had been waiting at Brookfield for safe conduct. They brought word of a massacre at Lancaster, and news of the death, finally, of Captain Hutchinson who had been ambushed at the time of the assault on Brookfield. Most disturbing of all was their news that the Nipmucks had harvested their corn at Winnimissette, and all of Brookfield's corn, too. The Indians would be well-supplied this winter. Better than the threatened towns.

Major Savage's first order called for the gathering of arms at the fort. Hampshire's Council of War protested angrily, they reasoned, they argued, they pleaded, they explained, but the strategy had been decided upon by the Council of the United Colonies in Boston: Major Savage had no choice but to follow directions. The Hampshire Council replied that the Eastern companies might do as directed, but they would do as they pleased. They would not join in the folly.

Major Savage headed a delegation of his own men, but they received no civility at the fort. In response to their summons, only a sullen squaw appeared at the closed gate. She shrugged that she might relay their demand to the sachems. When pressed, she claimed that the braves were out in the meadows. The delegation returned humiliated and empty-handed.

That evening, Hadley watched dismayed as a pair of drummers under Major Savage's direction marched to the edge of Great Meadow, opposite the fort. There they banged for attention. When a brace of sannups appeared at the bluff's edge, Major Savage's sergeant in a loud voice bade them come over and talk. In reply, the braves yelled back that the Major could come to them, and signalled and yelled obscenities that left the Valleyfolk muttering their disbelief.

The startling rejection set off a flurry of activity. Major Savage announced that the natives must understand once and for all that the patience of their easygoing neighbors had reached its limit. *All* arms at the fort would be taken.

Under cover of darkness, a company of volunteer militia moved across to Hatfield and bivouacked; an hour before dawn, militia companies from Northampton would join them; the teeth of the dragon would be drawn.

As the cover of night began to fade, Ham remained holed-up in his cottage, but Zech and the boys slipped away to join the anxious throng of villagers who moved into the copse along the border of Great Meadow. They watched the fort being stalked knowing no good would come of any skirmishing. In their concern for the stealthy figures creeping up the hill, barely visible in the brightening light, they breathed prayers entreating the ominous quiet there to continue. To their relief, no alerted figures suddenly appeared when the scent and finally the sound of the strangers should have aroused the dogs. DOGS — No dogs! Suddenly aware — heartsick, torn by doubt and despair, those watching in the distance knew before the gate gave way before the militiamen that the village was deserted.

Breathless and spent, some weeping, Hadleyfolk watched the militiamen swarm aimlessly about. Zech hurried down to the beaching place to intercept the first company of militiamen that crossed back to Hadley to stand guard while Hadley's younger men pressed on in eager pursuit of the flown warriors. One of the returning men, a friend of Henry's, hung back from Zech. The pained expression in his eyes warned Zech of more than he wanted to know: Warrwarrankshan had not gone. He and the dogs had been found with their heads caved in. Warr's "cousins" had dealt him their final insult: Indians never abandon *their* dead. Zech fled home to Biscuit, tied uncomfortably close to the shed by a tether too short for him to reach and chew. Biscuit yipped and leaped up to lick Zech's face in welcome, surprised and grateful at the prospect of attention; he had had so little, lately. He sensed Zech's mood, and hunched down and waited, trembling, trying to be patient and understanding while Zech struggled to unfasten him. It took a spell for Zech to loosen him; blinded with tears as he was, he could not discern the complicated turns of the thong that tied his remaining friend.

Zech led Biscuit into the barn. He threw himself down in the hay and drew Biscuit down beside him. Biscuit whimpered his sympathy before he settled down; he did not stir when Zech buried his face on his shoulder and sobbed out his grief for the loss of one he had loved so much; his loving, caring friend to the end of his life.

In broad daylight, the company pursuing the flown fort Indians could not miss the still-warm trail. Beside the swamp where Ham's men had held back the day of the search, the Nonotucks' crafty, visiting cousins waited.

Before noon, scattered and dazed survivors of Hadley's rash militia company began to stagger back to civilization. The day that had begun so stealthily with great expectations of triumph ended in stunned defeat. As dusk crept out of the low places of earth, the three villages in the midst of the river struggled to deal with the shock of blows dealt that day: the first awful toll for a generation's fumblings and misunderstandings.

The still, hot darkness could but mask the terror in the Valley. Each seaboard company had lost as least one life: a brawler who had spearheaded the chase, and eight others. Up and down the Valley, villagers lay awake and stared into the night, praying for deliverance. In 'Hamp, constable Tom Mason's only son lay dead; at Tom Dickinson's, Ike's new, rosy-cheeked bound boy lay mortally wounded, mercifully unconscious; Hatfield grieved for the youngest of Widow Fellows' three sons. As gently as they had been able to, distraught companions had carried Az Dickinson over the rough trail to Hatfield where Dorcas waited at his brother Nathaniel's dwelling. Torn as he was, Az would not see another dawn.

The Valley reeled in a state of shock, too overcome to recognize the first signs of further punishment: summer heat grown so oppressive and still it paled even brawny, weathered men and boys. Older folk began to speak with growing concern of a punishing storm thirty years before that had come in just such fashion. They dwelt on their helplessness, then, gathered together in blockhouses while roaring winds tore up trees and surging torrents changed river channels. Such an assault dealt as much harm as rampaging Indians.

Some women and children, defeated by Pastor's grim conviction that the attacks of men and nature were a judgment due, fell to sobbing helplessly. Old John Crow scoffed at the claim of doom deserved. Saints and strangers alike had been cruelly afflicted by the storm years before; not one had deserved such chastisement.

Townfolk no longer could gather together for consolation in one place. Indeed, Hadley's meetinghouse was not so much a fortress as a powder magazine with the town's supply of gunpowder stored in the loft. The plank building, dried out by fifteen years of weathering, had become a hulking tinderbox. One stroke of lightning could rend it to a formless pile.

Families trying to prepare for the onslaught, struggled in the dragging air. Ham led his household to the meadow to try to salvage as much hop as could be gathered in. What they left would be utterly useless. Chimney smoke not able to rise through the closed-in air, drifted across the common just above the trees, fragile pennants seeming to unfurl forever, omens of the battle to come.

Zech, working near a hedgerow, saw the first stir of life announcing the arrival in the Valley of the headlong, swirling hurricane. Dully, he watched the pointed leaves of a sheepberry bush lift as if weighted and turn slightly before falling back over drooping clusters of black berries. Soon all the leaves of the hedgerow began to move slowly; at first as if only experimenting. At the edge of the field, dust began to stir and rise in random, dry puffs; everywhere, young trees began to stir and rustle with a soft, soughing sound; and the stirring dust began to swirl in mad, little eddies. The first widely-scattered, hard-driven spattery drops of rain splashed the dust to the ground; suddenly Zech found that he could breathe more easily, as if the east wind and the rain were bringing relief rather than affliction.

Thanky stretched her face into the deceptively soft breeze and cool, refreshing rain. She thrust her chin high and inhaled deeply, gratefully. She held her head back beyond her shoulders so that the wisp of hair that had escaped the knot tied up on the top of her head fell free and did not blanket the nape of her neck. She turned her face slowly from side to side, savoring the relief that fanned her perspiring face. "It feels good, anyway," she murmured. "Even if we know 'tisn't, heh, Zech?"

Soon the steady, increasing rain drenched them to the skin. When they finally hurried from the fields, water glistened in every trench and hollow; the meadow had begun to look like a shallow lake.

Eastern volunteers had worked furiously trying to salvage as much fruit as could be harvested. Some pears could be cellar-ripened. Unless the storm shifted direction, there would be a surfeit of apples for cider and few in storage: once blown off the trees or damaged by the egg-sized hail that began to batter them and cover the ground, apples were good only for cider and apple-butter.

Before dusk, small trees began to turn and sway in the rising wind. A pair of Newbury volunteers who repaired from their camp on the common to Ham's barn, told him that the river must be churning to a tide like that in the ocean, if the usually unruffled meetinghouse pond was any example. Zech wondered how the waves on the river compared to the galloping, spume-edged torrents that swept downstream when spring freshets raged.

Darkness enveloped the village long before the usual twilight hours. After supper and evening prayers, those who usually slept in the barn stretched out on the commonroom floor, a safe distance from the fireplace. Everyone listened, fascinated, as the rain's steady pounding increased to thundering drum rolls. The steady beat lulled the younger ones to sleep in spite of their anxiety. At regular intervals, the wind died away, and when it began again, howled with greater fury. In the morning, with the coming of daylight, grey and distorted by the rain, the men hastily fed and watered the frightened livestock tethered in the barn.

The light of day took on an ominous glow, and taller trees began to turn as if trying to twist free of the assaulting east wind; everywhere, ancient elms and maples bent stiffly against their will.

Firelight relieved the closed-up gloom of the cottage. The young ones and Mungo, with Hope on his shoulders, leaned against the small-paned windows and peered at pelting rain through the cracks of shutters closed against the deserted world.

Zech found a spot of his own. He caught glimpses of massive, gnarled limbs tumbling reluctantly across the common, chased away from towering trees from which they had been sundered. Old trees succumbed slowly, majestically. Resisting a power greater than their own they crashed slowly, with sickening protest, tilting at first with only a cracking sound before being wrenched free and thrown mercilessly to the ground. Occasionally, a long piece of clapboard or shingle capered by drunkenly, end over end. In moments of calm, between pummelling torrents and fits of rending and crashing, an eerie glow lit the outside world.

As it had throughout the night, the rain abated only to gather power to renew its assault. Those indoors could hear nothing above the sound of rain slamming against the world without. The deluge continued to rush down the shutters and drape out the timid light. Rain soaked into the parched shingles of the roof until, swollen and saturated, they could absorb no more. Water began to drip from the ceiling and run down the fireplace rocks, a slender trickle spreading to a leaping, streaming, babbling stream. It hissed and steamed at the edge of the warm hearth where it surged into the cracks of the shrunken green-wood plank floor, leaving an ever-widening puddle in its wake. Even as abusive as the first day's onslaught seemed to be, the storm's climactic fury came Tuesday, at the close of the second day. The little house seemed to draw in its breath and cower around its inhabitants. Huddled close together in the circle of the firelight, they listened to the destruction being visited on the world about them and waited, spent and resigned, for whatever judgements should be meted out to them.

The young ones, exhausted after the first awe and excitement, readily gave in to pangs of hunger; they dunked bread chunks in mugs of cider before they finally slept, curled up where they were. Older folk chewed halfheartedly at bread and cheese, but could not rest even as fitfully as they had the night before.

With the first light in the East, Wednesday morning, the storm subsided. Weary watchers began to sally out into the pattering rain to discover what God had wrought. The rain stopped with the full light of day. Finally, the sun broke through the mist; it beamed as cheerfully and triumphantly as a child whose tantrum has succeeded. The hard-scrubbed village looked worn and refreshed at the same time. Trees hung limp, but cleansed, many twisted and broken; mounds of wet, green leaves piled against every obstacle. Beyond Ham's fence, a shed lay smashed among the litter in the

193

quiet common. Militiamen and settlers, men, women and children, milled about in the strange stillness. At first, everyone walked about aimlessly, not sufficiently recovered to begin to set the world in order. Many recalled especially grueling or awe-inspiring incidents. By instinct, all but the bedridden, extremely-aged turned toward the meetinghouse at the time once appointed for the now-discontinued Wednesday lecture.

Everyone knew the sort of text pastor would select for this occasion. No one paraded about. No one moved toward the meetinghouse unmindful of trial by wind and water.

In spite of the soggy condition, Zech lingered on the common while his father and Aunt herded the boys and Thanky into the dark and crowded gloom of the meetinghouse.

Pastor felt that those not members of his congregation had more need of his counsel than those within. He stationed himself on the top porch step. He found his support in the eleventh verse of the 39th Psalm: *When thou with rebukes doth correct man for iniquity, thou maketh his beauty to consume away.* When he finished the text, Deacon Smith moved to his side. The multitude bowed in prayer. The ancient deacon, his head thrown back, prayed long and fervently, his quavering tones crackling with emotion as he uttered thanks for deliverance from the wrath that had beset their world. Zech raised his head to study the ancient elder. In that instant a militiaman hurled himself toward the meetinghouse. The aroused dragoon caught the startled attention of others, instantly alert. He began to motion in the direction from which he had come. "Ind'ans! Ind'ans!" he tried to yell, but his wild incoherent motions told his message more loudly than his choked warning.

CHAPTER XXVI

The warning spread ahead of the messenger like a grass fire. Instantly, men grasped their muskets and began to hasten where he motioned. The few women outside scurried toward the already crowded building, hindering men trying to push their way out. By the time Zech reached the brow of the hill above the river, men were firing down toward the beaching place. The first militiamen had surprised a disembarking, war-painted horde. Astonished that an alarm of their approach had reached the gathered settlers, the warriors were fleeing at full speed. Excited militiamen plunged down the hill, shooting as they went. Surely they wounded some of the escaping assailants.

"If only we could have ambushed them!" Major Savage groaned as the war party skimmed out of harm's reach. He nodded solemn agreement with murmured prayers of thanks that the Hand of Providence had stayed total destruction of the gathering. The men all moaned as one, as the last war canoe disappeared around the bend in the river.

A youth on the shore turned, then, and stared up at the despairing men ranged up the hill. He yelled wildly at Major Savage: "I saw *him,* too! *I* saw him *myself!"*

The distracted throng caught its breath. Had he gone mad?

"*He* whispered to us that the Ind'ans was coming — down here!" The lad's tormented gaze swept the faces staring down on him. He began to gesture, throwing his hands about his face, as if indicating a beard, before he threw his hands to his left and pivoted about and pointed after the vanished Indians.

"Aye! I saw him, too!" an older man declared, and slid down the hill to stand beside the lad.

"Aye!" the lad declared, again. "*We* saw him!"

"Saw WHO?" Major Savage demanded.

"HIM! Like a ghost he was — so pale — "

Zech's heart flipped over; he could feel his knees begin to sag.

"HIM?" voices echoed uneasily, and pressed forward.

"Aye. Of a sudden — there *he* was — beside us. Praying we was — and he whispered to *him* — " he pointed toward the militiaman near Major Savage who had carried the alarm: "*He* told *him* — the Ind'ans are comin' — The Ind'ans are comin' — down below the ferry! And he pointed this way."

The amazed crowd stared at the messenger. Pale as death, he nodded agreement. "A ghost — he was — " he panted, his voice quavering. " — Or an angel — " he gasped. Overcome by anxiety, suddenly transported by that inspiration, he spread his arms wide and cried out: "An angel he was! Jehovah sent an angel to deliver us from the heathen!" Spent, he threw his hands over his face and began to sob uncontrollably.

Major Savage clapped his arm around the man's shoulders. He looked about, toward the dumbfounded gathering.

Peter Tilton found his voice first. "He must have seen a Hadley man," he declared purposefully, his words not coming easily, " — if 'twere not one from the East —"

" 'Twas no one from the East," the lad proclaimed, edging his way up the hill toward his elders. "I know the Eastern men, and the Connecticut men, too. He was not *like* one of us."

Major Savage glanced toward Elder Russell's nearby cottage. He looked about and found the stern old elder and his wife hanging back, stricken, at the edge of the crowd. He addressed Pastor, uncharacteristically silent at his side, for once not asserting himself as spokesman or interpreter. "Had your father been at home, he could have seen them coming — " he stated quietly.

" 'Twas no ordinary old man!" another Easterner protested stoutly, and another nodded vigorous assent.

Zech marvelled at Peter's and Pastor's self-control. Even as shaken as they were, they did not betray themselves. Carefully, he began to search out his father, to catch a glimpse of his expression. When their eyes met, he knew for certain that what he had guessed was true: the worst had come to pass — General Goffe had appeared to save the village.

"Surely they saw one of our elders," Peter counselled Major Savage. He put a sympathetic arm about one spokesman's shoulder. "And truly, he *was* an Angel of Deliverance —"

"Aye," Major Savage exclaimed, suddenly less concerned by who had brought the warning than by the danger of their situation. "We must post sentinels. We cannot let ourselves ever again be without a watch, and defenseless."

Those the Angel warned knew that the mysterious messenger was substance. He was a stranger, and strange in appearance. That first half-dozen rushing to the town's defense recalled remarkably human characteristics: his unusual height; his olive skin, in spite of his unearthly pallor; his face much like Major Lothrop's; long, triangular; his chin 'set-on-looking'; his eyes wide-set, burning, dark and dark-circled; his forehead broad; his brows unusually long and thin; his nose rather hawk-like; his mouth small, but the lower lip full; his dress that of a man of quality. He had shown authority, too, though he had kept his voice pitched to a whisper.

Zech knew they described General Goffe. The description did not fit General Whalley. He watched for Joe Kellogg to leave the council meeting that Capt. Pynchon called immediately. All the emerging men looked haggard; a special, studied blankness marked the weathered faces of those who *knew*. Well-remembered details had stirred old memories for Joe. Whereas those others tried to appear unaware, he looked stunned and hurt, too, because he had not been one to know.

Zech looked quickly away as Joe took a second look in his direction; he might betray himself if their eyes met: Joe might remember their conversation; he might wonder if General Goffe could have been in Hadley *that* long ago —

Furtively, Zech watched a Cambridge militiaman approach Joe; an older man, plainly a friend of yore. He tried to lead Joe away from Gail's side, but Joe grasped his wife's arm and held to her as if she were a tethering post. The man cupped his mouth and whispered confidentially to Joe.

Joe pulled back. Zech strode past them, pretending to be watching something afar off. "No — No — " Joe protested in a hoarse whisper. "No. It could not be he, Abe. No . . . No . . ."

With every breath, Zech prayed for the deliverance of General Goffe. Others prayed as fervently, while some began to babble about an Angel of Mercy, insisting wildly that Hadleyfolk must be the peculiar people spoken of in Deuteronomy, saved by God's Great Plan.

By dusk, everyone in Hadley knew that they had been shown great mercy that day: as twilight deepened, the sky to the north glowed red. The marauding horde had not been turned away from Deerfield, and without moonlight, no one dared hasten to Deerfield's defense.

At dawn, Major Savage dispatched Captain Beers and most of the able-bodied militia to Deerfield to bring back survivors, if there were any.

As if many had received revelations in the night, more and more men talked of the possibility that the Angel was either General Goffe or General Whalley. From the moment of his first realization, Zech was struck by the fearless conduct of those he knew had treasonously sheltered the Generals. They proceeded through the whole day without betraying themselves, as if they were as confounded as the first to spread the alarm — and, indeed, they were.

Throughout the long trek to Deerfield, men repeated the story of the Judges in bits and pieces. Captain Beers, the only one of the expedition who had known the Generals in England and Boston, protested that the Angel could not have been either of them. Zech was grateful for his blustering, persistent attempts to save Hadley from trouble.

Scouts returned from enemy territory about Deerfield and reported that the stockade appeared to have withstood the Indians' assault, but the village was utterly laid waste.

Zech was not ashamed of the tears that welled up in his eyes when the garrison militia and Deerfield men, women, and children began to pour out of the blockhouse at sight of their deliverers. He had no trouble spotting Jon, off in the distance; the white handkerchief on his father's hat, at his side, stood out like a beacon.

Jon explained with remarkable rapidity, for him, that yesterday afternoon young Jaimie Eggleston, out searching for his horse, had sighted scouts of the approaching war party. An arrow caught him, but he reached home in time to allow the villagers to reach sanctuary in the blockhouse.

The settlers slew two Indians in the first onslaught, before the warriors retreated and began to sack and burn the village. They did not sustain their attack as had Philip's men at Brookfield; perhaps their resolve had been shaken by thoughts of the

Englishman's God who twice in one day had saved settlers from destruction.

Jon led Zech to his mother. He told her that he had been billeted at Zech's before being sent to garrison Deerfield. Goody Plympton, a wisp of a crone surrounded by a bewildered knot of young ones, looked so careworn and exhausted she gave the appearance of defeat. When Jon explained that Zech would take her and the young ones back to his home in Hadley, and the garrison from Hadley would stay on at Deerfield to try to protect and harvest the ripening wheat, she turned a relieved look in Zech's direction and smiled faintly.

Accounts of Hadley's wondrous deliverance brought Old Sarge to attention. Jarred by the description of "The Angel," he gasped, entranced: "Why — that's — that's General Goffe you are telling of!"

Every eye within earshot turned on him, aghast.

"I ought to know!" Old Sarge blurted defensively. "I served him back in — That's — '' His voice trailed into stricken silence as he caught the horror in the stares of those who had not known General Goffe, or Old Sarge's connection with him, but did know of Hadley's perilous position.

As they parted company, Jon warned in a low voice: " 'Tis not go - ing to be eas - y back in Had - ley, Zech. You are con - duct - ing at least a hun - dred more mouths to feed, you know. We was able to save no ra - tions; the block - house had only a few days' sup - ply for the gar - ri - son, 'fore you got here."

"The wheat here looks promising," Zech tried to comfort.

"Aye. But 'twill burn eas - y," Jon answered bitterly. "3000 bush - els we have stack - ed all - ready. Right - ful - ly most is Maj - or Pyn - chon's you know. We are send - ing back all that can be car - ried, but 'twon't be near what's need - ed."

There was no choice. Hadleymen could return with either people or wheat.

"Since those heath - en did not burn the fields, 'tis ex - pected they will come back for it — when 'tis gath - ered in," Jon stated, tight-lipped. He turned a furious, accusing, smoldering glare in Zech's direction: a challenge for Zech to defend the Indians, now. Zech could not avoid Jon's gaze, but he could not forget Warr, either — or Sarah — or Benji — or — The challenging look between them held, painful and deep.

The passage home was slow and painstaking. The caravan moved in breathy silence through the steaming wilderness; occasionally someone whispered his conviction that if Old Sarge had *thought* first, he would not have made such a damning declaration.

In the cold light of the second day, Major Savage, a true Royalist, rejected the wish that an angel had saved Hadley. As Captain Beers' Deerfield-bound company disappeared from sight, he summoned the selectmen who had stayed behind on his orders. In the manse where they gathered, he inquired civilly regarding the harboring of enemies of the Crown. He did not need to remind his listeners of the dire consequences if word of the affair reached London authorities.

John Marsh, in all innocence, protested that their deliverer could only be a messenger from Jehovah.

"I will grant we are here now through the Grace of God," Major Savage conceded. "Had no one been at —" Perhaps he intended to name Elder Russell's cottage, but he hesitated, making no accusation. "If no one had been at a favorable location — none of us would be here, now." He studied the men facing him. They could see him accept the fact that conspiracy was not far-reaching. John Marsh did not feign ignorance. He did not know beyond what he knew happened yesterday. Peter Tilton spoke first, again. His gaze was as steady as it was worried. "None of us — in authority — saw who 'twas. Neither you nor I, nor any of us here," he reasoned.

Major Savage drew in a deep breath. He was plainly skeptical. He swept the staring townsmen with a searching gaze. " 'Twill go bad for all of us — if anyone outside the law is found amongst you," he said evenly. "No man could have got this far into the wilderness unaided," he reminded. "And what stranger could come alone into this Indian-infested neck of the woods in these times?"

"No man could hide in a town in such condition as this!" John Marsh protested, not dreaming what had been accomplished for eleven years.

"Not with such as Westcarr looking for ways to sell his soul for pounds sterling!" Philip Smith grumbled. Yesterday, men had talked of perceiving the evil Doctor's design in the Indians' strategy. "A whole village could not keep such a secret," Philip added in all sincerity.

200

Major Savage drew in another breath. "Well, we shall see," he announced finally, with a sigh: "We shall see — Even as you sit here, all likely places are being searched. Your houses, your barns, the magazine, the meetinghouse. No place sacred to you is sacred to men in my charge who would have it no other way than that a search must be made, according to the king's warrant, for one with whom you all are in sympathy."

The Hadleymen gasped.

After a shocked silence, Philip Smith muttered, unbelieving: "Humph, my wife will like *that* for a fact!"

His neighbors' chuckled relief eased the tension. Peter kept from sighing. He counselled: "Aye. 'Tis not a bad thing to do. 'Twill remove all doubt of any guilt —"

Major Savage gave him a sharp look. "If they find no one, I will have naught to report to higher authorities, of course."

Much later, Mr. Hawley, the Northampton schoolmaster, told Zech that Major Savage's searching parties should not have been blamed for not discovering that the boards of the closet floor between the two upper chambers at the manse could be raised, that there was space below, within a false cupboard beside the fireplace — directly behind where the Major stood — that was a sufficient hiding place for two men: a hiding place that never had been put to use.

CHAPTER XXVII

But that was much later — long after Zech hurried to Ike's trading post that evening. Most of the Eastern militiamen congregated at Ike's after chores, a last respite before lying down in their rags for another fitful night. The older men gathered first, and gradually the younger ones drifted into the yard. Zech wished that Henry was with him. He worried about Henry at Northfield; and Henry would have had interesting theories regarding yesterday's Angel, too. From someplace deep within him, he would have dredged up details that would have shed light on all that had happened.

Zech found Mungo wedged against the trading room wall, listening intently. He wiggled close to him and found the spot a vantage point for studying the faces of the others. An old man was droning: " — I thank God that I can look death in the face and not be afeared — "

Zech nudged Mungo. Mungo whispered out of the corner of his mouth: "Hugh Peter."

Zech knew the name should mean something to him.

"Hugh had the chance to recant, he did, but he were not that kind! Some of us knew him at Salem, you know."

Older men's heads bobbed in unison, their expressions grim.

"He was drawed through the streets on a sled, and spit on and made to watch Cooke die —"

202

Mungo whispered: "He were a Judge o' King Charles —"

"Oh - h - h - h — " A cold, cold chill slid down Zech's spine.

"When a rowdy upbraided Cooke, and ordered 'im to recant, 'e cried out: 'Friend, you do not well to trample on a dyin' man!' Then he were taken down, and Hugh dragged up so's 'e would 'ave a better view." The storyteller's voice dragged with distaste. "The executioner rubbed his hands together and he ast, 'Well, Mr. Peter, how do you like this?' Hugh, he come back quick — and dignified, too: 'I am not, I thank God, terrified. You may do your worst!' "

The second storyteller put in: " 'fore goin' to the scaffold, Hugh bent a piece o' gold and ast a neighbor o' ours t' give it t' 'is daughter as a token of 'is dyin'. 'Tell 'er my 'eart is full o' comfort,' he told 'im. 'Tell 'er, 'fore this reaches 'er, I shall be with God in glory.' "

An awed silence followed, before another witness added gruffly: "After Hugh was beheaded, and disembowelled, and drawn and quartered, his head were put on a pole on London Bridge for a long spell."

A resentful growl rippled around the yard. Suddenly, for the first time, the horror of tyranny became real for Zech.

"I heard tell," the first speaker went on, "that one who taunted Hugh was attacked by his own tame dog that day. Torn good he was, and good enough, too, I say!"

"I say," the voice of one Zech could not see, warned: "That those born and raised away from the misery we have known, know not of how uncivilized this world can be!"

"Aye!" a rough old man exclaimed, shaking a pipe at everyone. "A man can cut down a tree here and answers to no man save the one who owns the land, if 'tis not common property. But in England, right now, every log that's cut has a tax on it, no matter whose 'tis. And why? To support jest *one* of the king's dozen whores or bastards!"

"Twenty-eight, at last count, that I know of!"

"And some devilish form of taxation to support the spendthrift ways of every one of 'em. And more'n one kind for those he favors most."

"Well, enough wanted *that* way of life — they called the Stuarts back, did they not?"

A lad Zech's age, sitting close by, startled those around him by calling out: "Grandsir, tell 'em 'bout the trial!"

When others turned to see who had spoken, the boy bridled: "He was there! He's told me 'bout it, before!"

Those sitting close by nodded that they believed him. Mollified, the lad urged, again, "Tell 'em, Grand!"

The first speaker took a quick inventory of the interest; he shot a questioning glance in the direction of others who had been in the vicinity of the trial or had heard the tale many times before. He fingered his lip while he organized his thoughts. "I were one of the guards. *Me* in scarlet, *then!*" He paused as if he wondered now whether that other world truly existed. Slowly, his thoughts turned to his recollection. " 'Twas in the old hall — the walls was Spanish chestnut." He paused again, recalling the awe-inspiring scene. "That hall witnessed many a wild and wondrous sight, ye may be sure. Feastin' and trials — " he looked around to enjoy his audience's sharing of such events. Their annoyance at his wandering swung him hastily back to the subject.

"I were in the service o' Colonel Axtell," he related hurriedly. "He had charge o' the hall. In full dress uniform we were, the officers carryin' gold-headed canes — The windows is high in Westminster, and the light shown in and picked up scarlet and gold everywhere." He gestured, indicating the length and breadth of a hall beyond the confines of the yard. He pointed away from him. "There — was a crimson velvet chair with a judge's desk in front for the Lord President. And two smaller ones on each side. One for Mr. Lisle and one for Lord Say and Sele. At their feet lay the sword and mace. A table below, covered with turkey carpet was for clerk o' court." He stopped to get his breath, then plunged on: "There was railin's on each side o' the hall — separatin' the people from the soldiers, ye know. There was women in the galleries above. Some of 'em wore masks. As if they was at a play." He spoke the last with distaste.

"The benches for the judges ran half-way up the wall. Lord Cromwell and Henry Martin sat on the back row — under the coat of arms o' the Commonwealth. That seal replaced the Royal coat of arms — you know."

An oldster interposed: "I 'member, they blocked off the doors t' the taverns!" Graciously, since he was being allowed to carry the story almost alone, the original narrator nodded and repeated: "They sealed off the passages to the taverns, like he says. The Heaven and The Hell, they was called."

His tone a curse, the prompter reminded: "Later, The Lord Protector's head were on a pike in The Heaven!"

Another put in: "Aye, desecrated after he'd died in bed and was buried for two years!"

Another interrupted: "I have heard tell someone other than the Lord Protector was swapped around in the vaults for fear of that, and 'twas another's head in fact."

"Aye!" others about the yard breathed in agreement.

"No — " the first speaker said sadly. "I knew him. 'Twas his head —"

The hushed assemblage waited. "Right on the hour, the Lord President would enter the Hall from the Painted Chamber, wearin' a high-crowned hat that 'twas said was lined with steel. When everything was ready, the doors of Westminster Hall was thrown open and all int'rested citizens — without distinction — any desirous to come, and see, and hear — was welcome. How they flocked in, day after day!"

"The King said the court was only tryin' to bargain for their lives. And in a way, they was. He said he could not be duly called without his consent. He staked his life on that — on a king's never bein' tried by his subjects, be - fore."

"Aye!" from all about the yard.

"He had no notion of duty. He thought he was like God, who owes us naught. To him there was only the *Divine* Right of Kings. Up to the last meetin', President Bradshaw was willin' to let the King be heard — to come to some agreement with him — that the army would not be declared treasonous for tryin' to save the rights due them. But the King had no fear of his head — then. He did not understand treason — So, the Solicitor General prayed that the court should take the King's refusal to grant pardon to the Parliament leaders as a confession that *he held not sacred the rights of his subjects.* Now, that's TREASON! I tell ye, when the clerk read: 'to be put to death by the severin' of his head from his body,' the King were stunned! So were we all!"

So was everyone at the post. As if each one did not know every word of the story as well as the narrator.

"Well, the King seemed willin' to talk, then, but then 'twas too late, and not without reason. Never had he kept a pledge of all the many he had made before — so — why should anybody believe him, then? He'd told 'em what *he* thought of *them.* He'd had his day. He was removed."

After a moment's silence, the impatient prompter added: "Aye. In a *se* - dan chair. We hated them sedan chairs for a fact! 'e and Buckingham brought 'em back from Spain. Makin' beasts o' burden out o' men — such as animals always 'ad been. In Spain a man means less than a jackass. We had no desire to have England come to that!"

A strange voice inquired at the gate: "Is one called Zech here? The one who is a ferryman?"

Zech listened, too startled to reply. He could not imagine who wanted him, or for what purpose. Mungo nudged him before he called out feebly: "Here! I am here!"

He could feel himself blush as strangers around him watched him stumble to his feet.

"I am Chaplain Newell," a short, stocky figure told him. For everyone's benefit, he explained: "I must go over to Northampton. A dying militiaman there has asked for me. I am told you would be best able to take me over."

Zech caught back a sigh. He was bone-weary. It was dusk now. The mission could be fraught with danger. But he could not refuse. He nodded his willingness to go. Chaplain Newell handed him a chunk of sticky candlewood and Zech worked his way to the fire to light it.

"The moon'll be up in a bit, now," one of the watching men remarked sympathetically while everyone waited for the pitchy pine knot to flare up.

"That light bobbin' through the meadow could invite trouble," another volunteer muttered, bothered and thoughtless.

"There's little danger there's any of the enemy around tonight," Chaplain Newell admonished stiffly, his voice tight as a drum.

" 'Tis their way t' strike and run," someone agreed grimly and another said with an awe intended to be complimentary: "Jest the same, I would hate to chance the top o' my head —"

Zech knew they all were right. He tried to keep his mind blank as he gave the flickering light to the chaplain. The darkness had deepened while he lit the torch. He fell into step behind Mr. Newell who started down the common at a brisk pace. He made no effort at small talk. Silently, they passed the darkened houses. Both Joe Kellogg's and Old Mr. Russell's, isolated by the south highways as they were, had been abandoned at Major Savage's direction. Eastern volunteers watched at posts all about town. A pair challenged Chaplain Newell and Zech at the head of the beaching-place stairs. They appeared suddenly, silently, out of nowhere, though both Zech and Mr. Newell knew that they were about and had expected to be challenged.

At the river, Mr. Newell gave Zech the firebrand. Zech leaned toward the bow of the canoe and held the torch so it lit a pathway for the chaplain to follow across the smooth-flowing river. He listened to the water lapping against the bow and thought of Henry and the many trips they had made together; recollections of the Generals crowded in, too, and he lived, again, the unpleasant trip he had made *that* day with Joe and Dr. Westcarr.

He sighed, and shivered.

" 'Twill soon be more interesting," the chaplain whispered, as if to encourage him. Mr. Newell's tone — as well as his words — struck Zech as odd. He cocked his head and listened to the memory of what Mr. Newell had whispered. What was going on? Why had the chaplain said *that?* There seemed to be meaning beyond the words that had been spoken. Was this not the errand he had supposed it to be back in Hadley?

Zech began to prepare himself for anything Chaplain Newell might say.

But Mr. Newell did not speak again. Zech could feel his skin crawl with apprehension when they beached the canoe and climbed out. Beside him, the chaplain's heavy breathing sounded as loud as his own. They stood on the beach, Mr. Newell hunched over as if a burden had settled on him. They listened intently. They heard only night sounds, the continued monotones that assured them that nothing now disturbed the ways of nature within their hearing. No one had crossed the meadow recently.

Mr. Newell straightened, and thrust out his chin; he took the torch and motioned with his head for Zech to follow him into Old Rainbow Meadow. They trod the familiar way mechanically, but listened as no one ever had needed to do before. At the stile, Mr. Newell reached out and pressed Zech's shoulder, indicating he should stay where he was. Zech watched motionless as Mr. Newell suddenly, expertly, doused the light as he disappeared down the far side of the stile. He waited, breathless. Blood pounded in his head and drowned out all thought, he only heard his own labored breathing. In hardly more than a trice, Chaplain Newell scrambled back to his side. Zech had no idea how long they stood panting together in total darkness, trying to listen, before Mr. Newell pressed something into his hand. He recognized the sooty feeling and the lumpiness of a piece of charred wood. "Black yourself good, Zech," Mr. Newell ordered, whispering directly into his ear. "Your face, and neck, and hands. We will go along the hedgerow until the moon is up. Then we can see to do otherwise."

Zech and Mr. Newell rubbed the blackening on their fingers and begrimed their faces and hands. As Zech's mind cleared, he realized that anyone watching from Hadley would have thought they had gone on to 'Hamp, but Mr. Newell had extinguished the torch before it would have been seen there. Who would suspect Major Savage's chaplain of being General Goffe's ally? For surely all this secrecy and planning concerned General Goffe! He wished he could ask even one of the questions whirling through his mind. But he could appreciate the need for silence. Excitement began to buoy him beyond fear, or dread, or weariness. The time had come when he finally would *know.*

Chaplain Newell and Zech stumbled along the hedgerow, their speed increasing as they got the lay of the land and their eyes grew accustomed to the darkness, abating now as the moon rose. When they reached the woods' edge south of Old Rainbow, the moon was silhouetting the forest beyond Hadley.

"We will need the moon, now," Mr. Newell explained as they stood in deep shadows and watched the moon float free of a gentle hill to the east. It rose as golden-colored as a pumpkin and as big as a bushel basket; it flooded the meadow with soft light.

"Our friends wanted us here *before* the moon came out," Mr. Newell whispered as quietly as before. "The king's men expect that no one can move until the moon is up, so we had to get ahead of them. Major Savage's men are posted at the portage at the falls, and across the neck of both sides of the oxbow, too. So the river would be no good to us there. They have men on all the trails out of Hadley — and Hamp — and Springfield."

A chill straightened Zech's back. He could feel his eyes bulging. A wildcat's cry ahead of them congealed his blood.

"We're near no roadblocks, here," Mr. Newell assured him, but his hardly audible voice indicated he was taking no chances.

In the distance, a whip-poor-will called in the woods to the west. Mr. Newell responded, not loudly. He would not have been heard at the stile. The distant whip-poor-will sounded again. Mr. Newell touched Zech's arm and moved toward the call. Zech followed, beyond feeling.

They followed a trail made by turned-out cattle. In a few minutes, Zech could smell horses, before he could see them.

A shadow moved out of the deep gloom. "Good timing — " it exclaimed, pleased.

"Everything is in order, praise God!" Mr. Newell replied, equally pleased. "You know Zech — "

The slight figure had the advantage. Zech peered anxiously toward his companion in intrigue.

The figure maneuvered so that the moonlight fell on his face. Amazed, Zech exclaimed: "Mr. Hawley!" The Northampton schoolmaster grinned.

"I have been here since noon, when I was supposed to have gone home from Hadley," he told Mr. Newell. He asked Zech: "You know why you have been brought?"

Zech half-shrugged and nodded mutely. The schoolmaster nodded, too. "You have done a good work, being quiet all these years, Zech." He jerked his head southward. "He is waiting, yonder."

"I will await your return," Mr. Newell whispered to Mr. Hawley, as if dismissing him. Mr. Hawley nodded and shook his hand warmly before moving away, motioning Zech to follow.

CHAPTER XXVIII

They walked the horses quietly until they would have been well beyond the hearing of anyone along the river, then they mounted and followed the Westfield Trail a half hour. By then they were beyond where any Englishman ever had settled; finally, Mr. Hawley reined in and told Zech, "I am taking you well below the falls. You are to take General Goffe down to Capt. Bull's in Hartford. You know the house. Capt. Bull has directions for you, when you reach there." They rode on, and Zech recalled the night he had stalked the manse and had seen the riders return.

At a ford, Mr. Hawley halted again. " 'Tis not safe for horses beyond this place. Follow this stream to the river," he directed. "Stay on this side. Konaput's canoe is there." He took a snapsack from his saddlebag and passed it to Zech. "You will want this before morning." He clapped him on the shoulder. "Cross directly over the river. Our friend will be waiting on the north bank of the next brook downstream. You will cross back and keep to this side, in the shadows. You will need to bend your backs, but you will be in Hartford in good season. God be with you!"

"God be with *you!*" Zech prayed in reply. He did not wait to watch Mr. Hawley ride off with the horses. He could follow the trail swiftly in the mottled moonlight, steeply downhill and eastward toward the Connecticut. He was scarcely aware of the rustling sounds of night, or the fireflies, or the eyes that gleamed quickly at a safe distance then vanished, or the night birds that swooped silently on prey that saw or heard him coming and

210

foolishly stopped to listen and in that off-guard moment sealed their doom. Even the blood-curdling screams of the luckless small creatures as their enemies made their kill did not break his stride. He breathed a sigh of relief when he glimpsed the moonlight on the river. Konaput's canoe rested bottom-side up, above any sudden reach of rising water. Konaput, gone now, had supplied many Northampton families with fresh fish in the happier days of the past; this must have been his special preserve.

Zech felt a stab of excitement as the canoe cut across the moonlight's path on the river. He knew the territory. He was far from any habitation — English or Indian — any civilization — he had naught to fear, but he could not contain his dread.

He paddled quietly along the river's bank. At the brook's mouth, he let the canoe rest against the bank and waited, breathless. He heard a faint stirring on a knoll above him before he glimpsed a shadow slipping in his direction.

"Good Lad!" was all that was said. General Goffe eased himself into the canoe, picked up a paddle, and they shot out into the river. In another minute they were on their way downstream.

Never again would Zech know such an unreal, such a dream-like experience as the flight that night. Ever afterward to the end of his days, the moon's rising and the moonlight reminded him of the covenant he kept. For years afterward, whenever they were certain they were alone, he and Mr. Hawley discussed the gamy excitement, the exultation they had known while executing plans prepared for every conceivable emergency, plans that altered as years and seasons required. From Chaplain Newell's explanation of the location of Major Savage's outposts, Zech guessed that the Major's men were better watched than their prey.

Major Savage had not interfered with the zeal of those among his men who sought reward for finding the Angel. He had not suspected, either, that when he, and Peter Tilton, and Samuel Newell were watering their horses at the meetinghouse pond, and Peter directed Mr. Newell to call on Mr. Russell with all haste, that Peter was sending his chaplain to become part of the conspiracy to thwart him. General Goffe's friends had decided by then that as chaplain, Sam Newell could conduct Zech from town without arousing suspicion; they already had decided that Zech, so well-acquainted with the river, and already proven trustworthy, could, because of his youth, serve as guide for General Goffe's deliverance without attracting attention by his absence.

Throughout the trip, Zech marveled at General Goff's endurance, at the pace he set as they raced down the river — as if they were in fact being chased by the Devil. Always, before, he had welcomed the sight of another canoe to break the monotony; that night he prayed with every stroke that they would see none — none — none —

Dawn began to light the sky before the General guided the canoe into a stream above Hartford. Upstream, out of sight of the river, evidently at a spot clearly described to him, he nodded that they would beach. They smoothed away all signs of their being and tucked the canoe out of sight in the shadowy copse.

Zech tried not to stare at the worn face of his companion. While he tried to wipe away the charcoal with handfuls of wet grass, he kept seeking out the likenesses recently described. The General smiled wearily and nodded his thanks and relief again and again; finally, he motioned toward the village on the hill ahead of them. Painfully, for breathing was difficult after so much exertion, speaking softly, he directed Zech to go around, beyond the village, and come in on the inland trail. "Tell the watch, or any who inquire of you, that you are coming from Wethersfield. You are known by some in Hartford, so take care who you speak with. We cannot have you seen coming from Hadley — this time — Long before anyone will put this detail with others, your visit will be forgotten. When you get to Captain Bull's — you are to say —" He spoke slowly, distinctly: " 'Tis a long tale. I have been sent by the Commissary. Captain Bull will understand." . . . General Goffe had been a Commissary General with the Commonwealth government . . . General Goffe made Zech repeat the message twice before he clasped both of Zech's hands in his, in farewell. They exchanged a long look of wonder and appreciation before Zech began to make his way through the cold dewy meadow ways. As he left, Zech could hear the General trampling the bracken in a secluded spot — a resting place that soon would be dried and warmed by the rising sun.

Zech quailed at the thought of approaching Captain Bull. He had heard Connecticut militiamen tell how, early in the summer, Captain Bull had stood up to Governor Andros, the dupe that the Duke of York had appointed Governor of New York and "all territories in the parts." When Governor Andros tried to gobble up the Connecticut colonies as part of his territory, the Connecticut Assembly had stood firm: they had not fought off the Dutch two years before to make themselves a sacrifice to a worse tyranny. When Andros' flotilla started out to attack Hartford, it was Captain Bull who intercepted the Governor's sloop at Saybrook. He boarded Andros' flagship and read to Governor Andros the Connecticut Assembly's Proclamation of Resistance, the intention to retain its charter. Recognizing futility when it stared him in the face, Governor Andros had told the stalwart Captain: " 'Tis a pity, Bull, that your horns can not be tipped with silver.''

In spite of General Goffe's assurances, Zech expected that when he tried to deliver the General's secret message for the first time Captain Bull would not have a notion what he was talking about. How many years had passed since Captain Bull might have given thought to the message? He hoped that Providence would intervene somehow and he and Captain Bull might be alone; then he would offer a more direct message that, though it would not confound the Captain, would shock him no less than the General's. He hoped that he could just say: "Captain Bull, I have just come from Hadley — with General Goffe —''

To all appearances, the Wethersfield trail had changed but little since the last time he had walked it, beside Ensign Wilton's cart on his father's wedding trip.

Smoke was rising from the chimneys of Hartford village before Zech reached the first clustered houses. Two boys at a well looked at him curiously, but said nothing. After he passed, one of them laughed mockingly. Zech knew how bedraggled he must look. General Goffe had been right, of course. There was little chance anyone would recognize him alone under these circumstances, especially if he stayed away from the waterfront and the inn. When he arrived at Captain Bull's, servants were moving about in the yard. One lad much younger than he turned such a suspicious look on him that Zech hesitated at the gate. The boy held him at bay with his gimlet eyes and backed to the barn door where he called a burly hostler to his assistance.

"Who'd ye think you're lookin' for?'' the hostler demanded unpleasantly, assuming Zech to be a starving runaway.

The challenge roused Zech beyond the fatigue that had begun to sap his will, the weariness that had caused him to hesitate and appear timid as he arrived. "Captain Bull!'' he snapped back, surprised by his own churlishness.

"Who do I tell the Capt'n you are?'' the hostler inquired, his tone not so rough since Zech did not sound as fearful as he looked.

213

Zech caught his breath. He was beginning to feel addled. A wrong name could be troublesome, and he had given the matter no thought; nor had he been coached regarding the matter.

"I will present myself," he decided; his voice sounded to him as if someone else had spoken.

A woman appeared in the doorway, attracted by the loud talking. She looked baffled by the sight of such a caller at such an early hour. He was no local lad. Where had he come from? Full of doubt, she went to fetch the Captain.

Zech waited too weary to care. He prayed that the Captain would not prove too difficult. Eleven years was a long time!

Captain Bull, well-named in an aging, miniature way, arrived at the door, hastily clad. He stared at Zech from the kitchen door. Too many interested witnesses stood about for Zech to be direct. The statement General Goffe had instructed him to make came to his lips in a slurred rush: " 'Tis a long tale —" he began as distinctly as he could; with as much bravado as he could muster, he announced: "I have been sent by the Commissary!"

The Captain stared at him nonplussed. Not because he understood, but because he did not. "*What* Commissary?" Captain Bull bellowed, doing justice to his name; then, someplace within himself his own words stirred a response. Aghast, astounded, he cried out: "*The* Commissary?" He repeated, gasping: "*The* Commissary?" and Zech knew that the great Bull's knees were as weak as his own. "Come in, Lad! Come in!" he urged, overwhelmed. His roaring had quieted with concern.

Zech moved toward the Captain; the old man shouted bluffly for the benefit of all the ears present: "You mean Treat's Commissary, of course! Ha! You'd think *we* were well provisioned! Well! You've come to the wrong man, but if you've such a tale from Treat, I'll put you on the right track, right now, for a fact." Zech stepped past the Captain into the house; Captain Bull clapped his left arm about Zech's shoulder; his body shielded his right hand from the curious eyes outside. He gripped Zech's right arm and pressed it hard, reassuring him and unnecessarily warning him not to speak out too soon.

Zech nodded slightly, to let the Captain know he got his message. Captain Bull pushed him toward a trestle table where the woman who had first appeared at the door was setting out trenchers. "I've not eaten, you see, so you are just in time. Are you hungry?"

— "It's been quite a trek!" Zech answered, and glanced at the Captain who sent him a sharp look though he said quite gently, "You look weary."

"Aye — I am that," Zech agreed. As hungry as he was, he wanted nothing so much as to push back the steaming trencher and drop his head onto his arm and sleep.

Zech realized that the Captain had asked him a question. He realized, suddenly, how muddled he had become. Dimly, out of the numbness that began to creep over him, he realized that he had not slept since the fitful night after *the Angel* appeared — since this time yesterday he had trekked to Deerfield — then the swift flight down the Connecticut — and — He raised his head. The Captain looked befogged to him. Were his hands swelling —? Growing bigger . . . and bigger . . . and bigger? He was soooo weary. Whose voice, "Good . . . lad . . . rest . . ." weary . . . w . . e . . a . . r . . y . . . w . . e . . a . . r . . y . . .

CHAPTER XXIX

Zech began to awaken slowly, rousing from nothingness. Before he opened his eyes, he lay quiet and tried to decide where he was, how he had gotten there. After he opened his eyes, he lay quiet and stared at the unfamiliar striped coverlet wrapped about him. He moved his feet. They were bare. He was undressed? No. No. Just his moccasins off. His clothes were loosened, though. He frowned at the wainscotted wall beside the bed. This was not his home. Slowly, he raised his eyes to the low ceiling and let them follow the angle of the wall and ceiling to the corner toward his feet. A birthing room? Surely the kitchen was on the other side of the curtained doorway. He realized sounds from the kitchen had helped to awaken him. He closed his eyes and tried to think. He yawned. The featherbed seemed to draw him closer into its embrace. It felt good. Very good. Very . . . when he opened his eyes again, he knew he had dozed off. This time he felt more rested. He remembered Captain Bull. He studied the curtained doorway uncertainly. The curtains were drawn over the window, too. It was almost too dark to see, now. The last thing he recalled — He started up. The General! He had not told the Captain where to find the General. He started to flounder out of bed.

The woman he had seen — that morning? — lifted back a handful of curtain and peered in at him. She grinned sympathetically. "Awake, eh? Captain Bull says for you to rest and not to worry yourself, that everything's provided for. He said you'd want to know. Can't you rest more?"

216

Zech shook his head at the same time he dropped back onto the bed.

"What time is it?" he asked faintly.

"Near sunset," the woman answered.

"The Captain —?"

"Don't worry none 'bout Captain Bull!" the woman admonished. "I'm startin' supper now. You'll oblige me if ye stay out from under foot."

Zech stretched gratefully. The bed was very comfortable. He sighed. The Captain said not to worry. *Everything was provided for.* Including himself? How much would he be told — now? Where was the General now? Here? Someplace else? Would he, himself, ever feel lively again?

Zech's heart soared when he heard Captain Bull's voice suddenly inquiring regarding his welfare. An instant later the Captain loomed in the doorway.

"Awake, eh?" he boomed. "Good! Hungry, too, I'll wager!"

Zech struggled to a sitting position and tried self-consciously to smooth his rumpled hair.

"Major Treat's here," the Captain told him. "He came on from Milford as soon as he could. We've got everything under control. You are to go to Northampton with the Major — in the morning."

Zech's relief knew no bounds. Truly everything was provided for!

Zech could not see the old man's face in the shadow. He tried to keep his own expressionless. When he stepped into the kitchen, he nodded solemnly at the beaming gentleman standing by the fireplace: Major Treat, he presumed, who silently congratulated him with nods of appreciation that others might believe to be nods of recognition.

With the first dim light of morning, Major Treat's company left Hartford strung out in single file — each man ready to take flight to save himself and his mount, if need be. The men all thought Zech was of Northampton and had been in Hartford a spell before they arrived. Major Treat placed Zech just in front of him. Zech had expected to be told of General Goffe's whereabouts after supper last night, but he had learned nothing then, or since. He resented being uninformed. He knew that if he pressed for information he would be advised the continuing secrecy was for his own protection. His welfare had been of no concern when he could be of service! He had proved himself trustworthy; had he not earned the right to know what had come to pass since yesterday morning? He wondered what the reaction would be if he began to talk of the excitement he had known two nights before. These men would not believe that he had played a more important role than they could dream of. He decided that he would seek out Mr. Hawley and question him. The conspirators would not expect *his* assistance and then insult him by telling him nothing! Yet Mr. Hawley was hardly three years older than he, so he would understand his torment.

As soon as the company hove into sight of the hamlet across the river from Springfield, Connecticut men garrisoned there rode out to meet the Milford company.

Lack of cheerful signals and the men's rigid control of their horses warned of bad news to come. Major Treat's men quickened their pace; by the time the two columns came together the Connecticut column had closed ranks.

The grave-faced garrison sergeant bowed to Major Treat without taking his troubled eyes from the Major's face. His voice caught dramatically before he blurted, "There's ill news from up the river, Sir."

The Major's men sucked in their breaths. Zech could feel the Milford men's eyes on him as the Major asked, full of dread: " 'Hamp? Hadley?"

"Ah, — no — Northfield," the spokesman said grimly, and added: "Eight men killed there, Sir."

"Henry!" Zech cried out, half aloud; the Major shook his head convulsively, as if he could shake off the tragedy.

"How?" the Major pressed as quickly as he could.

The sergeant drew in his breath and swallowed, and cleared his throat, prolonging everyone's agony before he began, his expression solemn, his voice hushed: "The Council at Hadley judged that after what happened at Brookfield and Deerfield, the garrison at Northfield was not safe. On the day after Deerfield's families were brought down, a company of Essex militia was sent to Northfield with supplies — and to add to the garrison."

"Some said Northfield should be brought down, instead of supplied. For now, anyhow," one of the West Springfield men put in.

His fellow soldiers nodded their agreement, and the speaker went on: "Philip's Wampanoags went on — up to Northfield — the day after they attacked Deerfield. They caught a work party in a meadow.''

"One slain was a family man — leavin' eight young 'uns." (Sam Wright, of 'Hamp!)

"And a couple o' lads — up there from 'Hamp, but without their families.''

(The Janes boys, working for Joe Dick! Joe planned to go up and help Goodman Janes build a cottage there when he took up the rest of his family after harvest.)

"Did ye hear the name Bodwell?" Zech asked anxiously.

The spokesman thought a moment before he shook his head uncertainly. He went on: "The Essex Company — Captain Beers and his men — camped short of Northfield, goin' up. They wa'n't certain of the safety of the fort. They left their horses in camp and went along afoot. To scout it out. Within sight o' the fort, the Ind'ans beset 'em. More than thirty went out. Less'n half got back, that we heard of.''

"What o' Capt'n Beers?'' one asked, half in dread, half in awe.

"Gone — gone — gone — ''

After a stunned silence, a Milford man muttered; "After the Ind'ans fallin' on the settlements as they did, you'd think the militia would'a learned!''

"They thought they was takin' care!'' a West Springfield man defended, and everyone sighed.

The sergeant had a final blow to deliver: "The Ind'ans got the militia's ammunition carts. All the supplies.''

Someone behind Zech cursed, spewing out more profanity than Zech had heard in all his life before. Zech glanced at the Major, but he seemed not to notice. Zech could not keep his hands from trembling. He noticed others having the same trouble. Everyone stared about at his companions, pale and weak, before they began to straggle toward West Springfield's headquarters at one of Major Pynchon's farmhouses. There, Major Treat's company swapped horses and the Major reorganized his troops and sent a pair of garrison soldiers back to Hartford with news of Northfield's assault and a request for reinforcements — Mohegans if possible.

Before leaving West Springfield, Major Treat directed Zech in private to get ahead of his company as soon as he was in familiar territory so that no questions would be asked about his riding into town with the Milford militia. Throughout the nerve-wracking ride north, along a trail that the Indians favored, everyone scanned the sky above the drab duns and russets of the rolling hills for signs of disturbed crows or sudden flurries of partridge that might indicate a stalking enemy. Time after time as they rode, Zech caught himself fighting down spasms of grief that welled up within him and almost burst forth in choking sobs.

At Hurlburt's pond, the familiarity of the territory bore down on him; he signalled to Major Treat that he would be taking off. He dug his heels into the flank of his mount, and started pounding toward town.

He slashed across the ford at Mill River where men, splitting logs for the palisado that Northampton had decided to erect, halted in alarm, expecting him to stop. Later he learned that he had outstripped a sentinel watching from a knoll who tried to intercept him. He had flashed by too quickly to be recognized.

At Wilton's Post, the old Lieutenant emerged from his great-hall as Zech swung to the ground. The death's-head look of the old man shocked Zech.

"You got the General there safe, eh?" Mr. Wilton whispered cautiously in spite of the fact all able-bodied men and boys were engaged elsewhere and the yard deserted. His interest, his relief, his pleasure in the deed accomplished brought a momentary gleam to his sharp eyes.

Zech nodded and hesitated. He wanted to ask about Henry.

The old man realized his concern. He mourned, his voice cracking as he tried to comfort: "I've heard naught of your friend." He added, disconsolate: "Eben Parson was the first child born in 'Hamp, Zech."

"They all were not Essexmen, then, in the company?" Zech asked, wondering about all the boys he had grown up with.

"Well — in the company — aye. But they got settlers — first. The company was Essexmen — billeted at Coleman's and Grannis'." He paused and with great effort said, "You'll likely want to get on — to hear more. Others of Beers' company have been coming in. One got in just after sunup. He had been captured — and loosed from his bonds by a Natick —" He went on as if talking to himself: "They all are Eastern tribes — assailin' us. Nipmucks and Wampanoags." His tone became more alive as he added: "The one who came this morning told that they were drunk last night. Mourned a great Captain. That Philip, we hope! Without that varmint to incite them they would give up. Oh, some are bloodthirsty at times, but the Nonotucks never were vicious.

Not like the Mohawks. That's not their way. Not their way —"

Zech nodded soberly and played with the reins, uncertain what Lt. Wilton expected of him. Abruptly coming out of his revery, the old man reached for the reins and clucked in disgust at himself. He directed: "You run home, now. God bless you for bein' such a good lad! Your folks must be wanting word of you. Especially in such times as these!"

Zech could feel himself blushing wildly. He bowed his thanks to the old gentleman. Nothing was more heartening — nor harder to acknowledge — than genuine gratitude.

At the river, Young Joe Kellogg greeted him silently, absently, not aware Zech had been away. Zech picked up a paddle and marveled to himself that he had been involved in such a fantastic escapade as he had been, yet nothing of life about him had changed at all. He had not even been missed — Just to have gone to Springfield at a time like this ordinarily would rate a hearing — but he could not hint — or even admit — his absence, much less speak of any detail. He could only look as sad as he felt. He knew, too, that he must guard against showing ignorance of what had gone on in the Valley for the last two days. He might meet many friends and acquaintances before he reached home. Young Joe must not catch him unaware. He cleared his throat nervously and thought that being choked up would be a good excuse if Joe came up with something that overwhelmed him.

"Anything new since the latest?" Zech asked, as they shoved off.

Joe heaved a deep sigh in reply, and added reverently: " 'Tis strange — the ways of Providence."

"Aye," Zech agreed quietly. "I used to have such great sport with Eben and Johnny — 'fore I was old enough to go into lecture."

"There wa'nt many weeks difference, 'tween me and Eben," Joe said, able to identify himself more closely to the slain than Zech could.

After a minute's silence, Young Joe murmured, "It ain't easy — no matter how many sons a man has. But when there's only one — "

. . . That did not mean either Eben or the Janes boys . . .

" 'Twill be awhile — " Zech hesitated and then halted, fearing to go on.

"Aye. And I should not want to be the one to take such word to

221

so many. 'Tis bad enough here. Maybe worse where we know 'em. Some from the East did not have families. That makes it kind of sad, too, don't you think? Dying off in the wilderness — alone — you know —''

Zech cleared his throat, close to tears.

"Remember that Getchell one? He were a queer one, weren't he? A real old maid. The way he wore his hair long and fluffed out so. Always mincing along like a young maid in a new frock —''

Zech nodded and half-smiled to himself, remembering.

"Can't help feelin' sorry for Unwillin', either. Can't help myself,'' Young Joe went on, and Zech sighed, nearly overcome by anxiety. Had Unwillin' gone out? Was he hurt bad? The canoe touched the shallows and Zech tended to the business at hand, forgetting Unwillin' for the moment. Not until the morrow did he learn that Will Markham, Junior, had died, too. Unwillin' had put much store in his nephew. He had mourned aloud that one so full of life and so quick to learn did not carry the Webster name. He was "All Webster!'' Unwillin' was quick to tell everyone he could collar: Will, Junior, will bring great honor to the family, again, he promised.

As Zech climbed out of the canoe, Young Joe demanded: "How did you chance to get over in 'Hamp, anyway, Zech?''

Zech blinked. "When you weren't about, I guess —'' he bluffed brazenly. "Pa sent me early — I've been at Wilton's.'' Would Young Joe believe he had been gone so long — and so *far* — on *such* a mission?

Zech bounded up the hill to the common, wondering how the young ones in his family had been primed about his absence. What was he to do or say if Timmie or Mindie spotted him and came racing up demanding in some Royalist's hearing: "Zech, *where* have you been? Where *have* you been? You've been away two whole days!'' He had not been provided with a proper response for that.

No one even glanced at him until he was halfway up the common. It looked more crowded and disordered to him now, after having seen Hartford's less-troubled way of life. Suddenly, out of nowhere, Timmie hurled himself upon him, crying: "Zech, where have you *been? Where* have you been, Zech?''

Those within earshot grinned with distracted amusement. Zech laughed, relieved and excited. He made a grab for the little fellow and chided: "Seems like forever, eh?''

222

Timmie jumped up and down in his arms and tried to strangle him for proof of affection. Zech tore himself free of his assault while Timmie tried to explain excitedly — something about Hope's mouth — poor tongue-tied Hope's mouth.

Timmie squealed his incomprehensible tale while they threaded their way homeward. Hope, sitting on the doorstep, jumped to his feet at sight of Zech, and tried to grin. His eyes brimmed with delight as he stumbled forward holding his mouth carefully half-opened.

Zech stepped through the gate, full of concern. Hope stopped him short, an arm's length away. Carefully, he extended his tongue, well beyond his carefully puckered lips. He glowed with unbounded joy.

Zech stared, astounded. Hope's tongue was loosed! Hope's tongue was untied! "Hope! Hope! Hope! What happened?"

"That Mung' did't!" Timmie squealed again and again, dancing around Zech and Hope.

Zech knelt beside Hope and tried to peer into Hope's mouth. The seven-year-old nodded his wonder, his eyes full of tears, his mouth still sore and tender. Aunt appeared around the corner of the house.

Seeing Zech for the first time, her hands flew out in a motion of relieved welcome; at the same time, seeing his concern for Hope, her chin went up. Even as much as her eyes asked a dozen questions and at the same time warned him not to speak-out now, her lips trembled, and her eyes flew defiantly from Zech to Hope and back again. Overcome, she moved her head in little jerks that seconded Timmie's explanation. Evidently, Mungo had played surgeon and relieved Hope's unfortunate condition.

"He got him drunk!" she cried angrily when the words came. "He was a mighty sick young one! I was afraid he was going to die!"

Zech could only shake his head. The small body pressing against him, melting in his arms, told him of Hope's gratitude for what had been done for him.

Zech held Hope close for a long time. When Hope drew away, he beamed up at Zech and smiling grotesquely, raised his tongue carefully. He held his mouth open so that Zech could see what Mungo had done. Half-afraid, Zech murmured, "You will talk now, won't you?" The blue eyes danced, and the red mop nodded very cautiously.

"He was so sick!" Aunt protested, again. Zech patted Hope's shoulder as he stood up. He could imagine how sick Hope must have been. The very smell of that kill-devil! He'd touched it to his tongue once. Ack! How did anyone get it down? How it must burn on an open wound! But how else could the cutting have been done?

"Where's Mungo, now? Zech asked Timmie, avoiding Aunt's eyes.

"We don't know!" Timmie answered breezily. "Gone, we guess!" and Aunt disappeared into the house with a swirl of skirts.

Then Zech remembered that he had not asked about Henry, yet.

CHAPTER XXX

Major Treat left Hartford expecting to return immediately; word of Northfield changed his plans. He immediately directed a hundred Northampton-based militiamen to march up the river at daybreak. Even Pastor Russell did not object to such a mission on the Sabbath.

The tales of horror Major Treat's men brought back from Northfield exceeded those of Brookfield. Beyond Deerfield, they had found militiamen impaled on old wigwam poles and hanging from trees by chains through their jaws. All had been hacked up and scalped.

Major Treat's men wept as they began to bury their dead. One raised his eyes to implore Heaven for the reason — *WHY* — and distant, circling crows gave warning of skulking warriors. A few brave souls continued to dig as bait while their companions fanned out and lay in wait. They surprised a dozen warriors; only one Indian shot found its mark in the fray: a spent ball that braised Major Treat's thigh.

With the marauders dispatched, the Connecticut men gave up all thought of burying the dead. Full of apprehension, they hurried on to Northfield. Major Treat gave orders to abandon the blockhouse and the settlement immediately.

In the gathering dusk, the caravan started down the Valley laden with blankets, clothing, flax, and sacks of grain — only such as could be transported in addition to the women and children. Men

225

left their barnyard gates ajar and carried salt licks to coax the cattle to follow. Time could not be spared to drive the confused creatures. Disheartened, bewildered and prayerful, the long file of desperate settlers hurried down the Valley in the waning moonlight. They made their way unmolested.

Word of the arriving band reached Hadley at dawn; the able-bodied rode out to be of assistance.

Zech's pleasure at seeing Henry again knew no bounds. He beat Henry's broad shoulders in greeting, and assured him: "You can come back to ferryin' with me as soon as you are rested."

They walked to the Hatfield beaching place in companionable silence, listening to snatches of conversation flying around them about Hadley's 'Angel.' Zech found to his surprise that he would not be telling Henry of his flight with General Goffe. He had been anxiously waiting for Henry — for that purpose — but now he knew he would not tell. Even though he trusted Henry, who appreciated the Generals as much — more — than many, he found that he could not violate the confidence that had been placed in him. He could not make an exception. For the first time, he understood why his father had not spoken out four years before. Trust and loyalty and honor were more than words that could be manipulated or ignored at will; understanding them made the difference between a man and a boy.

In the morning, Northfield's neat cattle began to drift into town, bawling their protest at their neglect. Most were accounted for; the Indians must have left the country — again.

A week later, another quite different caravan moved in upon Hadley. Eastern militiamen going over to 'Hamp brought the news to Zech and Henry. With knowing looks, Henry's fellow militiamen told him: "Mosely's just come." "You should see the dawgs!" "Mosely 'n' 'is grey 'ounds is 'ere —!" " — Mongrels half as big as horses, too —"

Zech caught the undertone that went beyond criticism for bringing more animals — and such animals — with rations so short.

"Wait'll ye see him, Henry, he ain't changed one bit!" A Newbury man warned Henry.

"Why did you think 'e would?" Henry jeered. "What 'ud do it? 'ow many's 'e got with 'im? Men, that is?"

"Two — three score — at least."

" 'n' those dawgs!"

Zech could hardly wait for the Easterns to be off to Northampton so that he could press Henry for details: "*Who* is Mosely?" he asked, worried by the men's attitudes.

"Captain Sam-u-el Mosely. Sea Captain that is. Not militia."

"A sea captain — in Hadley?"

" 'adley's where the excitement is. 'e'd not be any place else."

"Do you 'spose he'll be staying in Hadley?" Zech asked.

"Ha! He'd not go any place else when Major Savage is 'ere to 'arass?"

" — He is not a friend of Major Savage?" Zech probed warily.

"Ha! 'is favored sport is bothering the Major near t' death!"

"I cannot imagine anyone purposely harassing Major Savage," Zech said thoughtfully. "Not with him knowing it, anyway."

"Well, 'tis not likely you ever knew anyone like the Capt'n, anyway. And you've not been missing anything worth your while."

"Seems strange the Council would send him here — If he and the Major —"

"If 'e put 'is mind to comin', 'e'd come, no matter what. 'is men are called Volunteers. And that's what they do. There's trouble 'ere, and they've volunteered to come and see it don't let up none! 'e pays 'em 'isself. 'e's 'ad many desertions at sea, but these landlubbers go with 'im with slim pay. They are that sort."

"Everyone seems to know him —"

"Aye. 'e came a privateer out'a Jamaica. Bought a cooperage in Boston, and married Gov'nor Leverett's niece, 'e did. 'e's never stopped sending out sloops. When the Dutch got too bold — piratin' — and the gov'ment did nothing, Ole Sammy took things in 'is own 'ands."

Zech frowned, troubled.

" 'e were still capturing Dutch this spring," Henry went on. "And Ind'ans. 'im and 'is Dutchman, Cornelius!"

"Indians?" Zech prompted timidly.

"Aye. After news of Swansey's massacre, Major Savage set out to investigate prowlers north of the seaboard settlements. Capt'n Sam rustled up this brisk band of 'is, then. He insisted to Major Savage that 'cause of 'is investment 'e should 'ave three hours on 'is own. 'e said if 'e wa'n't back in that time, the Major could 'ang 'im when 'e did come. Of course, Old Sam did not come back in three hours, but when 'e did, 'twere with tales of massacreein' a numerous tribe that attacked 'em. Later, 'twere learned 'twas friendly Nashuas fleeing to safety in Plymouth — 'cause they did not want to sack an' plunder with Philip. They surrendered to the Capt'n thinkin' 'e were a escort. 'e was, too! To Kingdom Come! Now, Jon knows that, for all 'is talk, but 'e cannot bring 'isself to judge a man like God does — by 'is 'eart, alone. Men like Capt'n Sam an' 'is Cornelius don't 'ave 'earts. They ain't fit to be called *men*. They ain't no better'n any snake that crawls.''

Zech nodded, repelled.

''Some Nashuas 'scaped 'is pillage an' got to Roxbury. That's 'ow the story got out. When 'e 'eard some survived, Cornelius took a mob an' went after 'em. But Pastor Eliot were with 'em. Now, 'e's got *real* strength. The kind Satan backs down to! Well, those Nashuas is safe for now. But I 'ave 'eard tell the Capt's tryin' t' git the gov'ment to ship 'em all to Spain. To be slaves. If they are shipped on one of 'is boats, God go with 'em. Only God would be able to 'elp 'em.''

The next trip across the river included a pair of Mosely's lordly ragtaggle Volunteers exploring the lay of the land. They talked to each other of the possibility of Northampton's being a better site for their headquarters, as if that would be a loss to Hadley. When Zech and Henry feigned disinterest and irked them, they tried to impress them by telling each other of comrades-in-arms who had run down a canoe in the Bay: Mr. Gookin, going out to the islands to help Indians, he was, the traitor! A pity friends rescued the varmit — They would like to have drowned! Mention of Mr. Gookin, friend of the Judges, distracted Zech from his intended indifference. One of the Volunteers, noticing Zech's sudden interest, warned: ''Capt'n Mosely frightens Ind'ans near to death — without doin' nothin'.''

Zech stared at him blankly, determined not to be intimidated; he shrugged, as if he did not care at all. Annoyed by Zech's response, the Volunteer pushed the canoe back into the water with a shove that nearly tipped it over.

The next group of passengers, regular militiamen, enlightened Zech and Henry. The story going the rounds told of Captain Mosely's being at a parley with Indians who did not know he was bald, and knew nothing of wigs. At the end of the conference, Captain Mosely swept off his wig and stuffed it into the top of his great boots. The flabbergasted Indians knocked each other down trying to get out of his presence.

By suppertime, Zech had heard so many flying tales of the flamboyant Mosely he could scarcely wait to get away from ferrying to judge for himself.

"You do not think you will find 'im with 'is men, now do you?" Henry teased as they started up to the common.

Zech shrugged.

"Ha!" Henry warned. " 'e'll be at 'eadquarters demanding 'is rights! If 'e don't 'ave any, 'e'll think some up! Ones nobody would think of but 'im. Not in a week of Sabbaths. Finally, 'gainst everybody's better judgement, 'e'll do as 'e pleases. See if 'e don't!"

Mosely's encampment of men and dogs teemed about at the south end of the common, setting up their camp. " 'fore too long they will no doubt throw a pike across this path and we will 'ave to pay a smart fee to turn it, to git by," Henry muttered to Zech. They walked along pretending to be unaware of the newcomers.

"We ain't rightly got room for 'em," Henry muttered. They were abreast of the invaders now, aware they were being studied with amusement.

"Hen - er - y Bod - well — " a voice mocked from among the strangers.

Zech faltered. He glanced toward the lounging Volunteers.

"Jon!" he exclaimed, stunned, and stopped in his tracks.

The youth he addressed grinned. "You know Jon, do ye?"

"Aye — " Zech struggled to keep from sounding awed or defensive. He had realized his mistake immediately. The Volunteer addressing him had to be Jon's brother, though.

"Jon was billeted at our house — " Zech explained. "Your mother and the young ones are at our dwelling now."

He expected Jon's brother's attitude to change, but if he cared at all about his family, he hid his feelings well.

"Don't have Jon with ye now, do ye?" he jeered.

Zech hesitated.

"Ahhhh — " Jon's brother scoffed. Zech began to move away. Jon's brother called after him: "When does the next canoe leave for Deerfield?"

Henry cut in: "There's many a bushel o' wheat up there to be brought down, Peter. 'Tis going to be 'andy, 'aving so many of you Volunteers to 'elp bring it in."

Peter Plympton spat accurately in Henry's direction. "We are scoutin' the enemy!" he announced haughtily. "We ain't bringin' in other men's gold!"

Henry grunted his contempt. He and Zech moved away, their gore rising. True, most of the crop was owed Major Pynchon for the purchase of land up the river. Wheat did not rust in Deerfield's virgin soil as it did now about Hadley. Men counted it a miracle the way it had survived the hurricane. And Major Pynchon had announced that the wheat was everyone's now. Since the attack on Deerfield, everyone watched the northern sky anxiously; clouds of smoke by day or a rosy haze by night could signal the end of the wheat by the torches of pillaging savages. Garnering it would be the Valley's salvation, with nearly a thousand extra mouths to feed, especially with supplies from the East cut off except by ship to Hartford — suddenly so far away.

For two days, Captain Mosely's Volunteers and their dogs boldly scoured the surrounding countryside. The Indians knew who to stay away from, they bragged, but Valleymen believed that Philip's men had moved toward the East, with the exception of the renegade troop that Major Treat's men had intercepted en route to Northfield. In Hadley, Hatfield, and Northampton, everyone tolerated the irritating Volunteers, but put more faith in their prayers that the harvest at Deerfield would proceed without interruption.

On Friday, Captain Lothrop led his company up the river as an escort to a cart train of seventeen wagons pressed into service to transport the grain to the lower settlements. Henry went with the Eastern militiamen; Mosely's Volunteers found more important undertakings off in another direction.

At Deerfield, the Hadley brigade found that the garrisoned men had harvested, and threshed, and bagged their grain without sign of Indians stalking the neighborhood. Old Sarge, an ardent admirer of Capt. Mosely, upon hearing that the Captain had arrived at Hadley and scouted the territory, maintained it was the Volunteers who had kept Deerfield unmolested. He told everyone that he and Captain Sam's father had been dragoons together in Old Essex, in the first skirmishes of the Civil War, conscripted by the Lord of their manor. He asked permission for Jon to be one of the teamsters to deliver the grain to Hadley. He directed Jon to urge Capt. Sam to make haste to Deerfield, and to plan to make his headquarters there.

Robert Hinsdale took charge of the cart train of grain and household effects being sent down to Hadley. A crude, burly Frenchman, Hinsdale had arrived at the Bay with the Great Migration. He had arrived in Hadley but a few years ago, a widower pursuing four sons who had pressed westward to escape his tormenting ways. Experience Hinsdale, his eldest son, had married Mary, a daughter of Liza Hawks, the flighty widow who years before had caused Ben Wait to be whipped for his offending verses. Rob Hinsdale's bluff ways swept the giddy Liza off her feet; she found soon enough that he was not the gentle soul of the sort that had married her daughter. In short order, she had Hinsdale called into court on charges that shocked the valley from end to end: so much so that the clerk of court who had entered many malodorous misdemeanors against Liza's wayward son, Gershom, and his delinquent friends, refused to put a summary of Liza's testimony into writing, recording the testimony of Rob's lascivious carriage as "too loathsomely obscene and exceeding nacious to an honest heart to hear or mention." Rob's four sons moved on to Deerfield then, and again he followed their lead.

Old Sarge, jubilant over the satisfaction of the harvest, and the excitement of knowing Captain Sam was in Hadley, waved the more than four score men off on their way down the Valley. The footsteps of the lead militia crackled the first crisp, white hoar frost of early morning as the cart train struggled away from Deerfield and across South Meadow. At the first ford, the wheels of the laden carts had to be levered from the softened ground on both sides of the stream. Up Long Hill, the going proved rough and slow, but no more difficult than expected. The oxen were fresh, equal to their loads. Long before noon, the sun warmed the straining men and beasts. Above Hatfield meadows, at the edge of the woods, not burned now for several years and grown thick with underbrush, the procession stopped while the teamsters decided how to cross what had become a swampy reach since the hurricane. In previous years, Muddy Brook had been forded at this place, and more recently a makeshift log bridge thrown across that had been swept away by the storm. The teamsters counted it strange that so few logs remained unburied along the banks. They had expected to salvage enough to support the wagons across the stream. While the teamsters probed for logs, Henry visited with Jon, relishing grapes from vines tangled along the stream. Everyone groaned when Rob Hinsdale overruled further search. The wagons would sink below the axles in this morass if there was naught to keep them up, but Rob would not hear of men going to fetch logs. The distance to likely trees was too far, and they had not the time. Frustrated and enraged, Rob ordered the train forward.

The first team splashed into the water; its wheels began to sink into the mucky bottom. Henry grunted. He would need to help with a lever. He turned aside, looking for a handy spot to rest his musket. He turned directly toward an onrushing band of Nipmucks, as if he had faced into the attack deliberately. He felt a hot bite . . . excruciating pain . . . in his left elbow. He reeled, but his fury surpassed his astonishment. He lunged toward a screaming, painted figure plunging out of the thicket toward him, swinging a smoking musket. Henry could not raise his musket, but using it as a club, he caught the Indian's advance full on. He smashed against the gaudy brave; his musket caught him below the chest; with his right foot, Henry caught the back of the savage's knees. They slumped sideways into the stream. Henry pushed the warrior under the cold, running water. He pounded the black head beneath him with his musket and pressed down the thrashing body. When his attacker lay still he threw himself into the brush, forgotten by the marauders besieging the cart train, murdering his companions. He collapsed, wanting to reach the shrieking slaughter . . . wanting to put it to an end. When he came to consciousness, through ebbing waves of sound, he heard volleys of shot . . . Did the battle still rage . . . or had help arrived . . . too late . . . too late . . . too late . . .

Later, while he sat in the sun or chimney corner at Ham's, nursing his pulsing elbow, piecing together the tales of that day, he knew that the shooting he had heard before he fainted again was Mosely's Volunteers. Ranging west of Hatfield, they had heard the din of battle and rushed to the defense of the wagon train. They surprised the Indians stripping the dead, plundering the carts, ripping open feather beds, and dumping all but the wheat into the brook. Ten to one, Mosely said his men were outnumbered, both as to men and their losses. But his men did not win the day. They engaged the enemy, but Major Treat and his company, bound for Northfield to establish a military post, attracted by gunfire, drove off the enemy. None of the teamsters struggling with the wagon at the ford escaped; only seven militiamen other than Henry survived to tell their tales: men who had been handy to the horses, or able to take refuge in the brush when the battle began. Major Lothrop fell with his men, and so did Jon.

In the morning, men from the fort rode out to where the brook had run red with blood the day before. In a state of shock, they buried seventy-one men in one dreadful grave: seven of Mosely's Volunteers, fifty-four militiamen, and one-half of the hopeful souls who had planted new homes in the wilderness village of Deerfield.

Even as the settlers buried their dead, Indians circled near the blockhouse at Deerfield. Boldly, as if help would come if summoned, the Deerfield watch blasted their trumpets and the warriors melted from sight. The men who had planned to hold the fort at Deerfield left the village then; for many seasons the ruins of the village would be but a fit place for owls. It was the third western village deserted within a month.

CHAPTER XXXI

Within a week of the massacre at Bloody Brook, Indians set fire to a house within sight of the fort at Springfield. Worried Springfield men already had begun to report the disappearance of Indians friendly to them, no doubt victims of their "cousins." Major Pynchon's wife, in charge of his enterprises during his absence at military headquarters in Hadley, became overwrought by Springfield's nerve-shattering existence; she sent word imploring her husband to return home. Immediately, he requested Hadley's council to release him from his duties. He reminded them that Springfield's crumbling palisado sheltered but few families. The time had come to repair the stockade and gather the village together within its shelter. He suggested that Major Appleton of Ipswich be put in charge.

In the meantime, Captain Mosely sent word to Boston that for the past two weeks his Volunteers had found signs that indicated Philip's men planned to rally in an encampment above the mill north of Hadley. He insisted that troops newly arrived to garrison Springfield should march to the assistance of Hadley and her neighboring villages. Before Boston returned a decision, he persuaded Captain Appleton to follow the strategy of the Indians at Bloody Brook. Under his and Capt. Appleton's direction, Springfield's and Hadley's troops would move out under cover of darkness and at daybreak strike the encampment with all the power and speed they could muster. Reluctantly, on Major Appleton's orders, Major Pynchon escorted his fresh garrison troops up the river from Springfield to Hadley.

At dusk, Monday, a message from Windsor arrived at Major Treat's headquarters in Northampton. Toto, the most trusted of the Mohegans, had reported to his English friends there that Philip's men had shown themselves about Hadley for a purpose. They were but few in number, and put in appearances in many places. They schemed to destroy the villages one at a time; to draw off the men at Springfield and attack it first.

Major Treat sent word across the river to Major Pynchon at Hadley, and immediately started down the Valley toward Springfield with his Connecticut Company. To avoid being ambushed along the riverside West Springfield trail, he followed the trail to Westfield, by which he had come. His company reached the Westfield fort before darkness stayed them. He planned to march to Springfield's relief at daybreak. But the season conspired against him, as the Indians had known it would. Thick, smoke-like fog peculiar to that section of the Valley in early autumn enclosed the Westfield fort so that the militia could only fumble along the Springfield trail, one man close behind the other, unable to see the third man ahead of him. They could only pray that the lead man did not go astray where pathways met, that the whole company would not be misled. They did not reach the Connecticut River, five miles to the East, until almost noon. By then the sun had warmed the earth and light breezes had blown the fog away. Nothing hid the destruction of Springfield from sight of the company that had expected to save it.

Triumphant Indians patrolled the holocaust on horseback, making obscene gestures toward the stricken militiamen who stared helplessly from across the river. The warriors already had driven back a canoeful of West Springfield settlers who had set out brashly to go to Springfield's defense. A volley of shot had hit one West Springfield man in the neck.

Major Pynchon's company, also delayed by fog, arrived in midafternoon. Three whooping braves dashed headlong toward the stunned Hadley company. Swerving at the last minute, they shouted: "The Englishmen's towns will go!"

Nothing outside Springfield's palisado survived the raid: flames consumed thirty dwellings and twenty-five barns and all other buildings, including Mr. Pynchon's mills. Families had not had time to gather their belongings together before thronging into the dozen small cabins within the patched-up stockade. Providentially, but one man and woman of those attacked lost their lives.

When word of the impending raid reached the fort, the lieutenant, Tom Cooper, rode out toward the Agawams' camp, believing he might be able to fend off the slaughter if he could reach his friends there. He was slain trying to keep the peace.

Two days after the sack of Springfield, the great Captain Mosely's scouts again discovered signs of the enemy north of Hatfield. This time they found no believers. The militia stayed at their quarters, and no renegade tribesmen attacked.

Captain Mosely's disastrous interference prompted the Council to restrict him and his Volunteers to scouting the post route to Brookfield. One day they rode into Hadley triumphant because they had met an Indian squaw who claimed she was en route to Hadley with a message for her daughter there. They had sicked their dogs on her and the beasts had torn her to shreds. The outraged town revolted against him. The squaw could have been Sarah's mother with a message. She might have had word that would help them all. Beside themselves with outraged anguish, Hadley's Council ordered the swashbuckling Captain and his company to be gone. But he only retreated. He withdrew to Hatfield. There the peril loomed so great that even the Volunteers seemed a lesser evil than no assistance at all.

Many times before the massacre at Bloody Brook, Zech had glimpsed Mungo about the common. He had felt jubilant when he'd first seen him, relieved to see that Mungo had not taken off as Henry had expected he would. He wanted to thank Mungo for freeing Hope, too. He tried to get to him, but Mungo always caught sight of him and slipped away, until Zech stopped trying. No doubt Mungo had convinced himself that the entire household shared Aunt's outraged indignation at the risk he had taken.

But Mungo appeared with the party that carried Henry to the house. Completely unconcerned regarding Aunt's displeasure, he contended with her to attend Henry. At first, they didn't exchange a word, but eventually they spoke accidentally. Now Aunt accepted Mungo. She could not, in justice, continue her coolness. Besides his care of Henry that could have become a burden to her, she could not deny that Hope's speech had improved. He did not talk as clearly as everyone else; habit too long established had taken a toll; but he talked so that other than family members could decipher what he meant. Some teased him now, telling him that they wished Mungo had not been quite so clever. Fortunately,

Henry enjoyed a constantly wagging tongue as long as it was attached to a pair of eager, listening ears. While Mungo attended to the needs of the militia's horses, Hope acted as his stand-in. He was good medicine for Henry, and Zech was certain that the tales with which Henry and Hope regaled each other more than made up for the hours each might have spent with others his own age.

Zech missed Henry's company, ferrying. He admitted it when Major Treat inquired after Henry, when he bid Zech farewell, announcing his plans to return to Connecticut. The Connecticut militia had become restless; Major Treat saw no point in his company's crowding in on their hosts; with proper precautions, the towns could protect themselves without so many militia to provide for. "Aye, I miss Henry, Sir," Zech admitted, his tone weary with a weight that oppressed him whenever he thought of Henry and what was to become of him. Henry no longer could ferry. His left arm hung useless. Zech's heart ached over the spasms of pain that gripped Henry and would for a long time. He was not the Henry, now, that he had been when he had come in August. Fever that set into Henry's wound had taken its toll; it left him gaunt and haggard. His dreadful brush with savagery haunted him. With no hope any longer for the future he had planned for himself, he had become a disheartened invalid quite dependent on Mungo who devoted himself to satisfying Henry's slightest whim. Zech was astounded to hear himself protest: "He had planned to be a smithy, you know. Now he must find a living he can manage with one arm. 'Twill not be a simple matter." He was so bitter for Henry!

The Major nodded sympathetically. "There's not too many things a one-armed man can do. There's talk of making grants up along the Kennebeck — to militiamen who were pressed, like Henry. Especially the injured men."

"Would his go to his master?" Zech asked quickly.

"Oh, no — 'twould be his. Only his."

Thought of wild, uncleared land came to Zech's mind and made Henry's injury seem an even more cruel affliction. The Major read his mind. Half-apologetically, he reminded: "He can sell his grant, you know."

Zech half-shrugged, half-nodded. Not having heard of the possibilities of grants for such as Henry, he had given no thought to the matter, had nothing to add.

"You know how remarkable men can be!" Major Treat reminded carefully: "Just think of *some* people." He meant, of course, the Judges and all their years as secret refugees. Zech knew what the Major expected of him.

"Aye," he countered quietly. "He will soon be one and twenty, and can be a freeman — " Bitterly, unexpectedly, he added: "I just hope he never must go hungry because his injury has made him so free he can not work at all!"

Major Treat looked taken aback. He tried to soothe quickly, firmly: "We must see to it that all that can be, is done for those injured in our service."

Zech's lips curled. He thought: Like the meager payment I got for services rendered? The satisfaction of knowing nothing! Everything and nothing!

Major Treat looked stricken. He hesitated, then clapped Zech soundly on the shoulder. He started to walk away, as if at each step he would turn back. Finally, he did stop and turn back. He called thoughtfully: "I am going through Hartford. You should be better rewarded than you have been, Lad. Next time you are in Hartford, be certain to stop at Captain Bull's. I am going to tell him that I told you to stop."

Zech's heart leaped. He could feel himself beaming. "Thank you, Sir," he stammered after the retreating figure. "Thank you, Major Treat!"

"What does he mean?" asked Gracie, who was ferrying with Zech.

"He is going to fix up something for Henry — or something like that," Zech answered glibly, and Gracie gave no further thought to the matter.

Foul weather soon began to add to the Valley's burden. Blustery winds bared the trees and the skies hung sullen and low. Everyone expected to take heart as autumn's drought-drab leaves began to disappear: Indians lost a valuable ally with the trees stark and without cover. The Hampshire Council decreed the villages would not burn the woods in November, though that was hardly necessary. Who would sally forth for such an undertaking? When fires appeared mysteriously north of the village, the Council sent out a company of nine militiamen and a Hatfield guide to investigate. They never returned. That put an end to scouting for any purpose.

Captain Mosely, exasperated by resistance to his strategies and charms, decided to turn his attention to the East. He did not leave before starting further controversy. Many settlers had become so disheartened that Major Appleton felt obliged to issue an order forbidding families from withdrawing from their villages to safer areas. Captain Mosely thought that not enough. He wrote to the General Court urging abandonment of the river villages. When he finally withdrew eastward, his company invaded Mr. Gookin's Indian village at Marlboro. In the absence of their protector he marched the Indians — men, women and children — to Boston, tied neck to neck. Within a week of his arrival in Boston, the Bay Commissioners sent a message to Hadley ordering the western towns to unite in one vast headquarters in Springfield. The message further directed that the Eastern militia should return home so that henceforth their large numbers would not be a drain on the settlements. The preposterous decision moved the Hampshire Council and the villagers to enraged laughter and tears. Major Pynchon returned a flat refusal to Boston by the next post.

Zech wondered, as he looked back on that winter, how the Valley had sustained hope at all. At the time, the very air seemed weighted by despair, yet on the slightest occasion everyone took heart. Within weeks of the tragic November ambush, when no further signs of Indians appeared about the Valley, the villages began to assume that they were safe until spring. A company of men went out of Northampton's new stockade to dig turnips in a field above where Mr. Newell and Zech had rendezvoused with Mr. Hawley; they worked without sentinels after storing their guns in a convenient spot. Convenient at least for the Indians who captured the precious, irreplaceable arms and pursued the careless farmers into the village. The raiders burned four remote houses and two barns outside the stockade before they retired. Next day, a small party of Squageages assailed Hamp's corn mill, but it was on guard. On the same day, a headstrong settler and his son, working in their meadow in spite of warnings, fell prey to a band of warriors.

That winter an Act of God — moving in a strange way — relieved many Hadleyfolk and Zech, especially, of a cause for anxiety. Early in the fall, an unfamiliar distemper struck the Valley. It started with what seemed to be a head cold, but about the time a head cold would begin to let up, the fever with this affliction became more intense and convulsive spells of a whooping cough set in. The wrenching, unrelievable coughing provoked choking and vomiting, and sometimes hemorrhaging. In Hadley, the disease began in the Barnard family and went from one member to another. Hannah Westcarr dragged on all winter, not recovering until spring from a lung fever and pleurisy that came of it; it left her mother a near invalid. With no one to help care for him, Dr. Westcarr became the first victim. Many had blamed him for the disease in the first place, some believing before the distemper struck him, too, that it was a devilish affliction he had visited on his wife's family.

In the next year, no household escaped the whooping cough completely. No doubt militiamen carried it from the East. Governor Leverett, puzzled, wrote of it there at the time Hadley began to feel its awful grip. At the Gillettes, Hope came down with it first. Zech and Serv escaped with light cases, but it sorely exercised Ham and Aunt for more than a fortnight. The wrenching cough tormented the little ones all winter. No one could help, and for hours at a time, at night, everyone slept fitfully because of the coughing. It was spring before they were shut of the torturing symptoms of the disease; then those afflicted could get away from chills and drafts and the irritating smoke of the fireplace and bask in the sun's warm, healing light.

CHAPTER XXXII

Before the first of December, half the militiamen left the Valley, Henry and Mungo among them. A wounded man such as Henry could not be kept in Hadley with supplies and provisions so short, though his medical care would not be better elsewhere. Medical supplies intended for the area had been mis-shipped and did not reach Hadley, but Mary Tilton, and Sarah and Sam Porter managed heroically. A surgeon who had been sent from the East to take Doctor Westcarr's place had become so jealous of the local nurses' successes, and had behaved in such a troublesome manner, the Hampshire Council had ordered him back to Boston with Mosely's Volunteers. As winter set in, the toll in deaths since the first of September stood at 145 — 43 of the number Valleyfolk.

Many flying stories claimed that the Commissioners in Boston were talking of surprising the Indians where they were known to be quartered for the winter, in a morass in the Narragansett section southeast of the Bay settlements. All the militia that could be mustered in the East would be needed for such an expedition; many Valley blades declared that they intended to join in the effort, too, though their Council ordered that they must stay home for the protection of their own villages.

Provisions began to be in such short supply throughout the Valley that families began to offer one cow for the wintering of another. Hadley's ancients began to talk, then, of returning to the Connecticut colonies from which they had come. Connecticut seemed a much safer territory. Connecticut's colonies had alarms in the hills occasionally, but from Mohawks, and that was another matter. The older settlers who talked of leaving Hadley reasoned that their heirs could more freely house militia and refugees without them about, and would be relieved of their care, too.

Old John Crow was the hard-headed prime-mover of what actually became a family affair. Just before the August siege, his wife, Betsey Goodwin, had died after a lingering illness. With the passing of her only child, the widow Goodwin no longer had heart to contend with Hadley's increasing dangers and hardships, and Hadley needed her rooms. Mistress Goodwin and Old John took with them his unmarried children, Dan and Nathaniel and their two sisters. When the Goodwins had moved up the river to Hadley, Governor John Winthrop, Jr., had purchased their mansion in Hartford as his official residence. Now the Goodwins left their solid, imposing dwelling in Hadley to Sam Crow and his wife, Hannah, Small Pockets' granddaughter. Small Pockets decided to go along, then, too. He sold his dwelling to John Lawrence, a Brookfield refugee, and rented his acreage to him. John White, widowed father-in-law to Sarah Crow, and John Marsh and his wife, completed the party. The Marshes might have stayed on in Hadley had not Jonathan stated his intention to marry Dorcas, Az Dickinson's widow. Jonathan and Dorcas would have need of a dwelling all to themselves.

The first snowfall at the time of the full moon put Old John's long-considered plan into action. The river had frozen early and had continued to freeze for a fortnight. With a safe covering of snow to protect against slipperiness, it could be a convenient highway for horses and could provide a quick passage to the south. Tribesmen were not apt to be about in this season, and any movement could be easily spied against the whitened wilderness. Because Zech knew the river, and perhaps for other considerations, too, Old John chose him to act as guide. Few knew the portages better than he, and his keen young eyes, with Dan and Nathaniel's assistance, could watch for tracks in the fresh-fallen snow. Dan, annoyed by Zech's importance, put on a show of command that he thought misled the elders.

As the sun broke through the half-darkness above Mount Holyoke and tinted the snow-covered world with a promising, rosy hue, the trekkers bid farewell to friends they never would see again. Garrison soldiers conducted the party to Springfield where they would request an escort for the next lap of their journey. Tracks of wandering deer; and families of moose and bear; and wildcats and catamounts alone, in pairs, and in family groups, crisscrossed the river, but they saw no sign of snowshoes or of moccasined feet, or of other travelers on horseback, who would not have been friends of the exodus. Zech's charges scanned the passing scenery constantly and prayed for the guidance of a faithful Providence in this time of affliction.

At Springfield, over a repast scant by comparison to bygone lecture-day hospitality, Hadley's pilgrims again bade brave farewell to friends of years past. A troop of young folk and militia accompanied the wayfarers to the Enfield rapids. Zech was anxious to be around that treacherous water and back on the river again before dusk of the shortening winter day closed in around his company.

After the Springfield escort dropped back, only the muffled plodding of the horses and their hoary breathing sounded in the eternal silence of the tranquil and sparkling, velvet world. At Windsor, friends joined the moonlight ride for the remainder of the trip to Hartford; a messenger from Windsor hurried ahead to rouse Hartford friends.

Throughout the whole journey, Zech had but one thought in mind: General Goffe. What would happen, now? Had Major Treat prepared the way as he practically had promised he would?

Since Zech's discussion with Major Treat, at the Major's behest, David Wilton and others had told him of General Goffe's sojourn in Hartford. No one in Hartford could harbor the General secretly for long, as had been possible in the isolation of Hadley's manse; too many strangers milled about and carried on business of every sort, with much coming and going. He had been hidden in a cottage at the edge of town until his conspirators decided on a likely explanation for his appearance in town. When Major Talcott married a widow newly arrived in New Haven, General Goffe conveniently became the new Mrs. Talcott's father, a Mr. Cook. He arrived in Hartford, supposedly directly from shipboard in New Haven. For reasons that satisfied their neighbors, Mr. Cook was to help with the Captain's trading, though business was slack because of conditions about the country.

Captain Bull waited at the river's edge with the Hartfordfolk who rallied to greet their old friends. Following the first frenzy of greetings, he claimed Zech. Now, Zech told himself, after all these years, his quest would be at an end. He felt confident. Almost as if knowing didn't matter, now. But it did, of course. He could not deny it. And now he was ready. In the scheme of things, as Ecclesiastes proclaimed, the appointed hour had come.

Captain Bull made no conversation as they crunched up the narrow pathway through the snow to his dwelling. Too many others were close by. They did not need to fumble for the latchstring in the dark entryway; the parting farewells of their friends, and their own loud stamping in the porch announced their arrival. The door swung open, and Zech gasped at sight of General Goffe standing just inside, tall, gaunt, a bit stooped, his hand stretched out in greeting. He was not dressed so much like a gentleman as General Whalley had been, and now, close at hand and without blackening, he did not look to be as ancient as Zech recalled General Whalley to be. His deep-set eyes and long, thin face crinkled with pleasure. He made Zech feel good, at ease.

"I believe you have met Mr. Cook sometime before in your travels, Zech," Captain Bull teased, as Zech, suddenly overcome by shyness, moved toward the General's outstretched hand.

"Ah — ah — I — " He did not know what he should say — how alone they actually were. Finally, he mumbled politely: "How are you, Sir?"

"Very well, thank you," Mr. Cook replied. He smiled broadly, and nodded, and moved toward the settle by the fire, indicating that Zech should do likewise.

"Mr. Cook was a bit wan for a time, having been confined for a spell, you know, but he's looking better, now," Captain Bull told Zech.

Zech sat down on the settle and began to remove his wet boots, satisfied that he would learn tonight what had been denied him all these years.

"Your trip was uneventful, I take it?" Captain Bull prompted indulgently. He handed Zech a pair of thick woolen hose that had been warming by the fire. He dipped up a trencherful of tantalizing venison stew from the kettle bubbling in the fireplace. He passed it to Zech as soon as he was ready. He served steaming mugs of mulled cider to each of them, before he seated himself comfortably, facing the fireplace. As he puttered along, he explained: "My lady's mid-wifing on the other side of town, this night. And Hannibal, out there, will not let anyone come within shouting distance. A loose dog is a worthy protection."

General Goffe gazed thoughtfully into his mug of cider. "Of course you remember the Nash lad," he said slowly, unhappily.

"Ohhh — Aye. Aye — " Zech blurted, distressed by a painful recollection he could not keep crowded to the back of his mind; more recent events had helped him *not* to remember, but the tolling of the new meetinghouse bell brought back thoughts of his jaunt to Aqua Vitae Meadow with Sammie Nash. They were slight lads, then, full of fun, and had been sent to catch Liz, the Nashes' young mare. It was spring, and the grass and trees were bright and new in the soft shades of gold that come before greenness, and all the smells were so fresh and sweet the young horses were throwing themselves down and rolling around, whinnying and cantering about as if drunk on the season. He and Sammie had run after Liz playfully, trying to catch her with the rope they had taken with them. When Liz was ready to be caught, she accepted the bucket of oats they had carried to bait her. They tied the rope around her winter-rough neck, then, and he had given Sammie a leg-up. As Sammie settled on her back, Liz shook her head in frisky protest so that she tipped the bucket from side to side as she ate. Sammie tied the rope around his waist while he waited; when Liz knocked the bucket over, searching for more oats underneath, Sammie pulled him and the bucket up behind him, and Liz jogged obediently toward home.

At the common gate, he slid down and let Liz and Sammie ride through; to tease him, and to let Liz run some more, Sammie dug his heels into the mare's lean ribs and spurred her on. At Goodwin's, the next house but one from home, Sammie pulled Liz up, and turned to come back. Someone had left the gate to Goodwin's ajar. Goodwin's dog — half wolf as some said? — part airedale, for sure! — tore silently at the cavorting boy and horse. It snapped furiously at Liz's heels. Startled, Liz bellowed and shied, and hurled Sammie from her back. Sammie clawed helplessly as he fell, screaming with terror. He tried to throw himself free of the rearing beast to whom he had tied himself. The attacking cur drove Liz lunging toward her own yard, dragging Sammie to where his mother stood watching, paralyzed by shock.

He would never forget the sight of Sammie's mother clutching the bloody, battered body of her dying child in her arms, or of her burly, blacksmith husband behind her, snatching at the crazed, panting mare, and falling unconscious across his wife and son.

He recalled little else of that day. Fortunately, his own dwelling had been too far away for his bed-ridden mother to know of the commotion before she knew that all was well with him. Later, Mary Tilton had led him across the common to her home, away from the milling excitement. She tried to quiet his frenzy with a nauseous concoction of posset ale in which she had boiled lettuce and some of her herbs; and she sent word to his family by Sarah that he was unharmed.

Hadley had a near riot that day. Goodwin's cur had been the cause of Dr. Westcarr's setting more than one broken bone. Usually calm family men, looking as evil and berserk as drunken Indians, had gathered in angry knots at the homes of selectmen and demanded to know what power granted Mr. Goodwin permission to keep that beast. Did some strange prerogative protect him that would be denied even the king in this settlement? Distraught men demanded action. But the selectmen took no immediate action. Baffled, everyone muttered that they did not understand. Some promised there would be an arrow in the brute's heart by morning, but it was a moonless night, and in the morning the beast slunk up and down Goodwin's yard on a long chain and dared everyone to try to carry out angry threats.

Tim Nash went to law against Mr. Goodwin to force action, but before the court found both parties equally guilty and fined them ten pence apiece, *'for negligence and improper equipage'* and *'for not restraining a savage dog'* — the beast disappeared. It surprised no one when children found the cur hanging from a sapling in what Hadleymen since called Hangdog Swamp. No one seemed to know how it got there, and no one ever heard a word of protest, either.

"We — my father Whalley and I — were dwelling at Elder Goodwin's, then," General Goffe told Zech, plainly reliving agonies of that long-ago day.

Zech stared at him open-mouthed. General Goffe explained hurriedly: "There was no excuse for the gate's being open. One of the Crow children had come into the yard on an errand. If the gate had been closed and latched properly, that terrible accident would not have come to pass." His words came in a rush, his tone full of regret.

Zech swallowed and stared into the fire. He did not want to discuss the affair.

"You see, at that time, Mr. and Mrs. Goodwin lived alone — and their daughter, Betsey Crow, next door. Susannah — Mrs.

Goodwin — was not well, and that was the excuse not to allow the grandchildren free run of her house. But after that — accident — it took such a toll of the Goodwins! — It became necessary for others to live-in with them, to help care for Mistress Goodwin.''

Zech stared at the old man, confounded by all the details that had to be taken into account. As if from a distance, he heard General Goffe explain: ''I did not tender my thanks to you — when we came down — as heartily as I would like to have, for all the long years you were silent. You might have talked more than just to Sam Russell. You can not know how apprehensive we were at first — how we prayed that you would not slip! 'Twould have been only natural if you had.''

CHAPTER XXXIII

Zech felt a stab of guilt. He said nothing. He did not move. After a moment, General Goffe went on: "That afternoon you ran into General Whalley — 'twas a shock to him. All the years of care could have come to naught in a trice."

Zech hardly breathed.

"We did go out-of-doors occasionally, on lecture days or during meeting, when no one *should* be about — " He half-smiled, not reproaching Zech. "That nook was a fine spot. Sheltered, and we could get sun there, too. For years, there had been little danger. We had an upper chamber with all our hosts, and kept to our rooms during the busy hours of the day, when outsiders might be about. After dark, in Hadley, when the moon was so we could, we rode out after the watch was past. Not only for exercise, either. We learned the lay of the land in every direction —"

Zech hoped he did not betray how much he knew of what the General thought he was learning for the first time. He hardly dared breathe.

"Of course, in winter, we could only walk up and down in the back yard, after dark. You can hear so clearly then that no one could surprise us. But we could not ride out after snow fell. Too many tracks would have roused suspicion. Pastor Russell rode out with us — of course —"

Zech nodded, urging him to go on.

"That afternoon that you met Father, he could not sleep. He had not been feeling well. As long as it was a lecture day, he thought it perfectly safe to go to our little nook to read. It was a particularly pleasant day, you remember? When I awoke — toward the end of the afternoon — Nero was making such a commotion! I went downstairs. Since Father had not come in, I supposed he was safe in the nook. It was possible to get there through the sheds. By force of habit, though, I peeked out the front and back, through the draperies. We always drew them when the Russells were away, leaving just a crack for us to see out of, but so that no one could detect us within. We were *always* cautious. So much depended on that! We did not trust to fortune at all — we thought. By the Grace of God, when I peeked out the back window, I could see you standing there with General Whalley —" For a moment, his anguish may have equalled the pain he had experienced knowing they had been discovered.

"Just think — if I had arrived through the shed — how could you have withstood the shock of seeing *two* of us?"

He looked at Zech and smiled faintly, and all three exchanged wild glances and rolled their eyes.

"Your father blamed himself. He thought he should have warned us that you would not be at lecture. But the chances of your passing through the back yard as you did —! Actually, all facts considered, 'tis a tribute to our guardians that your father took us so for granted. I was relieved to see it was you, Zech. I knew instantly that we could tell your father, and keep the situation in hand. If you had been anyone else — if you had been *anyone else!*"

Zech put his hands over his face. He writhed, remembering more than General Goffe suspected.

General Goffe went on: "The shock of exposure was too much for Father. He collapsed as soon as you departed." In answer to Zech's look of alarm, he scolded: "Do not blame yourself, now! 'Twas none of your doing, remember! Ours was the fault. We have only gratitude for you. For your silence these many years."

Each time that compliment was paid him, Zech felt flooded by confusion. He could not confess and destroy that feeling of false security — not even with Dr. Westcarr gone.

"The Moors came back within a while of your leaving. They helped me carry General Whalley in and get him comfortable. We had no idea how long he would live. Not long we thought, then. He was quite helpless."

Zech held his breath, waiting.

"He lived until last autumn, Zech — Four years."

Zech gasped.

"At first, we thought the end would come soon. Mr. Russell sent Jonathan and Mr. Lewis East with that message. We were not able to do much — not being able to consult with those who might be of service. Dr. Westcarr was the last person we could call on — and the older, sensible women, who might have cared for others so straitened — we dared not take into our confidence. How could we explain their continued presence at the manse even if they said not a word? Some would be most trustworthy, but their families would not have been accepting of what would have appeared to be gross indulgence of Mistress Russell's infirmities." He half-smiled. "Mistress Russell's complaints of poor health served us well through the years, but townfolk were not that accepting. Governor Leverett brought Lydia Fisher immediately. You remember Lydia?"

Lydia! Zech nodded.

"Her grandfather had been in the same way, and she understood the nature of the disease. She was an excellent nurse. He improved greatly under her care, though he never was completely well again. Then last year, he began to fail, but his understanding was good to the very end."

The three studied the crackling fire. Finally, General Goffe said: "I do want to commend you, Zech, for everything. For everything there *is* a season — "

Zech smiled, pleased.

"We learned when we were at Mr. Davenport's in New Haven that no detail was too small to be noticed. When we were at Guilford, a rogue there — Crampton — Dennis Crampton — reported that Squire Davenport put in £10 of provisions at once! 'Twas not our lives, after a while, that were at stake, so much as others — "

Zech nodded.

"Many provided as well as could be managed in New Haven, and we were two years at Michael Tomkins' at Milford with no one knowing we were about. We even stayed for a spell on the mountain above New Haven."

Zech's mouth fell open in astonishment. There was so much he had had no idea of!

"We had invested in farms at the Bay. Those known to be ours caused much trouble for Mr. Gookin, I have heard." He shot a reproving glance at Captain Bull who snorted and waved off any blame for not having reported unpleasant happenings.

"About that time, arrangements were being made for Hadley to have a school according to the Hopkins provision. Mr. Goodwin was one of the trustees of the estate. 'Twas he who deemed it wise for us to move to that remote area. At first it seemed like the end of the world to us, Zech!"

Zech smiled. Hartford had seemed that to Jack, the stableboy.

"At first, we made our home with Mr. Goodwin. Wherever we were, we wrote Ebeneezer as our address. It means Stone of Help, and that it was, everywhere we went." He stopped to puff on his pipe before he told Zech: "Your father conducted us to Hadley from Hartford, Zech."

Zech nearly pitched headfirst off the settle. He never had guessed that! No wonder his father had felt so protective of the generals! He stared at General Goffe, at his oddly unseamed face, tense now in the flickering light. He looked a bit weathered now. He could enjoy considerable freedom in another man's identity, as long as the rest of the world was cut off as much as it was. How long would it be, though, before someone recognized him — an ancient enemy, or an old admirer like Joe Kellogg, or a thoughtless friend like Old Sarge? Everyone fell silent.

Fatigue suddenly caught Zech. He batted his eyes. He wanted to pretend that he was not weary, but he could not. He grinned sleepily, admitting defeat. His companions smiled at him.

"You have put in a long day," both men said solicitously at the same time. They grinned, then, too.

Zech let his head drop against the side of the settle.

"You can sleep in the bornin' room, again," Captain Bull told him. He motioned toward the drapery beyond the table. "The bed is waiting there for you, again. Should bring back memories."

"Of when you were more weary than now, I'll wager," General Goffe added warmly. Zech yawned helplessly, and all but staggered toward his old haven.

Two days after he arrived in Hartford, Zech joined a band of Connecticut militiamen bound for Northampton. They found the Upper Valley in turmoil. Several companies of older Easterners had been returned to the Bay to take part in an assault on Philip's winter quarters in Narragansett country. Eastern youths from all companies and all Valleymen were left behind to erect palisadoes about the villages, and to do guard duty, and serve on night patrols in four-hour shifts that, in the opinion of the hot-blooded younger men, would never come to anything. Those left behind seethed at being denied a share of the excitement about the Bay.

While Valleymen struggled to erect a palisado, the combined forces of the United colonies and the Indian allies attacked the enemy in rough weather such as had seldom been equalled; gales along the coast left snow thigh-deep. Major Appleton led one thousand snowshoed men to Philip's palisadoed fort on a hill within the usually-safe confines of a swamp. Surprised in the night, the warriors who fled escaped only with their lives. The colonists lost eighty men. Some had been at Hadley; one was the father of Mr. Hawley, the Northampton schoolmaster.

Every settlement doubled its watch against the surviving warriors, roused to new fury. In the Valley, while Zech was gone, they put down their tools and Ed Grannis and Sam Barnard and several Eastern cohorts besieged a Hampshire Council meeting. They demanded powder and arms so that they, too, could hurry to the salvation of the East. The Council, beset by a host of worries, declared them mutinous and ordered twelve stripes well-laid on their naked bodies. Their comrades-in-arms rioted to protest the roughshod treatment of their spokesmen, and the Council ordered the protestors to be tried again at the next Council meeting.

At the second trial of the Valley mutineers, Frank Barnard interceded for his son, Sam, even as Sam angrily denounced him for doing so. Frank told the court he had ordered Sam to stay away from the meeting, but Sam was a freeman of three and twenty, and he had taken a club and had gone. Frank reminded the court of his ailing, grieving wife, smitten by losses and weakened by the cough and pleurisy. He reminded the court, also, that witnesses agreed that Sam did not join the fray; he pleaded that consideration be given his wife, a good woman, a devoted mother in a state of collapse from all the havoc of late. He claimed that Sam's whipping at his first sentencing had stayed him, that Sam should not be punished as an onlooker at the riot, however prepared he arrived on the scene.

The court commuted Sam's sentence to a £5 fine, and fined Tom and Nehemiah Dickinson £3 apiece; the more rowdy eastern leaders they bound to their good behaviour by £10 bonds. By spring, the restlessness subsided to muttering and complaining and an occasional malicious trick in defiance of authority.

Northampton, settled against dangerous foothills, had begun to palisado first; before freezing weather made their task impossible, Hadleymen began to dig post holes along the miles of town perimeter. The stockade would include all but Elder Russell's holding to the south and three small grants toward Hatfield. Hatfield, farther from the woods, enclosed only fourteen homesteads in the center of town, away from the river; there, everyone repaired within the gates when night fell. Late in January, during a prolonged thaw, a team of fine work horses and a sledge of Joe Kellogg's, hauling logs for the palisado across the rotting ice from a remote area, plunged into the river and were lost. Joe could take small comfort from the knowledge that the last trip had been made in spite of his protests.

In desperation, as winter closed in again, in February, and harsh, snow-laden gales lashed the Valley, men tore down the common fence and burned it as firewood. Shattered oldsters regretfully agreed that the sturdy fence rails would serve no better purpose than the protection of families they once had guarded in other ways. Men wondered, pained, how the horses, especially, could be saved with so little fodder gathered in. Everyone agreed, sorrowfully, that life never would be the same, again.

Word continued to arrive of further disasters in the East. One of Mr. Gookin's Christian Indians warned him that Nipmucks and Wampanoags schemed to fall upon the town lying northeast. Certain that to destroy the evil at the root was the only answer, the United Council sent six hundred men with long-arms to rally at Brookfield and fall upon the Nipmucks at nearby Quabaug. While the militia assembled, the Nipmucks laid waste to Lancaster.

Vexed militia stormed after the warriors who circled westward, retreating to old haunts in the Connecticut Valley, gathering captives along the way. The marauders crossed the Connecticut at Northfield; their English pursuers veered southward and joined Hadley's garrison.

A week later, stealthy warriors broke through Northampton's recently completed palisado in three places. Major Treat and his company, forewarned, had crossed from Hadley in the dark of the previous night or the assault would have proved a disaster to the settlement. Even so, the raiders left an old man and a young maiden and three militiamen slain, and set fire to a house before being driven off.

Thwarted war parties began to move south and terrify scattered areas in Connecticut. Simsbury families, warned in time, abandoned their village. A band of raiders, after alarming Windsor, fell upon a group of militia escorting a Longmeadow party to Springfield. They killed a man and maiden, and captured two women and their babies. Sixteen horsemen of Springfield, including Mohegans, roused by those who reached safety, set out after the escaping warriors. As the Springfield company came within sight of the raiders, the Indians murdered the babies and thought they had slain the women. Due to their haste, though they flayed the women's heads mercilessly with hatchets, both survived. One never would know reason again, but the other related that the Indians bragged of their camp above Deerfield as their chief fishing ground; they also claimed that two Dutchmen had brought them four bushels of powder and shot.

In April, Wappawy's prediction for Deacon Goodman came to pass. The Deacon took John and Young Richard to his Hockanum meadow to work with a company of soldiers to stand guard. According to Tom Reed, an Eastern dragoon, the party scarce arrived in the field when warriors lying in wait fell upon them and killed Deacon Goodman and two militiamen, and took him captive. Tom's captor, barbarously cruel at first, became so mellowed by Tom's fortitude, and perhaps by recollection of things past, that at length he set Tom free. Six weeks after his capture, Tom reappeared at Hadley in dreadful condition, but with worthwhile information: the Indians were indeed dwelling above Deerfield, on both sides of the falls. They had been fishing and planting corn and squash for three or four days. He had talked with many Eastern captives, for the most part in the care of old Indians and children; not more than sixty or seventy bucks represented the war party. They felt secure, though, and were scornful. They continually boasted arrogantly to each other of the great things they had done and would do. The night before Tom's escape, they had gone down to Hatfield and had captured its precious herd of over half a hundred cows and a score of horses that Hatfieldmen had penned together for safe keeping.

The Hampshire Council sent Tom's report to Hartford, requesting that it be forwarded to the Bay, then prepared to assail the Indians' camps at the falls. As their guide, the Hadley company chose John Gilbert of Springfield. But eighteen years old, and one of those fined at the time of The Riot, John had been captured at the recent attack on Springfield; through the assistance of Mistress Rowlandson, a Lancaster minister's captured wife, he had been able to escape. During his months of captivity, his war party had ranged the territory north of the settlements; he had come to know the Indian sites well.

Zech and Ham were among the more than eight score men, half of the number from the Valley, who assembled mounted at Hatfield on Thursday, May 18, under Captain Turner of Dorchester. The older men of the Eastern militia had fallen with Captain Beers, or had returned to their homes for the Narragansett expedition. For the most part, Captain Turner's company comprised lads of Zech's age. Captain Turner was not as hearty as the men he would lead. Since his arrival, he had reported his failing health to Boston in every dispatch; he advised that someone more able-bodied be sent to succeed him, but in the absence of a replacement, he remained in charge.

The company started up the Valley late in the day, planning to take advantage of moonlight. They did not halt until they reached a likely spot to reconnoiter, west of Fall River, beyond the Deerfield and Green Rivers. Scouts sent on ahead reported back that they found the recently captured horses under but light guard a half mile below the main camp at the head of the falls; perhaps lulled by the steady rumble of the turbulent, falling water, it appeared that the warriors slept without fear or sentinels.

Captain Turner's troops moved stealthily. They had no trouble overpowering the braves in charge of the stolen horses; quickly, they attacked their slumbering enemy, slaying many in the wigwams as they slept; many startled braves threw themselves into the river where dragoons shot them as they struggled toward the opposite shore. The swift-flowing current carried many to their deaths below the falls, but some reached safety on the opposite shore.

The militia scouts had not discovered a second encampment across the river. Roused by the tribesmen who reached them, the sannups from the second camp threw themselves into the melee. They attacked the exhausted settlers just as they began to taste their first victory. The march and the attack on the Indian encampment had seemed to Zech like a strange dream that might end in a trice; the final struggles and the flight became a nightmare, recalled only in flashes like illumination by lightning. The avenging warriors pursued the militia until daylight. Zech could recall, later, only his relief at sight of the common. He and his father reached Hadley tormented and spent, painfully bruised, but whole. Twenty-eight men did not return, including Captain Turner. Only one militiaman fell in the attack; thirty-seven fell victim to the disastrous Indian rally and the settlers' disordered retreat. Sam Crow and John Dickinson died while being carried home, and John Church never returned. An Eastern militiaman took the horse of Isaac Harrison, soldier son-in-law of Dick Montague, when he fell; he left him injured, sure prey of his enraged captors.

Jonathan Welles, severely injured in his good leg, riding with Stephen Belding behind him, witnessed that cowardice. They tried to go to the aid of Harrison. Jonathan's first recollection, later, was of fording the Green River on horseback and trying to climb a mountain. Riding had been a punishment for him since his jousting injury at play with Zech, and Dan, and Sammy Smith years before. Duty had buoyed him on the expedition, but as he began to recover from the shock of battle, despondency and weariness overtook him. Finally, alone, he no longer had strength to stay mounted. Convinced that he was dying and without further need of rations, he dismounted and freed his horse. Praying that the poor frightened creature might prove a godsend to someone more able than he, he sent it off with his supplies secure in his portmanteau. But resting revived him, and as dusk set in he started a small fire to drive off devouring mosquitos. He dozed, and his smudge fire spread out of hand, so that he had to flee that, too. Light-headed, his leg wound kept open by his constant struggles, he finally arrived at a swamp where he lay down, certain that the Angel of Death soon would comfort him.

This time, rest did not improve his lot. He stanched his wound with tow musket wadding and prayed to be released from his agony. At last he drifted off to sleep, expecting to meet his Maker. As he slept, his grandfather appeared to him in a dream. He told Jonathan that he would find a stream at the end of the swamp; that he should follow the brook 'til it joined a river at the end of the mountain; beyond lay a plain crossed by a trail that would lead him home. After reviving himself by inhaling a smoldering pine knot, and using his gun as a staff, Jonathan painfully hauled himself to the stream to which his grandfather had directed him. There, jubilant, but too weak to go on, he collapsed. He awoke to find a brave standing over him. Jonathan had dropped his gun as he dragged himself across a stream; it was wet and full of gravel. Useless. But from habit, he reached for it. Perhaps shocked by life in one who appeared so far gone, the warrior vanished.

Aware that other Indians would be along soon, Jonathan crawled from the path to a protected spot in an eroded gully, taking care to cover his trail. He lay there fainting and reviving for half a day while agitated sannups filed past just beyond him, returning from pursuit of the fleeing militia. After dark, in the waning moonlight, he followed the promised trail toward Hatfield. He arrived between meetings on the Sabbath, and the village received him as one returned from the dead.

The day after Jonathan's return, Hatfield's diminutive pastor, Hope Atherton, appeared at Hadley not knowing how he had crossed the Connecticut. His confused tale told of a gathering of Indians fleeing from him when he accidentally stumbled upon them as they powwowed. In after years, a surviving Nonotuck squaw related that Wampanoag braves ranging the territory after the assault on the falls told of their being approached by the Englishman's God — a little man in a black coat and without a hat, who came toward them moving as one who walks in a dream. His congregation and their neighbors accepted Mr. Atherton's survival and reappearance as nothing if not a miracle.

The Valley had need to believe in miracles just then, with Capt. Turner slain and Capt. Holyoke, his able adjutant, wounded so severely he lingered hardly alive and must die soon. One-third of the militia never accounted for were Valley men, many of them young fathers.

Left leaderless, volunteers scouted cautiously, trying to perceive the intentions of their enemies. They discovered gatherings of mixed tribesmen at the Falls and others at long-neglected campsites. Though warriors were reported in small numbers, they appeared to feel secure, repairing equipment and their squaws planting corn. If they continued their early plan, and assaulted each village in order, they could utterly destroy every settler in the Valley. No one took comfort from knowing that two pigs of iron and a forge had been pushed into the river during the attack on the Falls. Indians had other, effective means of destruction more natural to them.

Feeling bereft, Valley men fretted that they must not allow the Indians time or opportunity to unite. Anxiously they prayed and awaited a new Captain to lead them, and assistance from the Council at Boston.

CHAPTER XXXIV

Within a fortnight, Indians appeared again and set fire to Hatfield. One party of bucks placed itself to intercept aid from Hadley, another party lay in ambush along the Northampton trail. They took a toll of young lives, a half-dozen garrison soldiers. Before the attackers retired, they burned twelve houses and barns outside the half-completed palisado, including Ben Wait's, and drove off the village sheep.

When the report reached Boston, Captain Mosely petitioned the Bay Council for permission to besiege the encampment at The Falls again. But the Council appointed Major Talcott to take command. In the first week of June, Major Treat and two hundred and fifty mounted men and two hundred friendly Indians moved up the river from Connecticut. They arrived well supplied, with two tons of bread, more than a thousand weight of pork, twenty-six gallons of liquor, and a great quantity of dried peas. Major Treat found the northern settlements so bereft of supplies that within a week of his arrival he dispatched forty horsemen to Windsor to fetch more provisions, requesting that in future the bread be more thoroughly dried before shipping: what had been brought was found to be full of blue mold. At the same time, he asked that an extra barrel of powder and an additional three-hundred weight more of shot be sent.

Unaware of the arrival of reinforcements and supplies from the south, that Monday the Indians attacked Hadley again. A small party set upon three soldiers leaving the palisado through the south gate, expecting that their attack would divert the town's defenses away from their main assault on the north. Overwhelmed by the unexpected forces that rose at every point to drive them off, the attackers fled; the villagers pursued them for miles.

At the end of the week, a Bay company arrived to join Major Treat. Again, Hadley's common and barnyards teemed with strangers. Combined armed companies started up both sides of the river toward The Falls at the same time; as the last troops disappeared from sight of their headquarters, a long, warm, dry spell came to an end. Punishing thunderstorms crashed up and down the Valley; cloudbursts pummeled the soaked and bedraggled men for two days before dwindling to a steady, drenching rain. The disheartened militia found no Indians at their encampments. They returned to the settlements on the Sabbath, chilled to the marrow, their rations, their powder, and their arms wet and useless. A later scouting party returned to the deserted Indian encampments and burned the empty wigwams. With the assistance of Connecticut Indians, they uncovered underground granaries filled with corn and stores of dried fish. Grateful dragoons loaded the plunder into canoes they found hidden along the river's banks and hurried the provisions back to the hungry settlements; they left the squaws' growing corn trampled and uprooted.

Throughout the colonies, other militia companies dealt like destruction to other camps and crops, and gained succor from confiscated supplies. Throughout July, Major Talcott's Connecticut Company pursued Eastern tribes along a trail through the uninhabited western mountains beyond Westfield. Their "long and hungry march" ended in a battle on the Housatonnock River. There they surprised an encampment and slew many, and took more captives, though many escaped to the territory of Governor Andros, who gave them haven.

In the second week of August, word of Philip's capture arrived from the East. One meeting day a triumphant procession carried his head into Plymouth on a pole. Without Philip, with their camps destroyed and their caches discovered and removed, with unlikely prospects of more shot and grain, and with their numbers decimated and scattered, the Indian attacks slowed to a halting end.

Finally, unmolested for weeks, the militia captains declared their work done. They returned south and east. Of a sudden, the Valley found itself emptied of nearly a thousand men.

The villages had become accustomed to the discomfort of crowding. They still feared that some few determined warriors might attack, and they worried about their harvesting. They sent requests to Connecticut for garrison troops, but Major Talcott sent back word that he could not spare his men again. Connecticut's corn stood ready to harvest, too, and at this late date Rhode Island plantations were requesting assistance against diehard Wampanoag stragglers who had fled there, making trouble.

The Hadley Council issued orders forbidding the cutting and inning of corn and grass unless at least as many men remained in town as went out to work the fields; not more than fifty nor less than forty could go to harvest, and they were to dispose themselves in the best manner for security and safety; when work companies labored in Hockanum and Fort Meadow, no one went to Great Meadow; work alternated between the two places.

August passed without a sign of hostile Indians. Everywhere, men harvested their crops, wary, but undisturbed. Martial law continued; no one moved about alone; no party went unarmed; carpenters kept the palisadoes in good repair; the watch remained vigilant; but the hard winter continued to take its toll. The slow sad knell of the meetinghouse bell sounded too often before the coughing distemper for which many had first blamed Dr. Westcarr played itself out. In Hadley and Hatfield alone that affliction claimed the ancient patriarch, Nathaniel Dickinson, and two of his younger grandsons; Jonathan Welles' father and sister, who left three small children; Sarah Worthington, the mother of seven; Joseph Baldwin and an infant granddaughter; and John Cowles, once almost Ben Wait's father-in-law. John took with him his daughter, Sarah Goodwin, who risked the trip from Hartford to help care for him and her mother, who recovered. Bitter to the end that Esther had broken her word, Goodman Cowles excluded her when he gasped his will on his death bed. Aaron Cook's grandmother Westwood died of the cough, too, and Sam Gardner's wife and youngest son; and most unlikely of all, lively, much-indulged Sally Barnard who had taken such pleasure from life. Noah Coleman, Dr. Westcarr's half-brother, and his infant daughter, Mary, were the last victims to succumb. When Major Treat arrived in June, he brought word of the death of Mistress William Goodwin, in Hartford, where the disease had begun to take hold.

Again, when a light sprinkling of snow, following a long freezing spell, promised safety, Zech went to Hartford. This time he traveled with his father and a band of local militia. Two years had passed since he and his father had gone to Hartford to trade. Necessities had been transported by the militia. They would not risk another expedition until spring — and then only if affairs continued to appear settled. The trip reminded Zech somewhat of the Journey of the Elders the winter before, but this time there were no women to worry about.

Captain Bull's house looked deserted as Zech approached. Hannibal threatened him as he let himself through the gate, but when Zech called him by name, he settled down, muttering to himself. Zech tapped lightly on the door. When no one called for him to enter, he let himself into the porch. In the common room, the fire crackled a welcome, but no other sound interrupted the silence. A door to a new room at the back of the house stood ajar. Zech moved toward it; the aroma of tobacco, and hides, and spice told him plainly enough that it was the trading room. He did not realize how stealthily he had moved until he got to the door. He could see General Goffe sitting on the edge of a settle by the fireplace, unaware anyone was about. The firelight flickered over him as he leaned dangerously close to the fire to try to illuminate the pages of a book. Zech shifted uneasily. He cleared his throat lightly. General Goffe straightened slowly and lowered his book, listening intently. Zech tapped lightly on the door, and scraped his feet, and cleared his throat again; self-consciously, he stepped forward. The General peered toward him and smiled quizzically. "May I help you?" he inquired politely. Zech had been relieved to find the house deserted except for the General. Now he wished that he had looked around for Captain Bull first, or that Mrs. Bull had been at home to warn him of General Goffe's failing vision.

"This is Zech — Gen — Mr. Cook. From Hadley," he blurted out as soon as he could speak. The General's watchful expression broke into a broad smile of welcome. "Zech! What pleasure! Come in! Come in!" He blinked furiously and tried to focus on Zech's face as he rose and reached toward him. "Sit here by the fire and tell me first-hand about Hadley and what has gone on there —" he beseeched. "Tell me about everyone! Rob Treat is in and out, of course, but you know how that is! He has been so occupied with matters of great concern that I cannot press him for news of those I lived amongst so many years."

261

Zech dropped onto the settee, overwhelmed by his discovery. General Goffe, smiling broadly, nodded at him, urging him to begin talking. He did not look directly into Zech's eyes, and Zech guessed that the General thought he was hiding his dreadful infirmity from him.

For a moment, Zech could think of nothing to say. He had only one thought. What would become of General Goffe if he became blind? He could not escape, then, if he should need to! Zech wanted to weep. How could this be — after so much?

"Have you heard that Mr. Newell has gone to England?" General Goffe asked, when Zech did not speak.

"Ah, no. No," Zech exclaimed nervously. Apologetically, he reminded, "I have no way of knowing. I have seen no one —"

"Oh, aye, of course. Mr. Tilton knows, and Pastor Russell —"

Zech half-smiled at the thought of either gentleman informing him.

"He will see my family there," the General exclaimed. "Last spring, Mr. Richards, who brought us supplies for trading, visited with her —"

Zech wondered if Mr. Newell knew of the General's affliction. If he did, would he add to Mistress Goffe's burden by telling her?

"Major Treat told my father of your shop —" Zech began. He wished — he prayed — that someone would come right away and save him further distress. His discovery of the General's failing eyesight was proving too much for him.

"But enough of *my* business!" General Goffe declared. "Tell me about my Hadley neighbors!"

Zech took a deep breath and launched into an accounting of the happier details of incidents in Hadley. Few escaped mention; reluctantly, he admitted the deaths of so many in one season. He had to struggle against revealing his relief when Captain and Mistress Bull arrived home.

At Rose's tavern he was almost too bothered to notice a fresh-faced new girl who smiled a cheerful greeting and tried to engage him in conversation. He sat with his father and their friends and watched her at work, glancing often in her direction, but his mind was on General Goffe.

Dutifully, he returned with his father when he paid his respects to the General the next day. But aware of General Goffe's affliction, they took no pleasure from their visit.

When Ham's flotilla arrived at Hartford on the next expedition,

Captain Bull met them at the wharf. He urged Ham to come by his trading room, adding in a very offhand fashion that Mr. Cook had gone to New York before winter set in, that he had another daughter there whose husband was a trader, and they had a physician in the settlement who brewed a concoction of herbs very effective for one suffering with his infirmity.

Out of earshot of others ranging about, Captain Bull explained: "The General is with us still, but in hiding, again. We thought it best, with his failing sight, and all, you know. There are men up at Windsor who knew him in England. Rogues he shipped out — who came into the Valley with the militia. One — Jack London — has told that the description he heard of the Angel at Hadley answers to that of General Goffe. London is not now with the militia, but he has come back, and we fear it is to search out the General. So far, no one has considered it likely that Mr. Cook is not the father of Mistress Talcott, so we thought it best to remove him from sight while such trash as London is poking about. If he does not see him, so much the better. Mr. Cook will soon be forgotten by those who have no idea who he is. We will have him stay in New York with his imaginary daughter, getting imaginary treatment, for as long as can be. He has all the comforts that can be provided. At least he has had a few months' reprieve. And he is accustomed to such a way of life. Go up and see him, Zech. You, especially, he will be glad to see. You remember the details that escape us older men."

Zech drew a deep breath. Captain Bull gave him a sharp look. "His news from abroad has not been as cheering as we wish," he growled. "His uncle Hook, with whom his wife had been abiding, has died. At this moment he knows not where she is."

Suddenly, without any such intention, Zech found himself giving utterance to his fondest wish: "If only she could come over!"

The Captain gave him another sharp look, and Zech ventured "Have you heard from Chaplain Newell since he reached London?"

"I've not," the Captain answered gravely. "But you may be certain if anything can be done, the Chaplain is the one who will do it."

Hope welled up within Zech. "They could go to some village where they are not known — pretending to be someone's ancient parents just arrived — the way Mr. Cook was here."

263

" 'Tis all very easily said," Captain Bull answered levelly.

Zech sighed, and the Captain remarked: " 'Tis a strange Providence, when one who had only a desire to do God's will is tempted and tortured to the limit of human endurance while others with more weakness than strength are rewarded."

The older men exchanged a knowing look and nodded to each other. Zech guessed they were referring to the other Judge in New Haven. Captain Bull exploded to Ham: "Why! He is seventy, and I hear is now to wed a widow but thirty-one. He could yet raise a family!"

At the gate, Captain Bull warned Zech: "His spirits are beginning to droop, Zech. He hoped to hear more through Mr. Newell. Cheer him some, will you lad? You can do it!"

Zech found cheering General Goffe not difficult, though he would not have minded if the General chose to mourn to him a bit. It would have been a small enough service to lend a sympathetic ear to one such as he. But General Goffe wanted to forget himself, to talk of Hadley, and of his family, and what had been — once. Zech found his visit rewarding. The hardest part was *knowing* —

He was in turmoil by the time he returned to the tavern. This time he did not shun the smiling lass who had seemed so interested in him, his last trip. He had had enough of adversity of late. He wanted to be cheered up. Her name was Patty, and she was one of a large family in Stratford. She knew many people he knew, and she was full of flattering questions about the river trade and the brave towns up the river. As a lad, he had lingered at the tavern with his father taking in the news and excitement, but he had been no part of either; of late years he had repaired to Captain Bull's every possible moment. Now, for the first time, away from Hadley's overshadowing buckos, he became aware that he no longer was a mere lad helping his father and serving at the elders' beck and call. This was something new — this feeling of owning himself: much better than when he'd been waiting to see Biddy Strong again, after the trial. Patty and her interested ways made him feel other than he ever had felt before. *Now,* he was a man.

Before he left the next morning, Zech pressed a handkerchief into Patty's clinging hand: a brave knight's token of unspoken dreams and promises.

CHAPTER XXXV

A year later, as the Valley began to feel assured that King Philip's War had come to an end, Indians attacked once more. 19 September, a rampaging company set fire to the mill at Hadley, no longer defended, then coursed across the river to Hatfield. About an hour before noon, when many men were from home, some inning corn, the raiders attacked the dwellings north of the stockade. At John Allis', within sight of the stockade gate, one party torched his barn and scooped up his six-year-old daughter and visiting Gail Barthalomew, at play in the yard. At Obediah Dickinson's they left his cottage in flames and his wife wounded; they carried away his three-year-old son, and captured Obediah running in from the field. Next door at Samuel Kellogg's, they slew his wife and infant son and took off with his eight-year-old son who had witnessed his mother's murder; they left all the Kellogg buildings burning. They attacked Isaac and John Graves and two Springfield youths helping them fashion a cottage wall; they left all four dead amid flaming lumber. At Samuel Foote's, who had recently moved from within the stockade, they carried off his wife and a two-year-old son and three-year-old daughter. Across the common, other warriors slew Mary Belden, mother of seven, and set fire to John Coleman's dwelling; they slew his wife and baby son, left an eight-year-old boy wounded, and carried away a boy, six, and a lass, four. At John Welles', they killed his wife, battered two-year-old Elizabeth to death, and left an older child wounded. They took captive pregnant Hannah Jennings and her two youngest Gillette children whose father had fallen at the Falls Fight. At Philip Russell's they slew Betsey and two-year-old Stephen. At Ben Wait's they left everything in flames and carried away Martha and her three little girls, two, four, and six. Martha, too, was pregnant. In all, at Hatfield, the raiders left twelve dead and took seventeen captive, five being young ones without either parent.

At Deerfield, they picked up three young men: Benomi Stebbins, John Root, and Quentin Stockwell, and Betsey and Philip Russell's eight-year-old Sam, and Old Sarge.

Benomi Stebbins escaped his captors the next day. He brought back word that the murdering horde comprised twenty-three Bay Colony sannups and four squaws decamping to Canada. They had with them scores of women and children they had captured in the East; they had left them in Northfield while they assaulted the lower villages.

When the war party missed Benomi, a committee of warriors boldly presented themselves at Hatfield to parley for ransom for the return of their local captives. The braves demanded two hundred pounds and agreed to powwow a fortnight hence.

The Hadley Council immediately posted a request to Hartford for assistance. Major Treat started up the Valley posthaste with forty men, but by the time he arrived the renegades had fled northward.

Distracted with rage and grief, but heartened by generous donations toward the ransom that poured in from congregations in all Bay towns and the Connecticut Colony, Ben Wait and Stephen Jennings set off to try to intercept the sad brigade and meet the ransom demands.

With no confidence in their safety along the Mohawks' Trail, they went to Westfield and headed westward for the Housatonnock River; they reached Albany by way of Kinderhook, on the Hudson. Authorities at Albany gave the distraught men no satisfaction. They treated them ill and hindered their progress. Resentful and more determined, Ben and Stephen pressed northward on their own. In small villages beyond Albany, they learned the captives had been marched along that way. A day's journey above Albany, the New York constabulary overtook the Hatfield men. They dragged them back to Albany for questioning. They were ordered to seek permission for their mission from the Governor, Sir Edmund Andros, at Manhattan.

November was half spent before the men returned to Albany on their way northward; two months had passed since the carnage at Hatfield and Deerfield. Again, they received no civility from authorities at Albany, but a Mohawk with whom Ben had dealt during his early troubled years in Hadley befriended him. But for the Mohawk, the distressed Hatfield men could not have found their way through the barely-blazed wilderness.

The Mohawk conducted Ben and Stephen to Lac du Saint Sacrement which the British would later rename for King George. There he provided them with a canoe and a rough map of his own drafting. For days at a time, snow and ice and headwinds impeded their portage between Lac du Saint Sacrement and Lake Champlain; realization of the torment the expedition must have been for their wives and children spurred the men on. In December, they passed down the lakes to Canada, the first New England freemen to complete the journey. They arrived in Canada in January, in the dead of winter.

The French government put no obstacles in the way of the grateful men. Hampered by language barriers, they moved from village to village and found and ransomed those they sought who had survived.

266

They found Hannah Jennings first, in a wilderness settlement of ten shanties in the Richelieu River Valley, pawned for liquor to a French family. To their dismay they learned that little Sam Russell and Mary Foote, who had fallen ill, had been killed along the way, and defiant Old Sarge barbarously burned at the stake. Obediah Dickinson had been compelled to build Old Sarge's bier.

Within a week, Ben found Martha and their three small daughters; a few days later, their fourth daughter was born. They named her Canada.

As soon as Martha could travel, the party proceeded painstakingly to civilization in Quebec. There Hannah Jennings gave birth to a daughter, Captivity. Accompanied by a guard of eleven soldiers provided by the French governor, early in May the Hatfield company turned homeward.

Three weeks later, Ben wrote from Albany:

> To my loving friends and kindred at Hatfield. These few lines are to let you understand that we are arrived in Albany now with the captives and we now stand in need of assistance, for my charges is very great and heavy; and therefore any that have any love to our condition, let it move them to come and help us in this strait. Three of the captives were murdered — Old Goodman Plympton, Samuel Foote's daughter Mary, and Samuel Russell. All the rest are alive and well and now in Albany, namely, Obediah Dickinson and his child, Samuel Kellogg, my wife and four children, and Quentin Stockwell. I pray you hasten the matter for it requireth great haste. Stay not for the Sabbath nor the shoeing of horses. We shall endeavor to meet you at Kinderhook; it may be Housatonock. We must come very softly because of our wives and children. I pray you, hasten, stay not night nor day, for the matter requireth haste. Bring provisions with you for us.
>
> Your loving kinsman,
Benjamin Wait.
>
> At Albany, written from mine own hand. As I have been affected to your all that were fatherless, be affected to me now, and hasten the matter and stay not, and ease me of my charges. You shall not need to be afraid of any enemies.

Five days later, Ben's company left Albany; men and horses from Hatfield met their resolute neighbors at Kinderhook. The captives had been gone eight months.

Zech rejoiced that Major Pynchon dispatched him to Hartford with word of the reunion at Kinderhook. But his reception there tempered his mood. Patty was gone from the tavern to Young Tom Bull's. Recollection of Ben Wait's jilting, influenced by the Bull's wealth and Hartford, stayed Zech from seeking after Patty. How could he counter what Ben Wait had not been able to overcome with his singing, and music and light-hearted ways? Ben had turned every lass's head — or so it seemed. Zech felt so empty he ached. How could this happen to him, again? Then Captain Bull dealt him another blow: General Goffe was gone.

Captain Bull explained that but a few days before, General Goffe had been accosted at his home by that Windsor upstart, Jack London. He had reasoned that General Goffe and Mr. Cook, the trader who had left suddenly for New York, might be one and the same man, and might not be far away, either. By a ruse, he brought Dr. Howard of Windsor to Captain Bull's. Dr. Howard had known General Goffe in England; though he had heard of the Hadley Angel and knew of General Goffe's having been in the colonies, he did not suspect the situation. By sheer conscienceless nerve, London escorted the doctor directly to General Goffe's room at Bull's, and presented the General to him. Dr. Howard was not a treacherous man. He meant no harm and denied he recognized the General. He would not testify otherwise, if called upon. But that was small comfort. Things were in a bad way right now. Captain Bull made no explanation of the General's whereabouts except to tell Zech that he was safe, and again, the old familiar excuse: he would not be told more for his own good.

Zech started to protest. He was nearly one-and-twenty. No child! But he held his tongue. Protest would gain him naught. He did not linger in Hartford. He returned to Hadley with a heavy heart.

One crisp October day as Zech passed the Northampton schoolhouse, Mr. Hawley called to him. He dismissed the dozen boys of varying sizes who were laboring at their letters, and when the last lad had scurried away, took a brown, hand-sized volume from a handsome tooled-leather chest. He held the book toward Zech. Zech peered at it, studying the small gold oak-leaf design stamped in each corner. The fine kidskin leather felt as smooth as milkweed silk. Zech turned the book and studied the title printed in gold on the spine: *Baxter's Apologia.* His brows drew together. He looked to the schoolmaster for guidance. Mr. Hawley's look urged him to open the book. On the first blank page, inscribed in the uncer-

268

tain script, he read:

For a Gracious Guide
May God go with you always

In the lower right corner of the page, the same hand had written:

Ebeneezer
Hitherto hath Jehovah helped us.
1. Sam. 7. 12.

Zech's breath quickened. Ebeneezer meant the Judges! He glanced at Mr. Hawley for unneeded confirmation. He turned the next crisp pages uncertainly. He began to leaf cautiously past learned references and printer's directions, past the date of publication — 1654. His head jerked back when he reached the fourth page. He caught his breath at sight of the boldface type:

Dedicated
to the Commissary General
Edward Whalley

He began to tremble violently. Mr. Hawley lay his hand on his shoulder and steadied him. "The author of this book was General Whalley's chaplain during the Great Rebellion," he explained quietly. "He is a well-loved scholar — active still — He wrote this book when General Whalley was one of the dozen men ruling all England, during the Commonwealth —"

Zech inhaled deeply, again and again; overwhelmed by all he had experienced, he was unable to speak or think.

When Mr. Hawley spoke again, his tone had changed: "You remember about Jack London, of course?" he asked, warning of disaster.

Zech nodded, holding his breath.

"London was determined to expose General Goffe, you know. Though the authorities at Hartford conspired against him, he sought the aid of a neighbor, planning to spirit General Goffe off to Governor Andros. He went to Albany and got an arrest warrant."

Zech caught his breath. Mr. Hawley held up his hand to warn him not to jump to conclusions. "The one with whom London planned to conspire is a rough hostler, but no rogue. Aye. A man of good will and good conscience. He warned Major Talcott. The Major and Secretary Allyn charged London with maliciously intending to defame the colony — They ordered him not to leave

Windsor again without a special license. They know they have not heard the last of him, though. But London will not be able to prove his contention. The General is gone! Safely gone —"

Zech gasped his relief. Instantly, he wondered if he would be told more — this time. Mr. Hawley did not spoil the moment as the older men might have done. He explained: "All I know is that, for now, he has been taken to Long Island. To a section known as Buckram.* Peter Tilton has a brother and other relations there. A very independent lot, they are. There are Whalley families there, too, I have been told." He touched the book in Zech's hand. "General Goffe wanted you to have this as a token of his regard for you."

Zech held onto the book like a vise. In time, he realized he had begun to stroke the smooth leather as he recollected event after event of the last half-dozen years. He turned his gaze to Mr. Hawley, recalling *that* night.

Mr. Hawley smiled. " 'Twas exciting — " he mused. He added, hopefully: "I have been told that Mr. Newell is trying to make arrangements for Mistress Goffe to join her husband."

"Ohhh — I pray he has success —" Zech breathed. Unable to speak further at the moment, he began to turn page after page. A few pages beyond the dedication, someone had underlined:

Think not that your greatest trials are now over . . .
Prosperity hath . . . peculiar temptations by which it hath foiled many that stood unshaken in . . . storms of adversity.

Zech scowled. He looked up at Mr. Hawley and pointed to the passage. Mr. Hawley had read it. " 'Tis good advice for men of any Age," he murmured, "though of right our friends had need of no such admonition."

"I think not!" Zech replied tartly, and closed the book more abruptly than he intended. He stared at it, tracing the cover design with one finger. "Their trials never were over —" he said quietly. "Their struggles in the great councils were as great as any on fields of battle —"

"Aye — They were in a struggle not won by war —"

"Aye —"

" 'Tis written that 'tis the Truth that sets men free," Mr. Hawley reminded. " 'Tis an ongoing battle —"

Zech nodded and waited, head bowed, not knowing what to say

*Glencove

270

or how to take his leave. Finally, Mr. Hawley clapped him on the shoulder and without further speaking started him on his way. Zech turned back after a few steps, yearning to put his feelings into words. None would come. At last he took a deep breath, grinned sheepishly, shrugged, touched his forehead respectfully and, gripping his book against his chest as if to guard it with his life, hurried away.

Zech took Biscuit afield a few days later. He wanted to exorcise his troubled thoughts, put his mind in order. For the first time, he realized that his only solitary expedition abroad, before, had been when Benji had left him to make his way home alone — the day the Old Stranger had come into his life. The fragrance of ripening apples, when the sky was high and blue and the air crisp and teasing, always had brought to mind the great expectations he had known — starting out — that day. No doubt such recollections led him in the direction of the bee tree. He knew not what had become of Benji; since hostilities had ceased, no Nonotuck had returned to the Valley to dwell, and those who passed through on occasion claimed to have no word of him.

Zech found his way to where the bee tree had been — the broken trunk long ago reclaimed by the circle of seasons. There, Warr seemed like a presence with him . . . Warr, his near-relation, his good friend . . . his protector . . . Warr who had taught him to be a skillful canoeist . . . But Warr never had taken him fishing — or hunting — and they both would have liked that . . . Warr had abandoned him *that* day — had gone fishing . . . because settlers did not want their young ones to learn Indian ways . . . Zech snorted. He felt flooded by humiliation. *He* had thought the ways of the Indians strange! . . . Wise old Warr . . . Wise old Warr . . . He dropped to the ground and buried his face in his hands. Biscuit edged close to him and, when Zech lay his head on his, whimpered a bit as if he, too, were weeping inside.

Zech thrashed his way down to the brook where he and Warr and Benji had swum together and had eaten Aunt's cheese. That interval had been pure pleasure — just what he had wanted and expected of that day — then, suddenly, a new life had begun for him.

The Judges! — how they had changed everything — for how many —? for more than they knew? He wondered if discussion regarding their being in Hadley ever would be resolved — especially when much telling altered the facts so completely. Some believed

271

with unshakeable faith that General Goff had been an Angel of Deliverance, others wondered how anyone could have gotten to town just then for any purpose. Only a dwindling few had any idea that both Judges had dwelled in Hadley, and for how long.

Often Zech regretted he had not told Henry of the part he had played. He thought that someday he would take time out and find Henry and tell him of what had come to pass. Unlike those who dwelled on the mystery surrounding the Judges, Henry would talk of why the Judges had been refugees in Hadley. Like Joe Kellogg, Henry knew the importance of what the Judges stood for; others had learned what they knew second or third hand, they had lost sight of why men would dare treason: all the danger — To Henry and Joe the Judges were more than just romantic figures.

Henry came more and more to Zech's mind as troubled times moved toward decision. No one was prepared when Philip Smith returned from General Court and called a special town meeting. No Valley man was unmoved when Philip announced King Charles' decree that abolished all existing forms of government in New England. Henceforth, a governor of the king's own choosing would be appointed, a stranger who would select a council that would make known the king's wishes annually at the only known town meeting that would be permitted. The decree forbade gatherings for purposes of discussion. Men gasped, and blanched and shook their heads, unbelieving. Wednesday lectures would be seditious? TREASON, AGAIN?

To Zech, it was as if Henry, aware of all that Zech knew, was standing at his elbow, urging: "Now, Zech! NOW! You know why the Judges were here, Zech. Don't be silent, now. Not now! Not NOW!"

Zech, newly turned twenty-one, newly sworn a freeman, attending his first town meeting, was surprised to find himself standing in his place, the first on his feet. His voice, echoing across the shocked attention of his fellow townsmen, rang in his ears, unsteady because all eyes were on him. "We must not agree to this usurpation —" he cried out. "We are a people saved to govern ourselves. We must not agree — *ever* — to do otherwise. Carry *that* message back to Boston! We will *not* be a subject people!"

What turmoil the king's decree would bring to New England! Men groaned, knowing of the taxation and quit rents that would oppress them. With the expense of an extravagant court, again, this was History repeating itself. And those who had opposed the first Charles were either dead or gone away — without power or in-

272

fluence. The plight of New England's settlers became the burden of their prayers.

Zech talked long and earnestly with Joe Kellogg and Mr. Hawley. It was much as Joe had said long ago: being told only in words is not the same as being there. Much is forgot — left unrecorded. In fact, nothing was being recorded — out of fear.

Zech found himself talking of little else to his friends. They were losing rights that had been a matter of course at the beginning; from the first, New England men had governed themselves and each other. There would be no recourse to councils any more, though. Would Valley folk be taxed now as had been so foolishly proposed years ago? Such taxation could not now be beaten back by indignation alone. Here pony trains in the night would prove nothing, either. Everyone muttered and complained and worried about the new decrees; they mumbled "Tomorrow — tomorrow — tomorrow —" and blessed the distance across the broad Atlantic.

The underlined words in General Whalley's book haunted Zech: *Prosperity hath . . . peculiar temptations by which it hath foiled many that stood unshaken in . . . storms of adversity.* Few New England men had known the Judges, and most of those who had dared the wilderness for their cause were gone, their tales all but forgotten. If royal governors became oppressive, how many New Englanders would recall the years when to protest was a right? Would History repeat itself?

On his spring expedition, Zech went to Hartford intending to rouse Dan Crow's concern. Connecticut was as much a victim of the new decree as The Bay Colony, and Dan liked to be a leader in any cause. Surely Old John had told his offspring of the Judges and their stay at their Goodwin grandparents' home in Hadley, of the large part he and Squire Goodwin had played in the Judges' lives. He must have told them *why* the Judges had been in Hadley — why he, himself, had come to New England.

For the first time since his removal to Hartford, Old John was not waiting with Capt. Bull when the Gillette canoes swept up to the wharf. "Squire Crow is not well," Capt. Bull explained quietly. "And this latest news has been a blow to him, you know —"

Those old men understood!

Dan would be primed, for certain.

"Ham," Captain Bull exclaimed suddenly, his face stern, his tone chilling, "what kind of spell do you cast over your son that he

273

is in such haste to get back to Hadley?'' He laid a heavy hand on Zech's shoulder.

Ham stared at Capt. Bull dumbfounded.

"I understand 'tis not a lass there that's got his attention," the old man persisted.

Ham blinked. He had no answer for the old man. He and Zech exchanged troubled glances.

"Well, he should not consider Hartford such a great place to be *from,*" Capt. Bull scolded. "He should slow down a bit. Partake of some of our pleasures. There's a lass at my Tom's has an eye for him alone — pining away, you might say — and he flees the country leaving her to who-knows-what baggage that might take advantage of a slighted heart!'' His tone and expression became more teasing as he ranted on.

Zech gasped. His father, unprepared, shook his head as if stunned.

"She's a fine lass, Zech,'' Capt. Bull counselled, his tone grown merry and warm. "And you are one deserving of so fair a prize. I am telling you both, *now* — do not leave in such haste this time. Your coming is awaited at Tom's, Zech.''

Zech swallowed as soon as he was able to close his mouth. Both he and his father were scarlet and speechless. "You'll be around — *soon*?'' Captain Bull prompted Zech, pleased by the confusion he had created.

"Oh, — ayyee — '' Zech murmured in a small voice he scarce could hear himself. His father smiled, pleased, and clapped his shoulder companionably.

Zech stood a moment, bracing himself, trying to get his bearings. He would seek out Tom's dwelling, and brave the embarrassment he must face. But should he make unseemly haste — much as he wished to? And he had had another pursuit in mind when he arrived. He would tend to that first and *THEN* —

He followed Captain Bull's directions beyond the village to Old John's sawmill that had been put in Dan's charge. At first, Dan had come often to the tavern for small talk when he knew Zech was in town, but several seasons had passed since Zech had seen him.

Dan greeted Zech with pleased surprise. He began at once to extoll the extent of his riches: " 'Tis mine, Father tells me,'' he told Zech grandly, one sweeping gesture encompassing the solid, square mill building, and tranquil millpond and two-story shingled house beyond.

"Aye, I have heard,'' Zech nodded appreciatively. "I missed

274